"Rule number one in sharing the Christian faith with young people: don't patronise. Assume they are morally serious and intellectually curious; that they are in search of a structure that will carry the weight of their anxieties, passions, and imaginative energy. And if you start from that sort of point, the book you might well want to put into their hands is something very like this one—clear, respectful, challenging, candid, gracious."

—*Rowan Williams*,
104th Archbishop of Canterbury

"In this little book, East teaches about the gospel—he catechizes. But its epistolary format allows what could seem tiresome or didactic to become conversational and approachable. These letters tell the story of Jesus in many ways, from many different angles, and with a lightness of touch. They also convey what it might feel like to be a Christian and to think about the world in light of the story of Jesus. If you are someone who cares about young people or those of any age finding their way in the spiritual life—if you care about future saints—read this book and share it with others."

—*Tish Harrison Warren*,
author of *Liturgy of the Ordinary* and *Prayer in the Night*

"The letters that Brad East writes here are signed, 'Yours in Christ, a fellow pilgrim,' and that tells you most of what you need to know about this wonderful book. It's a warmhearted, clear-sighted account of life 'in Christ,' not pronounced from on high, but narrated by someone a little farther along the Way than the young people it's addressed to. This is a book to give to many of those pilgrims near the outset of their journey."

—*Alan Jacobs*,
Baylor University

"Sometimes catechisms seem to emphasize truth at the expense of life. The parroting back of doctrinal answers to posed questions, while often valuable, can be dangerous for those tempted to think of Christianity as the mastery of syllogisms rather than as the Way of the Cross. In this book, Brad East takes us along as he guides a young pilgrim in the path that is Jesus. Reading this will help you see your own faith with fresh eyes and will prompt you to be not just a disciple but a discipler."

—*Russell Moore,*
editor in chief, *Christianity Today*

"A personal, readable, informed, and confident exposition of the Christian faith—so confident, in fact, that it starts and ends with an invitation to martyrdom in the service of Christ! East's unwillingness to make Christ into a founder of a 'religion of comfortableness' (Nietzsche) is admirable."

—*Miroslav Volf,*
Yale Divinity School

"In this time of widespread unclarity, Brad East's insightful letters help us see what being a Christian might look like. A fascinating book that helps us see the fascinating character of our faith."

—*Stanley Hauerwas,*
Duke University

"Brad East does not cease to astound. This book is both spiritual meditation and pocket catechism—it instructs as it inspires, and its contents explain Christianity in a way both simple and profound. This is the kind of book to spread around everywhere: airports, homes, churches, used bookstores, universities, and so on. East has something important to teach each one of us!"

—*Matthew Levering,*
Mundelein Seminary

# *Letters*
## to a
# Future Saint

## BRAD EAST

WILLIAM B. EERDMANS PUBLISHING COMPANY
GRAND RAPIDS, MICHIGAN

Wm. B. Eerdmans Publishing Co.
4035 Park East Court SE, Grand Rapids, Michigan 49546
www.eerdmans.com

Book design by Lydia Hall

Printed in the United States of America

30  29  28  27  26  25  24      1  2  3  4  5  6  7

ISBN 978-0-8028-8387-2

**Library of Congress Cataloging-in-Publication Data**

A catalog record for this book is available from the Library of Congress.

*To the children I pray for daily by name—*
*my own, my brothers', my godchildren—*
*these letters are for you*

Show me O anchoress, your anchor-hold
Deep in the love of God, and hold me fast.
Show me again in whose hands we are held,
Speak to me from your window in the past,
Tell me again the tale of Love's compassion
For all of us who fall onto the mire,
How he is wounded with us, how his passion
Quickens the love that haunted our desire.
Show me again the wonder of at-one-ment
Of Christ-in-us distinct and yet the same,
Who makes, and loves, and keeps us in each moment,
And looks on us with pity not with blame.
Keep telling me, for all my faith may waver,
Love is his meaning, only love, forever.

—Malcolm Guite, "Julian of Norwich"


Be dead in life and you will not live in death. Let your
soul die strenuously and not live in weakness. Not
only those who, for the sake of faith in Christ suffer
death, are martyrs; but also those who die because of
their observance of his commandments.

—Saint Isaac of Nineveh


It is never too late to become a saint.

—François Mauriac

# Contents

one

# God Brings Life through Death

Jesus wants to possess your heart completely. He wants you to be a great saint. For that you will have to suffer very much, but then what joy will flood your soul when you reach the happy moment of your entrance into Eternal Life! My brother, I shall go soon to offer your love to all your friends in heaven and beg them to protect you. Dear little Brother, I would like to tell you a thousand things which I understand as I stand at the door of Eternity. But I am not dying, I am entering into life, and all that I cannot say to you while I am still here below I shall make you understand from the heights of Heaven.

—Saint Thérèse of Lisieux

*Dear future saint,*

I understand you want to be a Christian. Let me tell you a story.

There was once a very old man who was brought to the authorities and charged with breaking the law. His crime? He would not worship someone other than Jesus. When faced with punishment versus abandoning his exclusive devotion to Jesus, he chose punishment. When asked why he would make such a choice, he answered: "Eighty-six years have I served him, and he has done me no wrong. How can I blaspheme my King and my Savior?"

The man's name was Polycarp. He was born around the time Peter and Paul died, which was about four decades after Jesus's death on a cross. Polycarp was burned at the stake in the year 155 for refusing to offer a pinch of incense to the emperor, who at the time fancied himself a god, or at least deserving of worship.

I begin with this story for a simple reason. Being a Christian is many things. But among the most important is that it is costly. It costs dearly. It cost Polycarp his life. It will also cost you yours, however unlikely it is that you, too, will die a martyr.

The thing to realize, though, is that what it costs you, it does so without forcing your hand. It requires your consent. No one made Polycarp die for Jesus. He chose to do so. He chose to do so because for him it was no choice at all; he knew in his bones the words of Paul, that "to live is Christ, and to die is gain."

This is the flip side of the coin, the coin that here stands for the cost of following Christ. The flip side is that Christ is worth it. He is worth it all, because in him you gain all. What you cannot have apart from Christ is not worth having; what you gain in Christ is everything and more.

To have Christ is worth more than everything else combined, even the world itself. Even your own life. Imagine knowing, loving, and cherishing something more than your own life, so much so that you would willingly, even gladly, part with your life for its sake.

This is what it means to be a Christian. It is an adventure, yet just for that reason it is full of danger and loss as much as joy and pleasure. The joy, however, doesn't come without sacrifice; the light comes only after the night. But if you wait for it, if you wait in the darkness through all the hours of the night, yearning for the sunrise, for *this* sunrise, you'll never regret the loss of sleep. When morning breaks, you'll never tire again.

Yours in Christ,
a fellow pilgrim

**2**

*Dear future saint,*

I see you've drawn the obvious conclusion: that to live as a Christian means being, or being willing to be, a martyr.

Let me dispel any confusion: you are exactly right.

Martyrdom is the calling of each and every Christian. To say yes to Christ means saying yes to his cross. Which means that faith's first step is the resolve that life in Christ is more precious than anything else—including one's earthly life, since life in Christ outlasts earthly life. Or so Christians have always believed, in the confidence of faith.

But most Christians are not martyred in the literal sense. And martyrdom is not to be *sought*; Christianity is not masochistic. We do not hate ourselves or our lives. Both are gifts to be treasured. Observe that I did not say that Christ is more precious than one's *life* (though in a sense this is true). I said that *life* in Christ is more precious than one's *earthly* life. To follow Christ in this world is to pursue life above all, for Christ is himself life, the true life, and all life comes from him. As he taught, he came that we might have life—life in abundance.

Yet this very life, which is abundant life in Christ, is found in following him, and following him means living as a martyr. How should we understand this? How could it be true that the willingness to *lose* one's life is itself the way *to* life? How can a person be a mundane martyr, a martyr of the everyday, without being a martyr in the worst sense—sunk in self-pity, seeking perpetually to lose precisely in order to complain about everyone else always winning?

Let me offer three answers.

First, Christ calls us to count the cost. What he means is that, before we confess faith in him and pledge our lifelong obedience to him, we should understand what he means to ask of us, and what might result from our commitment. For what he means to ask is everything: all of us, all that we love, every virtue and vice, every desire, every habit and guilty pleasure, every ounce and drop of our lives. This is the cost. Are we willing to pay it? Are you?

Second, the way we pay the cost is death. Occasionally this means literal death—and we must know, up front, that death may be the price of following Jesus—but in every case it means what Christians call "death to self." Unless a seed "dies," Jesus says, it will remain just a seed. But if it "dies," it will rise to new life, growing and becoming fruitful. If we love our lives more than Christ, our lives will come to nothing; Jesus even says we will "lose" them. But if we unclench our fists, if we let go of our lives, if we confess that we are not our own, that we need and depend on God for life and for every other good thing—then, Jesus says, we will keep our lives, not only in this world but in the world to come.

Eternal life comes through dying to ourselves, for in dying to ourselves we live to God. Christ is the One who enables this; in fact, he shows us how.

Third, a clue to the daily martyrdom of the Christian life is found in the meaning of the word. "Martyr" comes from a Greek word meaning "witness." Jesus gives the name "witness" to the founding leaders and teachers of the church, called "apostles." Through them, Jesus extends it to all who put their trust in him. To bear witness means to show Christ to others, in what you say and what you do—in "word and deed." In her wisdom, the early church applied this general term "witness" or "martyr" to those Christians who bore *ultimate* witness to Christ, by giving their lives for his sake.

Their model is an inspiration for the persecuted among us: as one ancient Christian writer put it, the blood of the martyrs is the seed of the church. But it is also a gift to the rest of us, because their example should inform our ordinary daily lives. We ought to die to ourselves every day for Christ's sake. In doing so, we ought to show Christ to the world for what he is: the very Life of God, given freely for us human beings to share in, now and forever.

What could be more beautiful?

*Yours in Christ,*
*a fellow pilgrim*

3

*Dear future saint,*

You're curious: Just what am I up to in these letters? Let me tell you.

As you know, I'm a teacher and a writer. Put simply, I'm writing these letters in order to teach you what Christianity is, what Christians believe, and what it means to live as a Christian. I find myself worried that young people today, including young people who grow up in the church, do not know what Christianity is, what Christians believe, or what it means to live as a Christian. Reading and teaching and writing about these things is my day job, and instead of worrying or complaining, I'd like to help respond to the problem, if it is a problem.

I'm grateful, therefore, that you've struck up this correspondence with me. From what I gather, you fit the bill of the kind of person I have in mind. Raised in the orbit of church. Not unfamiliar with Jesus or Scripture. Not skeptical of them either. But untutored. And more than anything, hungry to learn more—to make the switch, in the Bible's image, from milk to meat: a sign of maturity and growth. No longer a child but approaching adulthood. Curious and serious, committed but ready to plant a stake in the ground.

You'll have to tell me whether you've been baptized. If so, then these letters are about living into your baptism. If not, then by the end, I hope you'll write to inform me the date on which you'll be plunged into the waters. Either way, we both know you're no longer a child, and you're uninterested in being a childish believer. You want the real thing. You want to know what Christianity means, what it *is*. I'd like to tell you.

Here's a word that will give you a sense of what I'm up to here: "catechesis." It comes from a centuries-old Christian term for *instruction*. Specifically, it means to instruct, or teach, or shape and form young persons, or new believers, in what it means to be a Christian: what is true and what is good; what to believe and how to live.

Traditionally, a catechism is quite short. Often it is written in a question-and-answer format, meant for parents or pastors to use with children. Typically it covers the basic story of the gospel (what's called the Apostles' Creed) as well as the Ten Commandments and the Lord's Prayer. There are many good catechisms out there; perhaps I'll point you to some.

This catechism is a bit different from those. I'm not going to follow the sequence of creed, commandments, and prayer—though I will certainly talk about each. And I'm not writing in a question-and-answer format, though I welcome your questions throughout.

I'm writing letters. Letters are more intimate, more conversational, than the formal overtones of a "religious book" meant for "religious instruction." I got the idea from an experience I had. In short succession, my godchildren (three of them) as well as my nephews (four of them) were baptized. For the days of their baptisms, I wrote each (all seven of them) a personal letter. The letter was meant to put into words they could understand, at least when they grew up, what was happening to them that day.

Writing and reading those letters was a very moving experience for me. (I hope one day it will be for them as well.) And it occurred to me: What if there were more letters, just like those, talking about this or that aspect of what it means to be Christian today? What if I could put those letters in the hands of young persons I know—even in the hands of my own children? (I've got four of those, too.)

So here we are. If these first few letters have piqued your interest, read on. If not, then put these letters away; ignore the whole correspondence. What I want, the one and only thing I want, is for you to come to know Christ—whether for the first time or, if you already know him, then with greater depth, richness, and intimacy. To know Christ is to love him. Life is nothing apart from loving him. Everything I say, everything I am writing to you, is because of that love.

As one of Christ's closest friends once wrote: "We love, because he first loved us." If you know anything in your life, know this: Jesus loves you. There is nothing more important to know than that. Everything else worth knowing begins and ends there, in the love of Jesus.

*Yours in Christ,*
*a fellow pilgrim*

*Dear future saint,*

I gave you the plan in my last letter. But what am I going to *write about* in coming letters? You're right to wonder.

Know now that there is no predetermined plan or structure. I'm not commenting on specific texts (though plenty of texts will enter in), nor do I have a set list of topics, or an order I want to follow. I'm writing to you about what matters most in the Christian life, and I'm going to discover with you just what that is.

But you'd be right to want to have some sense of what's coming. Let me give you the gist.

What Christians believe, confess, and share with others is called "the gospel." The gospel is the good news about Jesus. I'm going to say more about that soon. But for now I want to emphasize that the gospel is at the heart of what I'm writing because the gospel is the heart of Christian life and faith.

The gospel is not by and for individuals; it belongs to a community. The name of this community is *church*. The church is the people of Christ. No church, no gospel; no gospel, no church. Christ came to earth to form the church, a community of his friends and followers. I am going to beat this drum incessantly, so learn it now rather than later: The church is central to the purposes of God. The church is not on the periphery of God's plans. The church is essential to the Christian life. There is no such thing as Christian faith, Christian life, or even Christianity without the church. So we are going to be talking a lot about the church.

The church lives by faith in the gospel; the Bible is what tells the church about the gospel. The church therefore guards, treasures, and transmits the Bible across time. In this sense the church is a people of the book, and the Bible is the church's book. I'm going to have a lot to say about the Bible. Indeed, I've been quoting and alluding to it already quite a bit.

"Doctrine" is a word the church uses to describe very important teachings all Christians ought to believe. Some of these teachings concern what might sound like abstract matters: the nature of God or the creation of the universe. Some of them concern "morality," meaning how human beings are to live, to be good, excellent, or holy as the creatures we are. No doctrine is irrelevant to being a Christian, but some doctrines are easier to understand than others.

This shouldn't surprise us. We're talking about what matters most, in this case God, human life, and reality itself. We shouldn't expect it to be easy.

That's not to say, though, that you have to be an expert in Christianity, much less an especially smart or educated person, to be faithful to the call of Jesus to follow him. Some of the church's most beloved saints—holy persons we remember and revere for their example as disciples of Christ—were illiterate, unimportant, even unimpressive individuals, at least by worldly standards. The point about Jesus is that his standards are not those of the world. The way he measures, and what he measures by, is a shock and a scandal to the way the world normally works. At one point the Bible says that wherever the message about Jesus goes, it turns the whole world upside down. That puts it just right.

I want to tell you about the One (the only One) who has the power to turn the world upside down. By the end, I hope you'll come to see that when you follow Jesus—when you trust him and obey him in all things—it's not Jesus that's upside down. It's the world. Following Jesus is a matter of learning to live right-side up, sometimes for the very first time.

Yours in Christ,
a fellow pilgrim

*Dear future saint,*

Fine, I admit it: "what Christianity is, what Christians believe, and what it means to live as a Christian" is both vague and grandiose. Guilty as charged.

No one can put such things into words, much less into a brief series of letters. But something like it is necessary, else how could anyone be a Christian?

Here's an illustration. I can stand on a mountaintop and see the vista before me without claiming to "take it all in," memorizing every detail, with perfect accuracy and full recall of memory. Nevertheless, I'm not wrong to say *I see it.* Like Christianity, the power of such a view lies in its very grandeur: it overwhelms and conquers me. But the result is humility, awe, and gratitude, not frustration or resentment. Victory lies precisely in being defeated.

I want, in the coming letters, for you to have some sense of why people are defeated by Christ. If God grants my prayer, the living Christ will himself defeat you. As he said to his disciples ("disciple" means *student* or *learner*):

> "If anyone would come after me, let him deny himself and take up his cross and follow me. For whoever would save his life will lose it; and whoever loses his life for my sake and the gospel's will save it. For what does it profit someone, to gain the whole world and forfeit his life? For what can someone give in return for his life?"

Or in similar words, which he said just before his arrest and death:

> "He who loves his life loses it, and he who hates his life in this world will keep it for eternal life. If anyone serves me, he must follow me; and where I am, there shall my servant be also; if anyone serves me, the Father will honor him."

My prayer, therefore, my aim in these letters for you, is that you become a lifelong disciple and follower of Christ, preferring death itself to life without him.

You will be unable to do this without three things. The first I have already mentioned: prayer. The Christian life is defined by prayer. A life without prayer is not Christian. Jesus is never far from prayer; he constantly withdraws from public life, life with others, to be alone with the Father. All the more so should you depend on prayer.

Prayer is a kind of spiritual oxygen. Sure, you can try holding your breath. But it won't last long.

The second necessity is God's word. "By the word of the LORD the heavens were made," the Bible sings, "and all their host by the breath of his mouth." If you need God's breath to live, you need his word for sustenance. As Jesus says to Satan when tempted to turn desert stones into a meal (he'd been fasting for forty days), "Man shall not live by bread alone, but by every word that proceeds from the mouth of God."

God breathes his Spirit into your lungs through prayer; he speaks his word into your heart through Scripture. Let prayer to God and God's powerful word join hands to hold you in his care, throughout our correspondence and beyond.

Jesus also has this to say about making a meal of God's word:

> "Unless you eat the flesh of the Son of Man and drink his blood, you have no life in you; he who eats my flesh and drinks my blood has eternal life, and I will raise him up at the last day. For my flesh is food indeed, and my blood is drink indeed. He who eats my flesh and drinks my blood abides in me, and I in him."

This is a mysterious teaching about which I will have more to say in later letters. For now, it points us to two things.

On one hand, to feed on God's word is to feed on Christ, because Christ is God's living Word in human form. On the other hand, to feed on Christ the Word is to join him at the table or altar of his Holy Supper: the Eucharist, or Communion. This is the feast in which we hear the words of Jesus spoken aloud: "This is my body." "This is my blood."

We feed on Christ through hearing his word. But we are *fed by him* at the Lord's Supper. But where can we find the Supper? And with whom may we eat it?

Answer: the church.

The third and final necessity, then, is worship. To know God through following Christ means worshiping, in Jesus's words, "in Spirit and truth." You cannot follow Christ without worshiping him, and you cannot worship him without giving glory to his Father by the power of his Spirit.

How do you do this?

By joining with other believers, other followers and disciples, in public gatherings of prayer, song, Scripture, sermon, confession, encouragement, and sacrament. I have already said that the church is integral to the will and work of God. Let me now say: *Get yourself to church!*

It may seem simple; it may seem trite; it may seem unfashionable. It may even involve some measure of pain. But you can't have God without his people; you can't have the head without the body; you can't have Christ without his bride. And you can't journey, as a pilgrim in this world, to the kingdom of heaven without joining the company of pilgrims whose life together makes the journey possible. They *are* the journey. It's them or bust. We make it together or die alone.

Vote with your feet and find some fellow pilgrims with haste.

*Yours in Christ,*
*a fellow pilgrim*

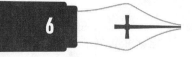

## 6

*Dear future saint,*

In later letters I'll elaborate on God's word as well as the church's worship and sacraments. Prayer, though, will be assumed throughout. It will be hidden, like the Spirit. Like breathing or blinking, it can become an unconscious and unreflective habit. That can be a good thing—I don't "think hard" about talking to my wife, I just talk to her—but since I want you praying constantly during this exchange of letters, I think it wise to say a bit more about it before moving on.

A man named Alphonsus de Liguori was a prolific Christian writer in the 1700s. He was so bold as to say that "without prayer no one can be saved." What did he mean?

At least two things. First: "Prayer is the only ordinary means for receiving God's gifts." In other words, we cannot receive what we do not ask for, and prayer is how we ask God for anything at all. Nor is prayer difficult. "What does it cost us to say: *My God, help me. Lord, help me. Have mercy on me!* Could anything be easier? This little thing is sufficient to save us if we are faithful to it." Communication is the basis of relationship. How can we be in relationship to God if we do not communicate with him through prayer?

Second: Prayer is necessary because it sustains us. Prayer puts us in contact with the Creator and Redeemer of all things. When we speak to him, he hears us. Liguori writes of one "church father" (the name given to the wisest and most influential of pastors and teachers from the church's first seven centuries of existence), a man named John Chrysostom, who said that

> prayer is as necessary for our salvation as moisture is necessary to prevent a plant from drying up and dying. Elsewhere [Chrysostom] says that just as the soul is the life of the body so prayer is the life of the soul and the soul without prayer emits a foul odor. He speaks of a foul odor because whoever fails to have recourse to God soon begins to rot through sin. Prayer must also be called the food of the soul. As the body cannot survive without nourishment neither can the soul survive without the nourishment of prayer, as Augustine says.

GOD BRINGS LIFE THROUGH DEATH

Prayer can take many forms. We ask God for what we want or need. We thank God for his many gifts. We praise God for his glory and beauty. We lament to God when things go wrong. We intercede with God on behalf of others.

Flip open the Bible to its middle, and you'll probably land in the Psalms. This book contains 150 prayers, songs, and poems addressed to God. Written and sung by the people of Israel over many centuries, it is both the prayer book and the songbook of God's people. As one theologian puts it, the psalms are a spiritual anatomy of the life of faith. They cover every emotion, every experience, the whole gamut of the human journey with God and toward God.

If you want to learn how to pray, look to the psalms. By this I don't mean that you should try to pray *like* the psalms, though that isn't bad advice. I mean *pray the psalms*. Make the words of the psalms your own prayer. Make the "I" of the psalms your "I." Rejoice and lament, petition and give thanks, offer praise and shout your anger. Monks recite all the psalms every single week of the year. That's a bit daunting for the rest of us. I myself pray through the whole Psalms every month. I read a few each morning with my coffee and a few each evening before bed. I start on day one with Psalm 1, and I end on day thirty with Psalm 150. I commend the same practice to you.

Here are a couple other practices to consider.

The first is called the Jesus Prayer. It goes back a thousand years. Like the psalms, it's beloved in monasteries, where monks live together in community. Its words are brief and to the point:

> Lord Jesus Christ,
> Son of the Living God,
> have mercy on me,
> a sinner.

This is a prayer meant for repetition. Standing in line for groceries, stuck in traffic, cramped on the subway, lying in bed: "Lord Jesus Christ . . ." Using prayer beads can help: one bead per recitation. Or you can time it with your breathing. Sit still in a quiet room. As you breathe in, recite (aloud or in your mind) the first two lines, then breathe out the last two lines. Over and over and over. Let this simple petition reach down into your very marrow, growing slowly to become a part of you, like a bone graft. Let it be woven into your heart and soul. The repetition is the point. Like saying "I love you" to a parent or a spouse, you repeat it countless times without thinking, not because you don't mean it but because you do. And in this sacred recurrence, God is present and at work.

Finally, we do not come to know and love the Lord because of anything wise or good in us. We do so because he draws us to himself in the grace of his love for us. We begin, then, not with what we think we know about him, but with prayer. The following words are the prayer of Anselm, a pastor from England born about a millennium ago. Make them, too, your own as we begin this journey together. Faith is not a destination. It is a starting point. No one knew that better than Anselm:

Teach me to seek You, and reveal Yourself to me as I seek, because I can neither seek You if You do not teach me how, nor find You unless You reveal Yourself. Let me seek You in desiring You; let me desire You in seeking You; let me find You in loving You; let me love You in finding You. . . .

I do not try, Lord, to attain Your lofty heights, because my understanding is in no way equal to it. But I do desire to understand Your truth a little, that truth that my heart believes and loves. For I do not seek to understand so that I may believe; but I believe so that I may understand.

*Yours in Christ,*
*a fellow pilgrim*

## *Dear future saint,*

An odd way to address you, I know: *Dear future saint.* I gave an offhand defi-nition of the saints a few letters back, but I've not explained my calling you one. What's going on?

"Saint" means *holy one,* in the sense of a holy person. It's commonly used in the church almost as soon as she comes into being. It's especially beloved of Paul, who uses it to refer to baptized believers in general. A saint is someone who belongs to Christ, having been cleansed from sin by the gift of God's Spirit. The saints are the Lord's people, sanctified—made holy—by the Holy One through his Holy Spirit.

So why do I call you a "future saint"? For three reasons.

First, although God begins to sanctify us in this life, the process is not completed until the Lord's return, which for most of us means not until death. Your present holiness is a seed planted in you by Christ through baptism; as your faith, hope, and love for him grow over time, watered by his holy word, so too will your holiness grow.

Second, very early in the church the term "saint" came to be reserved for a certain kind of Christian, following her death. A person was a saint (1) if the church had good reason to believe that her soul was in heaven with Christ; and (2) if that person's life on earth had been a particularly beautiful or reso-nant witness to Christ. As Christ himself taught, the dead are not dead, strictly speaking. They are alive with the Lord in heaven, awaiting the resurrection of their bodies. They cry out to God in prayer, as the book of Revelation shows us. In this way they compose a great cloud of witnesses, an image that comes from the book of Hebrews. These witnesses are women and men whose lives and deeds serve as testimony to Christ and examples for us to follow.

Another phrase that captures this idea is "the communion of saints": a heavenly fellowship of departed souls who pray for us, whose lives are a window and a mirror of God's own, who (you might say) cheer us on from the stands.

For this reason you and I could never claim to be saints in *this* life. But we may hope to become saints in the next. Or to switch the tense, we may hope *to have been* saints.

If it seems odd to use a term once used for all Christians as a designation for only some, think back to the word "martyr." Every baptized believer is a martyr in the original, literal sense: a witness or living testimony to the risen Jesus. This is how the book of Acts uses the term (building on the very first meaning of an eyewitness to the resurrection). Only those who die for Jesus, though, are martyrs in the special sense. Surely we are not wrong to honor them with this title! Nor are we wrong to do the same for the saints.

Third, then, I address you as a *future* saint with a famous quotation in mind, from the French novelist Léon Bloy: "The only real sadness, the only real failure, the only great tragedy in life, is not to become a saint." This is true. The purpose of human life is to become holy, because the purpose of human life is to know Christ. You cannot know Christ without becoming like Christ. And to become like Christ is to become holy. That is, to become a saint.

I want you to become a saint. And so I call you a future saint, because, with *Saint* Paul, "I am sure that he who began a good work in you will bring it to completion at the day of Jesus Christ." May it be so. And may these letters be one small nudge, used by the Lord to draw you toward himself.

*Yours in Christ,*
*a fellow pilgrim*

## Dear future saint,

I forgot something. Or rather, two things.

First: A word I am going to use and reuse throughout these letters is "tradition." I am wanting to introduce you to Christ, but my way of doing so is by introducing you to Christian tradition, sometimes called "the" tradition or "sacred" tradition.

You might have positive associations with that word, as many of us do. Family traditions, school traditions, holiday traditions, traditions with friends—that sort of thing. But you might not. You might think that tradition sounds like a dead letter, a human thing we do "just because," going through the motions in the absence of conviction or principle.

Sometimes this happens; the Bible has a good deal to say about loving God with your heart, and Jesus builds on that by saying that whatever comes out of a person comes from the heart.

But that's not what the word "tradition" means for Christians. Its meaning comes from the original Latin, which translates as "handing on." Christian tradition is what Christians have handed on as of most importance, from one generation to the next. This, the church teaches, is the work of God's own Spirit in history. We need not build Christianity from scratch in each new generation. We build on what came before us, on the foundations laid by our mothers and fathers in the faith. We aren't building the kingdom of God— God will see to that (in fact, it's already built)—but you might describe what we are building as a great household or palace, a single sustained construction project to be completed at the end of time by Christ himself, the cornerstone and capstone of our faith.

But we are not alone. It is Christ's Spirit who is building through us, by our hands and in our minds and on our lips.

Just this is what I want to impart to you: what wise and trustworthy builders (teachers, writers, saints, monks, nuns, pastors, priests, popes, bishops, missionaries, martyrs) have said and done before you and I came on the scene.

Second: In these letters we are working with words. This is no accident. Words lie at the nerve center not only of Christian teaching but of all human life, even the universe as a whole. I'll say more about this in a later letter.

But I want you to understand at the outset that words are not secondary or incidental in the Christian life. Christianity is a sort of language, and learning to *be* Christian entails learning to *speak* Christian. These letters are exercises in doctrine and storytelling and explanation, yes, but they are also grammar lessons. Faith has a grammar, and I want you to learn it—by heart—because faith's grammar is crucial to living as a Christian. In a word, I want you to be fluent in Christ.

I imagine that sounds odd. For the moment you'll have to trust me. Now to begin in earnest.

*Yours in Christ,*
*a fellow pilgrim*

*two*

# God Calls a Special People

And one peculiar nation to select
From all the rest, of whom to be invoked—
A nation from one faithful man to spring.
        . . . from him will raise
A mighty nation, and upon him shower
His benediction so that in his seed
All nations shall be blest. He straight obeys;
Not knowing to what land, yet firm believes.
I see him, but thou canst not, with what faith
He leaves his gods, his friends, and native soil. . . .
This ponder, that all nations of the Earth
Shall in his seed be blessèd.

—John Milton

*Dear future saint,*

Jesus is the center of Christian faith. And the first thing to know about Jesus is that he was a Jew. (*Is* a Jew. Tense gets tricky with Jesus.) This means that, before we can talk about Jesus, we need to talk about the Jews. As you'll see, to enter the Jesus story is to enter the Jewish story. This is not something you can choose on your own; you have to be invited to join. Fortunately, Jesus is the One who invites you.

The Jews are the people of God. Long ago, there was a man named Abraham who lived in modern-day Iraq, in the Middle East. The Bible tells us that God came to Abraham and told him to leave the house of his father and mother, to leave the land of his ancestors, to leave the life and work and worship that he'd known since birth—and to go. Go where? Due west, as it happens. Why in that direction? Not because there was anything waiting for Abraham down that road. There wasn't.

What awaited him was a future.

God makes a promise to Abraham. He says that he, God, will make from Abraham a great people; that this people will be God's people and he will be their God; that he will impart to this people a land in which they will live and flourish in the midst of other peoples; and that those peoples, every one of the world's nations, will find the blessing of God in this one people.

That's quite a promise. Not to mention that Abraham (called Abram at this point in the story) is an old man: seventy-five, in fact. Somehow an entire nation is supposed to come forth from this one elderly man and his barren wife, Sarah (called Sarai for now).

What would you do? Would you do as you were commanded? Don't overlook the fact that God doesn't make a request. He issues a command, without preparation or explanation. He plops down into the middle of Abraham's life and makes a promise that will change not only Abraham's future but the future of the human race. The Bible doesn't tell us what Abraham thought or felt. Once God is finished speaking, this is all that it says:

"So Abram went."

These three words are the beginning of the story of the people of God. In this sense they are the true beginning of the whole story: the story of Jesus, the story of the Bible, the story of you and me. For this is the one story

GOD CALLS A SPECIAL PEOPLE

23

in which everything has a part to play; it leaves nothing out. Quarks and electrons, gravity and evolution, Japan and Peru, marriage and farming, your parents and my pets, Columbus and Genghis Khan and Harriet Tubman: they all belong to this story, the story of Abraham. Why? Because the story of Abraham is at once the story of Abraham's children and the story of Abraham's God. The name of Abraham's children is Israel. The name of Abraham's God is the Lord.

Here is what Israel says about him: "The LORD our God, the LORD is one." There is, simply put, one God and one people of God. The God of the Jews is the God of the whole universe.

This is why the story begins this way. The one God, the only God there is, once upon a time came to one man, Abraham, and through this one man started a process that continues today. This process is the creation of a special people, a chosen people, God's beloved people. A people descended from Abraham, a man called God's own friend.

If you want to know God, start here. Start here because it's where God started. Start here because it's the only way to get where you want to go: life with the Lord.

Yours in Christ,
a fellow pilgrim

*Dear future saint,*

*Why did God choose the Jews?* Good question. Before I answer it, let me give you a glimpse of the big picture.

We may roughly date the call of Abraham to about two thousand years before the birth of Christ. Meaning it was about four thousand years ago. Now think about that. A solitary man and his wife, the father and mother to forty centuries' (a hundred generations') worth of people. Are the children of Abraham still among us? They are! Perhaps you are a friend or neighbor to a Jew. Perhaps you are Jewish yourself. A person is a Jew if his or her mother is Jewish, and the same for her mother, and the same for her mother, going all the way back to Sarah. Both simple and wonderful, I know.

If you ask me, the Jews are the first and lasting miracle of God. There was no reason to suppose that the voice Abraham heard was telling the truth, could make good on its promise. Later, when Abraham's descendants formed a small, insignificant, helpless nation in the eastern Mediterranean, surrounded by powerful and dangerous empires, there was no reason to suppose that they would last another century, much less twenty or thirty more. Later still, when those same descendants were crushed, defeated, and expelled from their homeland, would anyone have placed a bet on their surviving for millennia to come, scattered in exile across the world? Yet they did, and they do.

Empires rise and fall. Nations come and go. Peoples are born and die. But the Jews endure. Why?

Because God keeps his word.

And if God kept his word to Abraham, you can bet your life he'll keep his word to you. God's word to you is Christ, his only Son. And as Saint Paul once wrote, all the promises of God find their Yes in Christ. Christ is God's Yes to Abraham and Yes to Israel and Yes to you, too.

Abraham is the father of faith because when we set our hopes on God's promise in Christ, we are doing just what Abraham did right at the beginning. We are staking our future on God's word. There's no better decision you could make. The Jews are living proof.

*Yours in Christ,*
*a fellow pilgrim*

✝

*Dear future saint,*

I've not forgotten your question. But you've already raised another one: If the descendants of Abraham and Sarah are Jews, and the Jews are the people of God, then what does that make the rest of the world? What does that make *us*, if "we" are not Jews by birth?

Good question. There's one big answer I can only gesture at now, but there are a couple other important points to make as well.

To begin, everyone who is not a Jew—meaning everyone who does not descend biologically from Abraham, his son Isaac, and *his* son Jacob—is a gentile. A gentile simply refers to a person who is not Jewish. The Bible recognizes that there are all kinds of people in the world: Syrians, Ethiopians, Canaanites, Arabs, Greeks, Babylonians, and more. But unlike our culture, which uses the category of race or ethnicity to describe membership in larger people groups, the Bible divides humanity into two and only two groups: Jew and gentile. You are either one or the other. Every other category is secondary to this one. Why? Well, because it is a distinction that God himself created. And to belong to one or the other signals whether one does or does not belong to God's chosen people.

I realize this sounds odd to you. Does it also sound exclusive? Does it sound as though God did something rather unfair when he carved out a single family from among all the families of the earth to be *his*? The implication would appear to be that the *rest* of the human family—all the families that aren't Abraham's—are therefore not God's, too.

You're not wrong. How it appears is how it is.

Imagine yourself living four or eight or twelve hundred years before Christ, in eastern Asia or western Africa or northern Europe. You are born to a family or tribe, you go about your days, you try to be wise and just, you seek truth and piety as best you can. Do you belong to God's people?

No, you do not. Belonging to God's people, in this case, is a matter of birth— or chance, if you prefer to call it that—not choice. You either are or are not a member of Abraham's family, and Abraham's family is God's family. If you are not a member of the one, then you are not a member of the other. End of story.

Now—this is very much not the end of the story. For the good news about Jesus is that he opens up the family of Abraham to all the families of the earth:

to gentiles, as you now know such people are called. God promised Abraham that all the world's nations would find blessing in him, did he not?

If, then, you had to sum up the gospel with a single word, what would it be? My choice: *adoption*. Gentiles are adopted as *Abraham's* children, and all people, gentiles and Jews both, are adopted as *God's* children. To be adopted by one is to be adopted by the other. As the old children's song goes:

> Father Abraham had many sons,
> Many sons had Father Abraham.
> And I am one of them,
> And so are you.
> So let's all praise the Lord!

I'll have more to say about this later. I mention it now to avoid confusion.

But I hesitate to let you off the hook so easily. I want you to sit in the strangeness of God's calling of Abraham—what the church calls the "election" of Israel. It has long perplexed gentiles, whether or not they are Christians. Some have called it a scandal: the sheer befuddling oddity of God selecting a single people in the world as his own, seemingly to the exclusion of all others. Nor does God's promise to Israel have an expiration date. It's an everlasting promise. Jews will be Jews till the end of time. The descendants of Abraham, Isaac, and Jacob will always possess a unique and incomparable relationship to the God of Abraham, Isaac, and Jacob. You might describe it as the status of the firstborn. Some of us may be in the family, but we are younger or adopted siblings. We had better accept this as a fact rather than wish it weren't the case. That way lies anxiety and resentment, not gratitude or affection.

(As it happens, the Bible is full of stories of older and younger sons, riven by envy and division. These stories almost never end well. One way to think about God's work in Christ, to make us all children of a single Father, is that it is his final act to reconcile perennially estranged siblings. He wants us to get over ourselves and get along, once and for all!)

This picture of God may challenge how you thought of God beforehand. If so, that's good. God isn't an idea. He's alive, more alive than you or I. Because he's alive, he has a certain character, and this character doesn't always line up with our expectations. If you want to know God, then you have to *get* to know him, just like any other relationship.

But here's one more thing about him. At a point later in the biblical story, Moses is speaking to Israel, reminding the people about God's choosing of Israel when he called Abraham. Moses asks: Was it because the Jews were especially impressive that God chose them? Or morally upright? Or numerous, or powerful, or deserving? No. That's not why.

Moses gives the real answer: "Because he loves you."

We are not told why the Lord loves Israel. But this is just how love is. Why do you love the people you love? If you listed all their good qualities, would that add up to an explanation? I don't think so. Love is mysterious. God is likewise mysterious. But he is a God of love. In fact, the Bible says, he is love. This is why he chose Israel. Because he loved them then and loves them still.

If you know this, deep in your heart, then you will be well on your way to knowing and loving God for who he really is.

*Yours in Christ,*
*a fellow pilgrim*

*Dear future saint,*

You're beginning to see why we are talking about this. Abraham and Israel are not a history lesson. Or, if you want to put it that way, then when we talk about the Jews we aren't discussing someone else's history. We are discussing *your own family history*. The Jewish people are your people, even if you're not a Jew. The Jew Jesus makes this possible. More, he makes it a reality.

The major point for now is this: If you want to know God, you must know Christ. If you want to know Christ, you must know the Jews. If you want to know the Jews, you must know the Bible. This is one reason why the Bible is so important to being a Christian.

But let me put the point a different way. To know God in Christ isn't just to know *about* the people who produced Jesus. That sort of knowledge will get you only so far. A scholar can know about Jesus and the Jews the way an astronomer can know about distant solar systems. Such knowledge is good, but it's not what we're looking for here.

We want the real article: up close and personal knowledge of the one and only God there is, the God who created the universe, the God who made you and me, the God who loves us all and who—in the words of Saint Augustine, a great Christian teacher—is nearer to us than we are to ourselves.

To know God means, in short, to be part of God's people. We come to know him through being one among *them*. It is as though God made himself the head of a vast household, the Father of a great family. If what we want is access to him—better than that, a relationship with him—then we need to dwell in his house. We need to join the family.

As you've seen, the Jews are the family of God, because they are the family of Abraham. Before I explain how it is that Jesus is the way gentiles join Abraham's family, I want you to catch a glimpse of why God called Abraham. He was starting a family. This family would be different from other families. It would be a family founded on knowing and loving God. With God at the head of this family, other families might take notice. They might peak over the fence, wondering what life was like inside the house.

They might even knock on the door.

*Yours in Christ,*
*a fellow pilgrim*

GOD CALLS A SPECIAL PEOPLE

**13**

*Dear future saint,*

We face a fork in the road. One way goes forward, the other backward. First we'll go forward, into the life and history of Israel, then backward, into what happened before Abraham.

I'm sure you already have some sense of what happened with God and Israel after Abraham, but I want to give you a snapshot in any case. Once I've done this, we'll look over our shoulder at the how and the why, which will begin to loom large in the story.

The story in question runs from Abraham to Jesus. It's found in the Old Testament, which makes up three-fourths of the Bible. The Old Testament is a collection of writings that together form the sacred Scriptures of Israel. It is very important that you have clear in your mind, here at the start, that what Christians call the Old Testament is not a second-class citizen compared to the New Testament. It's not less important or insignificant. It's not about some other people. It's about your people. It's not about some other God. It's about your God. The God of Christian faith is the God of Jesus, and the God of Jesus is the God of Israel. The God of the New Testament is one and the same as the God of the Old Testament. How could it be otherwise? There's only one God, and God doesn't change.

Roughly speaking, the Old Testament consists of three groups of texts. They're called the Law, the Prophets, and the Writings. You'll find reference to these all over the New Testament, on the lips of Jesus and the apostles. So much so that C. S. Lewis calls the New Testament but "a tissue of quotations" from the Old Testament. Reading the latter, you realize "how constantly Our Lord repeated, reinforced, continued, refined, and sublimated" what came before him, and "how very seldom He introduced a novelty."

Why? Because in the first century, the writings we now call the Old Testament were simply *Scripture* for Israel, and thus for Jesus and the apostles. The first generation of the church had no inkling of a New Testament, much less of a need for one. They had the Law of Moses; they had prophets like Isaiah, Jeremiah, and Ezekiel; they had the psalms of King David and the proverbs of King Solomon. Jesus and the apostles taught the early church how to read these writings in service of faithful Christian living; in turn, the early church saw how these writings mysteriously foretold the coming of Jesus and the good news about him.

Think of the Old Testament as a map. Maps always have a legend or key. Jesus is the key that opens the Old Testament for gentiles; Jesus is the legend for understanding the terrain: the terms and symbols, persons and events that fill the scroll spread out before us. Almost like a treasure map from a novel or movie.

There are riches to be found. You just have to know where to look.

*Yours in Christ,*
*a fellow pilgrim*

## 14

*Dear future saint,*

Here is a sketch of Israel's story, beginning in the twelfth chapter of Genesis, which is the first book of the Bible.

God calls Abraham, and Abraham obeys. He goes to a land he knows not where, for reasons he knows not why. Eventually his special calling by God, the unique promise God made to him, is expressed in a ritual. This ritual seals the relationship between God and Abraham: it binds them together forever. God will forever be *Abraham's God*, and Abraham's descendants will forever be *God's people*. This binding relationship is called a "covenant." (The sign of the covenant is circumcision, an indelible mark in Abraham and his sons forever. The scope and implications of the circumcision commandment will reappear in a major way later in the story.)

Sometimes a covenant is like a contract: you hold up your end of the bargain and I'll hold up mine. This covenant is different. It's unconditional. Recall that God doesn't make any requests or stipulate any conditions for Abraham. He makes a promise, issues a command, and off Abraham goes. What God does with Abraham is create a new future—almost out of thin air. It's a future God vows to make himself. And as I've said, when God makes a vow, he keeps it. God is faithful.

So this covenant isn't subject to negotiation; there's no fine print, nor are there escape clauses for either party. God and Abraham are stuck with each other. The election of Israel is, in the words of Saint Paul, *irrevocable*. If this is a deal, there are no takebacks. If it's a marriage, there are no divorce proceedings (much less a prenup). As you'll see later, God doesn't believe in divorce, and here God walks the walk: he would never and shall never divorce his beloved bride. He is love and he is faithful. Whatever Israel might do—whatever you and I might do—he will never leave. Never.

In one sense this is the whole story of the Bible, the Old Testament included. For this reason many Jews and Christians have found the essence of the Bible's story in a curious little book called the Song of Songs. On its face, the Song is a love story between a man and a woman (it's told from her perspective, in her voice). In a deeper sense the characters in the book stand for God and God's people. Try reading it that way sometime. Here are three things you'll walk away with.

GOD CALLS A SPECIAL PEOPLE

First, the love between God and Israel is a passionate, intimate business. God isn't lifeless or loveless; nor is his relationship with Abraham's children. It's a rather stormy affair.

Second, the love between God and Israel is a cycle of pursuit and distress, possession and loss, desire and disappointment, climax and frustration, fulfillment and bereavement. It's back and forth, to and fro. In this world, life with God, love for God, is never a matter of final arrival. We're always coming up short. We're always left wanting, panting for more.

Third, the love between God and Israel is, in the end, invincible. It is unquenchable and therefore unbreakable. The Song says that love is stronger than death. Indeed it is. The gospel of Jesus is one long expansion of this simple claim. Death cannot defeat true love. True love is God's love for God's people. No matter the slings and arrows of this life, no matter our pain or sorrow in this world, nothing—*nothing*, not in heaven or on earth—can separate the people of God from the love of God.

For some of us, this truth is like rain in the midst of a drought. For others, it is difficult to accept. Some part of us resists it. Whichever describes you, I pray you receive it for the good news it is. Know God's love in your own life, in your heart and mind and soul and body. There is nothing sweeter.

*Yours in Christ,*
*a fellow pilgrim*

*Dear future saint,*

Forgive me. I told you I would give you a sketch of Israel's story, but the love in the story—for it is a love story, a divine romance, a cosmic drama—carried me away from my task. Here's the story in a nutshell, best as I can tell it. (I'll be skipping over a lot, mind you; the best way to learn the details is to read for yourself, ideally with others and under the guidance of a pastor or parent or trusted older believer.)

Sarah, Abraham's once-barren wife, gives birth to Isaac, the son promised by God to this elderly couple. Isaac grows up and marries Rebekah, who gives birth to twins: Esau and Jacob. Jacob carries the line of God's promise forward; in fact, he receives a second name: Israel. From him come twelve sons, whose names are the names of the twelve tribes of Israel. This is why, when you read "Israelites" in an English translation of the Old Testament, the original Hebrew has the phrase "the sons of Israel." For the people of God are, at one and the same time, the twelve tribes of Israel and the twelve sons of Jacob—for Jacob *is* Israel, and his sons stand for all his future children. (This relationship of "standing for" is an important one in the biblical story and in the Christian faith. One person can stand for another, before God and before other people. We'll be coming back to this.)

By a winding path, Jacob's sons and their families—which, you now understand, just means the whole of Israel—end up in Egypt. For a good while they live and flourish among the Egyptians. But at some point the Egyptian people forget to show them honor and affection, and they begin to be oppressed and exploited. Eventually they become slaves. Yet God has not abandoned them. The Bible says that God hears their cries and "remembers"—keeps faith with—his covenant with Abraham. Accordingly, he raises up a great leader named Moses to deliver and teach his people. God shows himself to Moses in the wilderness (this is the burning bush, which you may know about) and commands Moses to go to the Egyptian king, called the pharaoh, and to say to him on God's behalf: "Let my people go!"

A great contest ensues: a contest between the God of Moses and the gods of Pharaoh. Now, are the gods of Egypt "real" gods? I'll say more about this later, but there are two things to say now. On one hand, no: there is only one God—only one all-powerful, all-knowing, all-good Source and Savior of everything in the universe. On the other hand, yes: there *are* other powers besides God that exist beyond this world that nonetheless act in it. Some are good and some are evil. We would do well to interpret "the gods" in this way. In which case God really is doing battle in Egypt. He really is showing Egypt, and Israel, and even the world, who's boss. Because if Israel's God can't lay waste to Egypt's gods, how could he be the one true God that Abraham and Moses say he is?

God wins in short order. He displays his incomparable power to rescue Israel from slavery through ten plagues that frighten and devastate the tyrannical Egyptians. At last Pharaoh relents: he lets God's people go. And go they do, liberated from their chains by, the Bible says, the Lord's "mighty hand" and "outstretched arm." Pharaoh gives pursuit and chases the people to the Red Sea, where God miraculously parts the waters for them to walk through on dry land. Pharaoh and his army are drowned in the depths of the sea.

God's people are free.

This event is called the exodus. It is one of a handful of founding events in the history of Israel. First comes Abraham's calling. Then comes God's emancipation of Abraham's children from "the house of bondage," as Scripture calls it. Then comes the Law of Moses. I'll tell you about that in the next letter.

The thing to grasp is this. We have learned that God is love and God is faithful. Now we see that God is mighty to save, for he is the great Liberator and Deliverer. Israel knows him as Savior and Rescuer, the breaker of chains who responds to the suffering of his people. The loving and faithful God hates injustice and smashes the bonds of servitude. He *frees*.

At the Red Sea the women of Israel lead the people in a song that shouts their joy and thanks to God their Redeemer. In every age and place since, people have joined in this song of freedom, for wherever the news of Jesus goes the news of the exodus goes with it. In a sense they are the very same news: the liberating God has come down, drawn near, to liberate his people. For this is just what he always does, since it is who he is at the core. We gaze on his face in Jesus. The God who raised Jesus from the dead is the God who first brought Israel up from the grave of slavery in Egypt: the God of Moses.

Sing a song of praise to the Lord! Sing with Miriam and Moses the song of Israel's joy:

> "Who is like you, O LORD, among the gods?
>   Who is like you, majestic in holiness,
> terrible in glorious deeds, doing wonders?"

No one and nothing, is the answer. And so we sing:

"The Lᴏʀᴅ is my strength and my song,
    and he has become my salvation;
this is my God, and I will praise him,
    my father's God, and I will exalt him."

Amen.

*Yours in Christ,
a fellow pilgrim*

GOD CALLS A SPECIAL PEOPLE

*Dear future saint,*

The God and Father of Jesus Christ is the God of Abraham and the exodus: the One who elects Israel as his people and delivers them from slavery in Egypt. What comes next?

I left something out in my sketch of the story. When Moses goes to Pharaoh, speaking on God's behalf, he doesn't just command him to free the people. He says: "Let my people go *so they may worship me.*"

That makes a difference, doesn't it?

God liberates Israel from bondage with a purpose. This purpose is to know him, to love him above all things, to worship him alone. Remember: he is their God, they are his people. Freedom *from* chains, freedom *for* God. Now is the time for a second covenant.

So the Lord leads Israel to Mount Sinai. There Moses ascends the mount and meets and speaks with God. Storm cloud, thunder, and lightning descend. The voice of God issues commands to the people through Moses. He says: Do these things, and you will be blessed; do not do them, and there will be consequences. The people agree. Between God and Israel a covenant is ratified, only this covenant is conditional. It's an if-then agreement. And it's centered around what the Bible calls "Torah," meaning the Law of Moses.

Broadly speaking, the Torah is the first five books of the Bible: Genesis, Exodus, Leviticus, Numbers, and Deuteronomy. Specifically, it consists of comprehensive regulations for how God's people are to organize their life in common: marriage, children, eating, hygiene, clothing, animals, war, politics, ethics, worship—all of it. Some of these laws may seem obvious to you: don't murder, don't steal, don't lie, don't commit adultery. Some may seem "ancient" or "tribal": here's how to sacrifice an animal in the temple, here's what to do when a woman is on her period, that sort of thing. And some may seem strange or arbitrary: don't eat pork, don't eat shellfish, don't work on Saturdays, circumcise baby boys on the eighth day after their birth.

So what's this all about? What's God up to?

I've got a one-word answer for you: *holiness.*

Over and over, God tells Israel that they shall be holy as he, the Lord, is holy. Holiness is the number one job description for Abraham's children.

The people of God must be holy, as the God whose people they are is holy. If they're not holy, then what makes them different from any other people?

To be holy is to be set apart. It means to be *other*, different, distinct, unlike the rest. God is holy because there is no one and nothing like him. There are no other actual gods, and if there are "gods," then they have nothing in common with him. God is all-good, all-knowing, all-powerful, all-just. Everything comes from him. Everything is for him. He is love. Nothing remotely compares.

Israel is supposed to be similar. Whatever peoples or families or nations there may be in the world, Israel should stick out like a sore thumb. People should look at Israel and cock their heads. They should wonder, "What's up with *them*?" It should be crystal clear who God's people are just by looking at the world at a glance. There are gentiles and there are Jews. According to Moses, you should be able to pick the Jews out of a crowd. They should stand out.

This is what Torah is for. In everything that makes a human community human, Israel's election as God's people should shine in their lives like neon lights. What they eat, how they work, how they marry and bury, how they raise children, how they treat others, how they worship God. All of it, together, is a cue to the gentile world: *We are different. We know God. If you want to know God, too, know him through us.*

Israel, according to the prophet Isaiah, is meant to be a light to the gentiles. Moses says Israel is a priestly kingdom. What does a priest do? He stands between the people and God, representing each to the other: God to the people and the people to God. What the Torah shows us is that part of God's purpose in calling Israel to be his people is to use Israel as a kind of mirror to show himself to the world. When the world sees Israel, they should see not just *difference*. In Israel's difference they should see *God*. Israel says to the world (and with a straight face!): You can't see God, but if you have seen *us*, you have seen him, too. Israel is the moon to God's sun, reflecting the divine light to a world blanketed in darkness.

This is why Torah is a gift and a blessing. It's the charter of God's holy people. Should they obey, the world will come to know God because of Israel. As Jesus himself put it: "Salvation is from the Jews."

Yours in Christ,
a fellow pilgrim

*Dear future saint,*

It's somewhat unfair of me to say this, but you fell for the bait. You wrote what so many Christian versions of Israel's story end up saying: *Things didn't go as planned.*

The thought may come naturally, but it's a dead end. Here's why.

First, because it's God's plan. In this sense, everything happened "according to plan"—granting that God's ways are not our ways and that God's plan permits and incorporates our faults and failures in the service of goods we neither understand nor anticipate.

Second, because your phrasing makes it sound like Israel was nothing but a failure, and that's nonsense. Israel's history is like the history of every other people, because it is an altogether human history. It contains glories and triumphs alongside defeats and disasters. The note of tragedy, if there is one, comes from our elevated expectations. We want God's people to *succeed.* We want victory, through and through, not the mess and muddle of human beings.

Third, because there *are* successes in Israel's story. Joshua and Ruth, Deborah and Joseph, Samuel and Hannah, Elijah and Amos, Jeremiah and Esther: these are only some of the heroes—better, saints—that fill the pages of Israel's Scriptures. They are the great cloud of witnesses that surrounds the people of God as they journey into the future. They are the models of faith to whom we look for encouragement and inspiration. Indeed, the church has long believed, following the teaching of Jesus, that they are not merely dead in the grave but alive in heaven with the Lord. They aren't just cheering us on. They're praying for us, every one of them, every day of our lives.

That doesn't sound like failure to me.

Does this mean Israel lived up to God's glorious Sinai vision of holiness for his people? No. She fell short. I'll get to that in another letter. But for now I want to warn you against a terrible temptation some Christians are prone to: namely, using Israel as a foil. What do I mean by this?

I mean thinking of Israel as the *negative* example by contrast to the *positive* example of the church. As if the Jews got everything wrong whereas Christians get everything right. Surely you see the problem. Christians get just about everything wrong, too! Nor did the Jews fail to get some things right. Which means it's not them versus us. It's them and us, together. Where they succeeded, we hope to imitate their example; where they failed, we look to learn from their mistakes. In all things we think of them as our mothers and fathers in the faith, our predecessors in God's great family. Jesus and his apostles certainly thought of them that way. You and I should too, as should all Christians—especially gentiles. We're adopted, after all. We should show respect for those who came before us and made our lives possible.

Yours in Christ,
a fellow pilgrim

*Dear future saint,*

Here's what comes next, albeit on fast-forward.

After leaving Sinai and approaching the promised land—meaning the land God promised to give to Abraham's descendants—the people balk at the idea of seizing it. They fear the power and numbers of its inhabitants. For their lack of faith, God punishes them: the generation that left Egypt will die before entering the land; they will wander in the wilderness for forty years before entering and taking the land. Yet there is grace in judgment. God provides food in the desert for his pilgrim people: manna from heaven, together with quail.

Once the time is up, a man named Joshua, the successor to Moses, leads the people into the land. They walk across the Jordan River on dry land just as they had across the Red Sea, which God parted when they came out of Egypt. Following the battle of Jericho, they begin to possess and settle the land promised by the Lord to the family of Abraham. As they do so, the Lord fights for them; it is *his* land to give to whomever he chooses. And just as he issues judgment on the land's current inhabitants, so he will one day issue a similar judgment on Israel, expelling them, too, from the land.

For some years the scattered tribes across the land are ruled by "judges," leaders who rise up on special occasions, in response to need or threat, to defend the people or make decisions. This is a disorderly and violent time. The people want peace, justice, stability. They want a king.

Samuel, a judge and prophet, is distraught. For God is Israel's king. Is not their request for a human king a rejection of God? It is, God says. They shall have their king, and they shall see what human kings are made of. Yet there is a deeper plan at work. The people's rejection of God will turn out to be their salvation. Though they mean it for evil, God means it for good.

At this point we are about a thousand years before the birth of Jesus. Before I fill in a few of the details, let me give you the big picture.

First, Israel becomes a great kingdom. Then it divides in half in a kind of cold civil war between north ("Israel") and south ("Judah"). A foreign empire, Assyria, comes and destroys the Northern Kingdom, despoiling its people and carrying them off into exile. The Southern Kingdom withstands the onslaught, but little more than a century later another empire, Babylonia, does the same thing to them. This second exile appears to be the end of God's people. Yet how can this be, if God's promise to Abraham holds true?

It can't. It is as intolerable for the Lord as it is for Israel. Once again, therefore, God delivers his people. God raises up *another* empire, Persia, which conquers the Babylonians. Not only this, but the Persian emperor, a man named Cyrus, decides to send the exiled Israelites back to their land. You can imagine how they felt about that. It was a miracle, pure and simple. God's faithfulness knows no bounds. Even when all hope is lost, the good news of God's love resounds like a thunderclap. God does what only God can do: make a way out of no way, something from nothing, life from death.

The return from exile is like another exodus. The people return rejoicing. One psalm describes it:

> When the LORD restored the fortunes of Zion,
>      we were like those who dream.
> Then our mouth was filled with laughter,
>      and our tongue with shouts of joy;
> then they said among the nations,
>      "The LORD has done great things for them."
> The LORD has done great things for us;
>      we are glad.

This happens a little over five hundred years before the birth of Jesus. From here till Jesus, although Israel is grateful to be back in the land, life becomes rather dismal. Things are not as they once were or as they ought to be. One empire after another conquers the land and occupies Abraham's inheritance, usually exploiting the poor and insulting the Lord. After Persia come the Greeks (about three hundred years before Jesus), who are replaced by the Romans (just sixty years before Jesus). It's as though these great powers are exchanging the land of Israel like an unwanted gift.

Put yourself in Israel's shoes. How angry would you be? How resentful? What would you be willing to do, if the result would be kicking out these pagans who mock and manipulate your way of life? Would you be willing to take up arms? What would you ask God to do? Would you trust God to keep his promises? Would you lose faith in them?

This is the world into which Jesus is born. When Jesus comes on the scene, his land and his people are under imperial occupation by Roman soldiers. They are required to pay taxes to the Roman emperor, called Caesar, with coins inscribed with Caesar's image. Do you know what Caesar calls himself, what titles they write under his image? *Son of God. Savior. Lord.*

The great American writer Herman Melville once penned a novel, *Moby-Dick*, in which a character sees the world as one great cosmic joke. The suffering, the horror, the chaos: it's all absurd, from top to bottom. It makes no sense, and the joke's on you if you try to make sense of it. It's a fool's errand, an exercise in futility.

This is how you might feel, living as a Jew in the promised land. Staring down at Caesar's "divine" image on a coin in your hand, a coin you're made to pay just to have the right to live in the land. Land that belongs to *you*, by God's gift, not to these pagans from across the Mediterranean Sea. It's a bad joke.

So what are you going to do about it? Better yet: What is God?

*Yours in Christ,*
*a fellow pilgrim*

## 19

*Dear future saint,*

Unfortunately, and despite your wishes, the cliffhanger I left you with isn't ready to be answered just yet. I want you to sit with it for a while. Before we answer the lingering questions—before we see how God answers them—we have other matters to address.

One such matter is a final comment on Israel, filling in a few of the remaining gaps. Then, once we've done that, we need to look over our shoulder, as I promised a few letters back. There's something very important we haven't spoken about yet, and its importance has begun to haunt the story I've been telling.

But first I want to say a word about the kings of Israel, followed in the next letter by the prophets who opposed them and the priests who ministered at God's temple.

Saul is Israel's first king. But he's a failure. So the Lord instructs Samuel to anoint Saul's successor, a young man named David. Anointing is a symbolic act; it involves pouring oil on someone's head as a sign of divine favor or royalty, or as an appointment to some important task. To be anointed is to be chosen by God, to stand in some special relationship to him, to be charged with a mission and an office. Not only kings are anointed in Israel; priests and prophets are, too.

David is a mighty warrior, on fire with passionate love for God, for Israel, for power, for women—not always in that order. After consolidating his rule in Jerusalem, which he makes his capital and home base (though he was born in Bethlehem, from the tribe of Judah), and after building a magnificent royal palace for himself, it occurs to David that he's done things in reverse. Here he is, living in luxury, while the Lord has no equivalent dwelling place. Ever since their time in Egypt, when a minister of Israel has sought to meet the Lord or offer sacrifices to him, he's done so in a tent, called the tabernacle. Its mobility was appropriate so long as Israel was on the move. But now Israel is in the land. Shouldn't the Lord have a home? And isn't David the right one to build it for him?

You'd think so; but God has other plans. A prophet named Nathan comes to David with a word from the Lord. He says: You suppose that God is in need of a house, and you are the man for the job. But God does not need a house, and he does not need you. But because the Lord chose you and loves you, he is going to build *you* a house. Not a house of cedar and gold, but a royal house: a dynasty.

Nathan says to David: Just as God made a promise to Abraham that his children would for all time be God's chosen people, so now God is making a promise to you that *your* children will always and for all time be kings over Israel. Like the first promise, this second promise is unconditional; it is a covenant between God and David initiated and maintained entirely from God's side. The kings of Israel will be sons of David; the "seed" of David will rule over Israel, from now till kingdom come.

Think for a moment about the very first sentence of the New Testament. The book is the Gospel according to Saint Matthew. Here is the opening verse of the opening chapter: "The book of the genesis of Jesus the Anointed, son of David, son of Abraham." Do you see? All this family history, all this talk of Israel, is absolutely crucial to knowing Jesus.

Jesus is Abraham's son, which means he is a Jew. Jesus is David's son, which means he is king of the Jews. And Jesus is anointed, which means he is chosen and set apart by the God of the Jews for a special mission or task. The Greek word for "anointed" is *christos*, or Christ; this is a translation of the Hebrew word *mashiach*, or Messiah.

Hence: "Jesus Christ" isn't a first and last name, like Rosa Parks or Jane Austen. It's a title, like Mahatma Gandhi and Queen Elizabeth. Matthew wants us to know from the start just who this Jesus is and what we should expect from him. He even gives us a hint, with the little word "genesis." It could be translated "lineage" or "genealogy," but it also suggests that whatever God is up to with Anointed-King Jesus is a radical new beginning, akin to the first book of the Old Testament, also called Genesis. If that book recounts both the creation of the world and the creation of Israel, what is God up to in the life of Jesus? What is his mission?

The questions keep piling up. We'll answer them soon enough.

*Yours in Christ,*
*a fellow pilgrim*

## 20

*Dear future saint,*

So much for kings. Two more groups to learn about.

One is the prophets. As Israel lived in the land, it had need not only for political leaders but also for religious leaders. A prophet was an Israelite who conferred with God and brought God's word to God's people. Sometimes this word was one of comfort or joy. Often it was one of judgment and rebuke. Rarely were prophets welcomed, for prophets were gadflies, willing to say anything so long as it was the truth of God. Accountable to God alone, prophets were often lonely, ostracized, and ignored. Occasionally they were arrested, punished, or killed. Being a prophet could be a miserable bargain.

Nevertheless, the prophets were at the heart of Israel's life, and their witness is the backbone of Israel's Scriptures. Since Moses and David spoke God's word to God's people through the Law and the Psalms, Jewish memory accorded them also the status of prophet. In this sense the entire Old Testament is one great prophetic testimony. When the New Testament refers to the writings of Israel as "all the prophets," this is why.

The second group you need to know is the priests. What is a priest? Depending on your experience with church, you may or may not be familiar with priests. Most Christians, past and present, have been led and taught by Christian priests—in which case, this may be old news to you. But if not, let me tell you.

In a previous letter I described the role of a priest as standing between God and the people, representing each to the other. A prophet does this, too, but in terms of *speech*: what the people have to say to God and what God has to say to the people. When a priest stands in the gap, it isn't about words. It's about sin. Sin and sacrifice.

What does the work of the priest look like? To the people, the priest represents the Lord's holiness, which is glorious and majestic in its spotless beauty and unstained purity. To the Lord, the priest makes offerings and sacrifices on behalf of the people's *unholiness*, their sins and stains and errors and evils. By God's mercy these offerings and sacrifices impart to the people what they need and desire in relationship to God: innocence, blamelessness, cleanness, purity, uprightness, holiness. They are washed and cleansed of every sin. They may stand in the presence of the Lord with a clear conscience.

GOD CALLS A SPECIAL PEOPLE

I wonder how this strikes you. It might strike you as odd or distant; why should burning up grain or killing an animal alter the standing of human beings before God? Or perhaps it strikes you as true to life: you recognize the strange alchemy of substitution, when one thing stands for another, or when one person's act makes good another's wrong, or when the voluntary loss of something you value works to "set things right," to make a balance where before there was imbalance.

In any case, sacrifice is a universal human practice, always and everywhere bound up in people's relationship (happy or complicated) with the gods. It should tell us something important, that God did not withhold sacrifices from his people but instructed them how to sacrifice rightly. This the priests did at the temple, day in day out, year after year, so long as the temple stood. (God did end up dwelling in a temple in Jerusalem: only it was built by David's son, King Solomon, not David.) After the first temple was destroyed and a second one built just like it, the priests got back to work.

In the time of Jesus and his apostles, temple sacrifices were a fact of life, taken for granted. Indeed, the apostles quickly began to use the language of temple and sacrifice to describe Jesus and what happened to him. Later they called him a priest, though a priest outside the usual mold. But if he wasn't an ordinary priest offering animal sacrifices in the temple, then what sort of priest was he? And what was it that he had to offer?

More questions. Keep asking. We're getting closer.

*Yours in Christ,*
*a fellow pilgrim*

**21**

*Dear future saint,*

You want to know about sin. The last letter closed with a reflection on priests and sacrifices, and sacrifices are offerings for sin. I've not yet homed in on the word "sin" in these letters. I told you, though, that something was haunting our story. This something was sin. Sin is what requires a backward glance. We need to know what sin is and where it comes from. Recall that the story of Israel and Abraham begins in the twelfth chapter of Genesis. We've yet to look at the eleven chapters that come before Abraham's arrival on the scene. Let's do that now.

As we do so, we must be vigilant about avoiding two great errors. Both errors make sin fundamental for understanding God, humanity, and the story of the Bible. Sin, however, is not fundamental. It is not the ground of our being, the source of our life, the invisible thread that runs through creation from beginning to end. That ground, that source, that thread is God. God *alone*. We know we have made a mistake if our words suggest that sin is foundational in a way that displaces God. On center stage is the Creator of heaven and earth. Sin is uninvited. It's unwelcome. It's an enemy and an interloper.

So this is one way the error runs: giving sin the starring role in the drama of creation rather than the Lord, who brings creation into being. Another version of the same error is to suppose that the story I've told in the previous letters, the story about God's election of Abraham and love for Israel, is merely God's way of responding to sin. No doubt God *does* respond to the problem of sin through his beloved people. But calling and caring for his people cannot be reduced to a plan to respond to sin. To do so misses the point entirely. To say that God chose Israel *solely to solve a problem* contradicts the Bible's teaching that God loves Israel for her own sake, as a husband loves his wife or a father loves his child. It undercuts and belittles the claim that Abraham was the friend of God. Are you a true friend if you see your friend as nothing but a means to an end?

No. Just as God creates the world out of love for its own sake, so God elects Abraham's children out of love for their own sake. He has plans and purposes, to bless them and to bless the world; if he didn't, he wouldn't be much of a *divine* father and friend—not to mention husband. But even as he executes mysterious and glorious plans for Israel and through Israel, the Lord remains her lover, and she (to use biblical language) remains the bride of his youth.

Don't forget this as we turn to creation and, later, to sin.

Yours in Christ,
a fellow pilgrim

# *three*

# God Creates the Heavens and the Earth

May God who, after having made such great things, put such weak words in my mouth, grant you the intelligence of His truth, so that you may raise yourselves from visible things to the invisible Being, and that the grandeur and beauty of creatures may give you a just idea of the Creator. For the visible things of Him from the creation of the world are clearly seen, and His power and divinity are eternal. Thus earth, air, sky, water, day, night, all visible things, remind us of who is our Benefactor.

—Saint Basil of Caesarea

## 22

*Dear future saint,*

The opening words of the Bible read: "In the beginning God created the heavens and the earth." What do they mean?

First, God is the Creator of everything that exists. Whatever there is, it comes from God. Put differently, if it isn't God, then God made it. This includes living entities (humans, chimpanzees, velociraptors, gnats, pigs, hawks, humpback whales, cedar trees, sunflowers), lifeless phenomena (rocks, rivers, air), whole ecosystems, matter itself. Everything in the universe, past, present, and future, has God for its Creator. Nothing is excepted.

Moreover, this includes whatever *isn't* in our universe. Suppose there are other universes: God is the Creator of those, too. Suppose, as the Bible teaches, that material universes are not the only realm that creatures live in. Call such a realm beyond our world "heaven." Angels and archangels and every manner of spiritual being dwell there. God made them. If they exist—and we ought to take for granted that what exists surpasses our wildest imaginations—then they come from God. When we call God "Creator," this is just what we mean. It all comes from him.

Some of us take this for granted. My children have never known a day in their lives without the self-evident certainty that every sunrise, every bumblebee, every man, woman, and child they stumbled upon was created by God. It's good they know this. But things we know without reflection can become "old hat" after a while. Don't let that happen to you.

Right now, consider that every atom in the cosmos comes from a single all-powerful Being who made every one of those atoms for no other reason than pure love. The great Italian poet Dante Alighieri wrote that divine love is the soul or animating fire of everything in existence: he calls it "the love that moves the sun and the other stars." What made our sun? Love. What made all the stars in the sky? Love. What made you? Nothing but love. All-powerful, all-consuming, shining, dazzling, fiery love.

To understand this even for a moment will have us down on our faces in adoration. A classic hymn describes this experience as being "lost in wonder, love, and praise." When you contemplate what God has made, do you find yourself lost in wonder and praise? You should. I certainly do. I can barely fathom it without tears coming to my eyes. The same God who brought this earth into existence brought you and me and everyone we love into existence, knitting us together in our mothers' wombs, fulfilling a plan he had from all eternity. What else can we do but worship him? There can be no end to our thanksgiving.

*Yours in Christ,*
*a fellow pilgrim*

## 23

*Dear future saint,*

No, I am not done with creation! It is a simple truth, yes, but it contains fathomless depths. So there is more to say.

Start here. To call God Creator is to say that he *alone* is Creator. My wife is the mother of our children, as I am their father. They have two sources, humanly speaking, not one. Or think of a collective project: a document or mosaic or piece of architecture. Many hands combine to produce it. It has no single source.

Not so with *the* creation. Creation considered as a whole has one and only one source: God. There is no second power alongside God that helps God's creative action. The opening chapter of Genesis says that God spoke the universe into existence. This is a helpful image, because it shows us, on one hand, that God required aid from no one for this particular job; and, on the other hand, that it was an utterly peaceful activity. God, we may say, sings us into being. He breathes forth a poem, and the poem is us: galaxies, planets, molecules, continents, animals, people. It is a beautiful poem, a glorious song, and somehow we are alive and in the middle of it.

(We do not know whether there is life, much less intelligent life, elsewhere in the universe. Either way, Christians know what to say. If there is *no* such life, then glory be to God: he has seen fit to populate a single planet in a single solar system with creatures made in his image! What a thing. And if there *is* such life, then glory be to God twice over: he has seen fit to populate his cosmos with many types of creatures and many kinds of life, all a reflection of his majestic and lovable generosity. Should there be such life and should we meet them one day, we will be meeting fellow creatures of the same Creator. Only one more occasion to thank him for his goodness as our common Lord.)

A further point: Apart from God and "prior" to creation, there is nothing but God, for God alone is the Creator and God alone exists (to borrow another phrase from the Bible) "from everlasting to everlasting." Most Christians I have known, including young children, grasp this point, but I want to be as clear as I can be about it.

Since her beginning, the church has taught that God creates "from nothing." What does this phrase mean?

Basically it means what I have already said: that everything apart from God comes from God. Put another way, there are only two categories of anything

GOD CREATES THE HEAVENS AND THE EARTH

in existence: God (called Creator) and everything else (called creatures). God has no source—he is not made, he is beyond time, he is self-sufficient, nothing threatens him—whereas creatures do have a source: God. So there is God and there is everything else, all of which comes from God. A pebble is a creature; an angel is a creature; a shark is a creature; a black hole is a creature. Think of something, and if it's not God, it's a creature. If it's not God and it's not a creature, it's not anything at all; it's a no-thing, which is nothing.

This is what the church means when she teaches that God creates "from nothing." It's not that there's a dark gooey something that God uses to make the universe. It's a denial: God *doesn't* create *from anything*. God neither needs nor uses raw materials. He speaks, and when he speaks, there *is*: "Let there be light; and there was light: and God saw that it was good." You and I need *stuff* to make *other stuff*. God doesn't. That's what makes him God.

In this sense, only God can create. We are, as J. R. R. Tolkien puts it, "sub-creators." We imitate God's creative activity whenever we write stories, paint portraits, make music—surely this is why children are incessant and delighted artists. They want to be like God! And in the best way.

Yours in Christ,
a fellow pilgrim

## 24

*Dear future saint,*

I understand why your first thought is the so-called big bang. That's not a bad mental image for the opening chapter of Scripture. But it's not quite what the church has in mind by the doctrine of creation from nothing.

God's act to create the world isn't a onetime event faraway in the deep cosmic past. If the universe began with the big bang, then, yes, that is the work of God; but, no, that isn't all Christians mean when they say "God is the Creator." Think of the world less as a wind-up clock and more as a long novel. The novelist is the author of the entire story, start to finish. What she does is bring *the whole narrative* into being. Page 500 is as much her creation as page 1. She is the source of the whole, not just the beginning, and not just while writing it.

The analogy is imperfect, but apply it to God and creation. God didn't just snap his fingers once upon a time. God *is* the Creator *of the whole.* "The whole" isn't just spatial (the "whole" universe, from one side to the other); it's also temporal (the "whole" span of cosmic time). Whenever this universe comes to an end, whether it's next year or ten billion years from now, *only then* would we (from our perspective in time) be able to say, "God is the author of that single entity called 'the universe.'" Only then would the story be concluded; only then would the last page have been written.

Now instead of a novel, think of a song. A song (not a recording) exists only so long as it is being sung. A song requires a *singer.* Creation is a song and God is the singer. It exists because he sings it—because he *is* singing it. If he weren't singing, we could not and would not be (*being*) sung. But we are sung. So his creating is like one continuous act of singing.

In sum, God *sustains* the universe at every moment of its existence. Which means that God, because he is Creator, sustains *you and me* at every moment of *our* existence. This is the point. God is our Creator right this minute, and he will remain our Creator to the end of our lives. It isn't something over and done with; it's not something that ever stops. God will remain our Creator even in heaven. For we will never cease to be creatures in need of his loving power to hold us in being, to impart life to our souls.

We are, in a word, absolutely dependent on God. This is what it means to be a creature. This is what it means that God is Creator. He does not need us. We need him. To need him is to recognize what we are and who he is. To love him is the only reply we have in response to the infinite gift he has given us. There was no need for you or me to exist, to be born and live in this world. Yet we do. Because he loves us.

This brings us to a final point. Because the Creator is God and because God is love, what God has made is good. God makes good things and only good things. When you look out at the world, you are looking at something good in itself, for it comes from God and is held in being by God. *To be* is good; *to be* is to be good. Whatever is, is good. Everything God has made is worthy of our reverence, devotion, service, and love. Every instinct humans have ever had to worship creation is rooted in wisdom. Creation cries out to be adored. What the Bible teaches is that we are to adore it *in God*. This means to give it honor, not as though it were worthy of worship, but as God's beautiful handiwork. As God's great gift. As God's good creation.

(There is an old line attributed to J. B. S. Haldane, an atheist British scientist from the twentieth century. It says that, based on the evidence of the universe, if there is a Creator, then he possesses an inordinate fondness for beetles and stars. Why this is supposed to be a "gotcha" line is beyond me. Clearly God *is* fond of beetles and stars. Are we supposed to think they are not worthy of our own fondness?)

There are many lessons to draw from all this; here are two. If you have trouble seeing the good in your neighbor, you are forever forbidden from denying this goodness to her, for you know that God is her Creator. God treasures her with the same burning affection that led him to make whatever you find most lovable in the world: a parent, a friend, a particular song, a favorite novel, the Grand Canyon, Niagara Falls.

But perhaps this isn't your problem. Perhaps you have trouble seeing the good in yourself. Perhaps you look inside, or in the mirror, and wonder whether there's anything good there. God be praised, let me be the one to tell you the answer.

You are God's beloved. You are God's creation. From before all time God knew he would make you, because he chose to make you. No one forced his hand. He chose because he loves you and wanted you to be one of the many unique and wondrous creatures to fill his good creation.

I can hardly write these words because of the sheer inexpressible joy they communicate. It is almost too good to be true. But it's not too good; or if it is, it's true regardless. *You exist because God made you, and God made you because he loves you.* Copy that sentence on every scrap of paper you have; scribble it on your hand; memorize it as a mantra. There is more to say, but everything else builds on that and assumes its truth.

If it weren't true, we'd be lost.

*Yours in Christ,*
*a fellow pilgrim*

## 25

*Dear future saint,*

Most Christians for most of Christian history have, whenever gathered together for worship, recited a creed together. A "creed" is a brief statement of the core of Christian faith. It comes from a Latin word that begins the statement: *credo*, "I believe." The Nicene Creed opens this way:

> I believe in one God,
> the Father, the Almighty,
> maker of heaven and earth,
> of all that is, seen and unseen.

And this is just how the Bible begins. Whatever exists, whether or not we can experience it with our senses, whether or not we can measure it with our devices, God is its Maker. Everything comes from God. God is Creator.

I want to linger for another moment on this important confession. Because you might mistake the teaching as primarily about us, the creation. Which it is: it is about us. It tells us some of the most important things we need to know about ourselves. You and I are made by God and for God. Our home is in God. We are beloved. We are dependent. We need God, every second of every day, if we are going to be happy or good, much less both. Very little is worth knowing more than this.

But we don't put trust in ourselves; we don't confess faith in creation. We believe in *God*, and the God we believe in is *Creator*. This means that coming to understand something about our nature as created beings means coming to understand something about the nature of the God who created us. Let's think a bit more about him, then.

I have said the following: God is the source of time and space and matter. He is the source of this universe, any other universe that might exist, and heaven itself—wherever creatures like angels dwell, whatever it means to say they dwell there. But not only *things* come from him. *Meaning* comes from him: intelligence, action, emotion; goodness, truth, beauty. Everything comes from God, which is just another way of saying that everything *good* comes from God. As the letter of Saint James (a man who knew Jesus before he went to the cross, for he was called the Lord's own brother) puts it: "Every good endowment and every perfect gift is from above, coming down from the Father of lights with whom there is no variation or shadow due to change."

In short, we learn some very important things about God when we say that he is Creator of heaven and earth. What do we learn?

First, God is all-powerful. This is what the word "almighty" or "omnipotent" means. Don't think of God at the end of a line of increasingly strong entities, as though just before God there is a being *almost* as strong as God is. God isn't merely the most powerful being. His power is on another level entirely. It's off the map; it breaks the scale; it's immeasurable and therefore incomparable. To say that God is all-powerful is to say that he lacks peer or rival. There are no threats to God. He is unthreatenable. He is wholly secure. Nothing can harm or interrupt God's plans or desires. God gets what God wants. He is the Lord.

Second, God is infinite. He has no limits. He is not hemmed in. To be God is to be boundless: there are no constraints or boundaries or restrictions on God, certainly not from the outside. For whatever is "outside" God comes from God. Nor is God like a human inventor, who may realize that his invention has evolved beyond his power or knowledge. That's not the way it works with God.

But I want you to see here what God's limitlessness means for creatures like you and me. When human beings give, we tend to lose what we give. If I give you a dollar, the dollar is no longer mine. If I give you a book, the book is no longer in my possession. If I give you my spot on the bus, I'm no longer sitting in it; you are. This is just what it means to live as limited (or "finite") human beings.

But this isn't how it works with God. God gives from an endless bounty. Because his resources are unlimited, he's never at a loss. He never runs out of what he's giving us. He just keeps on giving, and giving, and giving. His Being is like a bottomless well; we keep drawing up water to drink—cool, refreshing, satisfying water for parched lips after a long day's work—and the well never goes dry. The water keeps coming.

Third, then, God is generous. He did not have to create this world. No one made him. You and I did not need to exist. The theological word for this is "contingency." We are *contingent*, meaning we are not necessary. God exists necessarily, meaning God could not *not* exist. He wouldn't be God if he didn't exist. But he is God, so he does: always has, always will. For this reason the Bible calls him the One "who was and is and is to come." God himself says that his name is "I am that I am" or "I shall be what I shall be." God *is*.

Some Christian teachers have said we should think of God as *Being itself*, whereas you and I are just "beings": lowercase and in the plural. But that's not nothing. It's good to be a creature. I'm certainly happy I'm one. I'm glad to be alive. God didn't have to make me, or the people I cherish, or the stars in the sky, or the birds in the air, or anything else. But he did. He did because he wanted to, and he wanted to because he is love. Imagine God, if the comparison is not too much of a reach, as a bottle of champagne. What happens when you shake it up and pop off the cork? It explodes! It shoots out and up and everywhere. It runs over every which way. This is what creation is like. God is so *full*, so *rich*, so *much* that he simply runs over with being—and out come quarks and quacking ducks, moons and minerals, newborns and narwhals.

When I think of it, I want to sing. So do God's people. In the Psalms we read this:

> The heavens are telling the glory of God;
>     and the firmament proclaims his handiwork.
> Day to day pours forth speech,
>     and night to night declares knowledge.
> There is no speech, nor are there words;
>     their voice is not heard;
> yet their voice goes out through all the earth,
>     and their words to the end of the world.

The psalmist captures it perfectly. As usual, when you spend even a little time reflecting on God, you find yourself falling to your knees in praise. Get used to it.

*Yours in Christ,*
*a fellow pilgrim*

## 26

*Dear future saint,*

I imagine you've been sitting on this question for a while. "Faith and reason." "Religion and science." How do we relate these things? What does it mean to call God the Creator in a time when scientists have unveiled for us so many extraordinary mysteries and beauties and truths of the universe—where it comes from, how it works, what it's made of? Is God an attempt at an explanation that has now been replaced by better explanations?

The first thing to realize is that there is not and can never be "conflict" between "faith" and "science." Notice how abstract these words are. We should know what we mean by them if we want to know what we are talking about. If by "faith" we mean "things Christians believe," then it is obvious that some things Christians believe are going to be in error. Christians are human beings, and human beings lack perfect knowledge about reality.

If by "faith," however, we mean "the gospel," or "the good news of Christ," or in greatest detail, "what God has revealed to the church regarding himself and our salvation"—then, no, the truths of "science" will never be in "conflict" with this. Why?

Well, again, it all depends on what we mean by "science." Individual scientists might not believe in the gospel; that's a given. Some individual scientists might suppose that the conclusions they draw from their work imply or demonstrate the falsehood of the gospel; that's also a given.

What I want you to see, though, is what science truly is and why it neither will nor even could conflict with, much less disprove, the Christian gospel. Put differently, if Christianity is true, science will never uncover knowledge at odds with it; if Christianity is false (which, as you know, I deny; but this is a hypothetical), science would not be the way we would know it.

Science is something people do. It's a human activity of knowing. Accordingly, science has certain things it can seek to know and certain ways of knowing them. Just like human beings in general as well as other ways of knowing, science is limited. It has a specific scope. The kinds of things it can know about are called "empirical." Empirical things can be measured. They are known by the senses or detected by instruments, devices, and machines made by us for that purpose. (You might include math, which is not per se about empirical things, but we'll leave it aside for now.)

Over the last few centuries, scientists have shown a dizzying ability to produce human knowledge about empirical things. Christianity has no interest in denying or obstructing this. In fact, Christianity—Christian writings, Christian ideas, Christian institutions, Christian ways of imagining the nature of the world—is one of the main wellsprings of scientific investigation. Whatever we can know about the world through the methods of science, so long as it is done in moral ways and to moral ends, is all to the good.

Christian teaching about God as Creator, however, isn't the sort of thing that scientists can investigate by their methods. Whether or not God created the world is not a piece of information that might result from completing a math equation, looking through a telescope, or carbon-dating an artifact. It's just not that sort of question. In technical terms, it is a philosophical or "metaphysical" question. Scientists are not competent to answer it, because it lies outside the scope of their ways of seeking knowledge about the world.

Here's one way wise thinkers have articulated the difference I'm getting at. Scientists ask: How old is the universe? How did it begin? What is its extent? Is it expanding or contracting? What is it made of? What is its future? What are probable answers to these questions?

Here is what theologians and philosophers ask: *Why is there a universe at all?* That is, why is there *something* rather than *nothing*? No amount of empirical research can answer this question, or even take a single step toward answering it. It's a different question altogether than the ones scientists ask.

This is why saying "God is the source of the universe" or "God created the heavens and the earth" is, first, a theological statement; and, second, a confession of faith. It can be neither proved nor disproved by empirical methods. All claims about God are like this.

This also helps us to see that "God" is not a bad answer to a scientific question. God isn't a category mistake. Ancient philosophers and theologians were not stupid. They knew that whatever *material* factors make the universe what it is, the mere existence of these factors, even if we knew all of them, could never tell us *why* they are or what they are *for*—or, ultimately, *how* they exist at all, rather than simply not existing.

Abraham's children know the answer to such questions, whatever the scientists may say. The answer is that the Lord God made the world and upholds it in existence for the sake of love and his own marvelous glory. Believe it or not, this is the only kind of answer apt to the question. And it's the answer Jews and Christians have been giving for three thousand years and counting.

*Yours in Christ,*
*a fellow pilgrim*

+

## 27

*Dear future saint,*

There are many benefits of realizing that theologians and scientists speak in different registers. One is that you can revel in the wonders of scientific knowledge with a free and happy conscience. Every time a Christian learns from scientists some empirical fact or feature about the world, she should cry out, *Ad maiorem Dei gloriam!* To the greater glory of God!

Another benefit, at least for some believers, is being freed from a picture of the world that can feel like a burden or restriction. This picture we will call "scientism." Scientism doesn't mean believing reputable scientific work. Scientism means believing that science and science alone tells us true things about the world. Such drivel doesn't call for much debunking on my part; you already know that science can't tell you what love is, or the value of a newborn child, or why Rembrandt's painting of the prodigal son is beautiful, or why the death of God's saints is precious in his eyes.

Nevertheless, many educated Christians today feel as though a very powerful entity called "science" sets the terms for what they're allowed to believe while remaining a reasonable person. No one wants to be a fanatic, a zealot, a fundamentalist, a weirdo. No one wants to be deplorable. Scientism becomes a sort of unspoken or unofficial form of social pressure hemming us in, telling us all the silly things we shouldn't admit to believing. Ever so slowly it closes the circle on anything we might believe that science can't confirm.

Now, eventually this circle will close on beliefs like "resurrection" and "incarnation" and even "God." At that point, there are no Christian beliefs left. You're no longer a Christian if you've given up faith in those. What's the point then?

Fortunately, scientism is not true. So you don't have to feel the pinch of its straitjacket. It's not in charge of what are sometimes called "supernatural" beliefs. Science is about the natural world. What is above or outside of the space-time continuum falls beyond its range of competence.

So let me put in a word for a little weirdness here.

The Bible testifies on its every page that the world God made is teeming with life. This life is not only yours or mine, or the life of our planet. The catchall term here is "angels." Traditionally angels are understood to be intelligent spirits whose native home is not this universe but elsewhere. By "spirits"

I mean, or rather the church teaches, that angels are not composed of matter. They are "supernatural" or "spiritual" and thus not the kind of thing a scientist might study. Yet on occasion they interact with our world, even with us. Again, open your Bible to a random page, and likely as not, you will be staring at a story in which angels are up to stuff in our universe.

Some Christians think talk of angels is a holdover from a mythical past, before science and enlightenment and the modern world came along. That's bogus. If God is the Creator of anything and everything that exists; if God became a human being like you and me; if Jesus, that human being, died and rose to new life; if the gospel is true; if the Bible that gives us the gospel is trustworthy—why in the world would we not believe in angels? Why would they be somehow beneath us?

Besides, doesn't it make more sense, logically speaking, if we humans (or we earth-creatures) aren't alone in existence? Isn't it reasonable that the infinite and all-powerful God made creatures whose mode of existence surpasses our ways of knowing? Doesn't it *fit* that reality is full to the brim and overflowing with life rather than limited to our lowly globe or our little old universe? Don't the presence and activity of spiritual beings who sometimes interject themselves into human affairs make better sense of the innumerable stories, testimonies, memories, folk songs, and religious teachings of every human society and culture we know of than the alternative?

I think so, anyway. As have God's people from the very beginning. The cosmos is populated. Science isn't going to tell you otherwise. Use the eyes of faith. You'll be surprised what you see.

*Yours in Christ,*
*a fellow pilgrim*

**28**

✝

*Dear future saint,*

I get it. Things have gotten spooky. We're not in Kansas anymore. Let me give the last word on creation to someone with far more credibility than I possess.

Julian of Norwich is one of the wisest teachers in the church's long history. She lived a little less than seven hundred years ago. She was an "anchoress," a title that means she withdrew from public society in order to be alone with God: to fast, to pray, to worship, to know the Lord with an intimacy that forsakes all others. Like a marriage. In effect, Julian married Christ and spent the rest of her life utterly devoted to knowing him more deeply—till death.

Only in this case death wasn't a parting from her lover. It was her final union with him. (Remember: life through death.)

While Julian was still young, she grew terribly ill and felt herself to be near death. During this time she experienced a series of visions. Once she recovered she recorded these visions with painstaking detail, then years later, after much prayer and contemplation, she expanded on these visions—she called them "showings"—with profound theological insight. What she wrote is one of the most beautiful Christian writings in the English language, indeed in any language.

The work is called *Revelations of Divine Love.* You should read it. Lend Julian your ear as we meditate on the goodness of the Creator and of his creation.

Julian describes her first "showing" or revelation this way:

> Our Lord showed me a spiritual vision of his familiar love. I saw that for us he is everything that we find good and comforting. He is our clothing, wrapping us for love, embracing and enclosing us for tender love, so that he can never leave us, being himself everything that is good for us, as I understand it.

When Julian says "familiar," think "family." The way "kind" has roots in "kinship": *kinder* is German for children; there are "kinds" of species; and kindness is a sort of gentle affection, as between friends or family members.

Here is what she says next:

In this vision he also showed a little thing, the size of a hazelnut in the palm of my hand, and it was as round as a ball. I looked at it with my mind's eye and thought, "What can this be?" And the answer came to me, "It is all that is made." I wondered how it could last, for it was so small I thought it might suddenly have disappeared. And the answer in my mind was, "It lasts and will last forever because God loves it; and everything exists in the same way by the love of God." In this little thing I saw three properties: the first is that God made it, the second is that God loves it, the third is that God cares for it. But what the maker, the carer and the lover really is to me, I cannot tell; for until I become one substance with him, I can never have complete rest or true happiness; that is to say, until I am so bound to him that there is no created thing between my God and me.

You see what Julian wants to show us. Not just the earth but the whole universe, in fact *whatever at all* God has made, is like nothing so much as a hazelnut. It is a small thing, of little consequence in itself, held in the palm of God's hand. Yet God does hold it. And he holds it because he loves it.

She goes on to remark on what she calls "the littleness of all created beings." This is the glory and the frailty of God's creation. When understood as God's handiwork, it is a treasure and a delight; when preferred to God its Maker, it is an idol and a fantasy. For God alone satisfies us. As Julian writes, "When a soul sets all at nothing for love, to have him who is everything, then she is able to receive spiritual rest." And so she concludes:

Our Lord God also showed that it gives him very great pleasure when a simple soul comes to him in a bare, plain and familiar way. For, as I understand this showing, it is the natural yearning of the soul touched by the Holy Ghost to say, "God, of your goodness, give me yourself; you are enough for me, and anything less that I could ask for would not do you full honor. And if I ask anything that is less, I shall always lack something, but in you alone I have everything." And such words are very dear to the soul and come very close to the will of God and his goodness; for his goodness includes all his creatures and all his blessed works, and surpasses everything endlessly, for he is what has no end. And he has made us only for himself and restored us by his blessed Passion and cares for us with his blessed love. And all this is out of his goodness.

In these words we hear an echo of Saint Augustine, writing about a thousand years before Julian a famous prayer addressed to God: "You have made us for yourself and our hearts are restless until they rest in you."

It is simultaneously a small and a great thing to be God's creature. Small, because we are nothing compared to God; great, because God loves us, and in his depthless love he has made us and made us good—which means, in some mysterious sense, sharing in his own goodness. He is our beginning and end. We are the hazelnut; we are held in his palm. This is enough.

More than fifteen years after her visions, Julian wondered what it all meant. What did her Lord mean to say to her?

Happily, she received an answer:

Do you want to know what your Lord meant? Know well that love was what he meant. Who showed you this? Love. What did he show? Love. Why did he show it to you? For love.

From this reply Julian sees that

God loved us before he made us; and his love has never diminished and never shall. And all his works were done in this love; and in this love he had made everything for our profit; and in this love our life is everlasting. We had our beginning when we were made; but the love in which he made us was in him since before time began; and in this love we have our beginning.

Julian's soul is now in heaven with the Lord Jesus, her lifelong love. At last, she is happy. Happiness, she shows us, is resting forever in the Creator's love. It is the simple secret of eternal life.

Rest in it yourself. You'll have a small taste of Julian's happiness with Jesus even now.

Yours in Christ,
a fellow pilgrim

# *four*

## God Creates Human Beings

God is good, or rather the source of all goodness, and one who is good grudges nothing, so that grudging nothing its existence, he made all things through his own Word, our Lord Jesus Christ. Among these things, of all things upon earth he had mercy upon the human race, and seeing that by the principle of its own coming into being it would not be able to endure eternally, he granted them a further gift, creating human beings not simply like all the irrational animals upon the earth but making them according to his own image, giving them a share of the power of his own Word, so that having as it were shadows of the Word and being made rational, they might be able to abide in blessedness, living the true life which is really that of the holy ones in paradise.

—Saint Athanasius of Alexandria

## 29

*Dear future saint,*

In the Bible's account of creation, there is a sequence. First God creates habitats, environments, spaces. Then he fills them. He fills the heavens with the sun and moon and stars; he fills the sky with birds and the sea with fish; he fills the land with animals of every kind.

Last of all come human beings. Here is how Genesis puts it:

> Then God said, "Let us make man in our image, after our likeness; and let them have dominion over the fish of the sea, and over the birds of the air, and over the cattle, and over all the earth, and over every creeping thing that creeps upon the earth."
>
> So God created man in his own image, in the image of God he created him; male and female he created them. And God blessed them, and God said to them, "Be fruitful and multiply, and fill the earth and subdue it; and have dominion over the fish of the sea and over the birds of the air and over every living thing that moves upon the earth."
>
> And God said, "Behold, I have given you every plant yielding seed which is upon the face of all the earth, and every tree with seed in its fruit; you shall have them for food. And to every beast of the earth, and to every bird of the air, and to everything that creeps on the earth, everything that has the breath of life, I have given every green plant for food."
>
> And it was so. And God saw everything that he had made, and behold, it was very good.

There is so much to say about this passage from Scripture. Every part of the Bible contains truths whose depths are fathomless, but these few verses are one of those places that call for whole books to be written, every year of the church's life, for centuries on end. And this is just what has happened. You can read tome after tome plumbing the depths of these words. In this letter I can barely go beneath the surface. Consider this a snorkel expedition. What you glimpse far down in the deep I encourage you to explore on your own.

That said, let me draw out a few of the most important parts of this passage.

Begin at the end. The drumbeat of God's creation of the world is that he sees it is good. But now, with human beings as the crown of creation, he beholds it as *very* good. You can take this to mean that humanity is the point of creation, or the highest part of creation, or perhaps that creation was incomplete until we were created. Regardless, creation is now finished, with human beings the last of the animals to be made. And it is all very, very good.

I called us "animals," and that's significant. According to this narrative, human beings are created on the same day as lions and giraffes, dogs and cats, horses and elephants. We are animals. The philosopher Aristotle knew this; the sciences confirm it; but Moses got there first. The human creature is an animal. We aren't angels. We belong to the animal kingdom. We have bodies and appetites, we eat and sleep, we mate and procreate, we are born and die. Whatever else we may be, we were created animals and we shall always remain animals. It's our nature.

This word "nature" is an important one. Though it's a normal word people use in daily life, it actually has a technical meaning in Christian tradition. "Nature," theologically speaking, doesn't mean "the natural environment." It means "what God has made." That's nature in the singular. In the plural, the word "natures" refers to the character of particular entities or species as created by God. In other words, "human nature" refers to what God made human beings to be, just as "canine nature" refers to what God made dogs to be and "feline nature" to what God made cats to be (and so on). This might seem mere semantics, but the implications are important.

First, nature is good, because it comes from God. Whenever people use "human nature" to refer to something bad, faulty, evil, or problematic in our behavior, that's not how the church talks (even if we understand what they mean). For the church, the nature of human beings is simply what and how our Creator made us and wants us to be. This includes, among other things, our purpose, our happiness, and the rightness (or wrongness) of our actions.

Second, nature is a gift. What I am comes from outside me. It is bestowed upon me by God, my Creator. I am not my own; I belong to the Lord. I am not self-made; I am made by him.

Third, nature can be known. What I mean is this: Human nature, though it is a marvelous mystery, need not be a black box, totally closed off from our knowledge. The church has long taught that we can come to know certain fundamental elements of human nature through the use of our minds, observing and reflecting on human experience as well as the character of existence to draw important conclusions about who we are, what it means to live well, and even about our relationship to God. But we can't know everything that way. We need God himself to teach us. And so he does: through the life of God's people; through the Bible; above all, through Jesus.

The term for this teaching is "revelation." Revelation means to show forth something previously hidden or unknown. Think of a wedding in which the bride, at the height of the ceremony, has her veil removed. The groom beholds her face in all its shining beauty.

This is what revelation is. God unveils his face to us, in all its dazzling glory. He shows himself to us. He does it in mighty actions to save; he does it in covenants with Abraham's children; he does it through words of instruction and consolation. But most important he makes himself known in Mary's son. For to see the face of Jesus is to see the face of God. To know Jesus is to know God. As Jesus says, "He who has seen me has seen the Father."

Because Jesus is the love of God in human form, to see and know Jesus is to see and know, for the first time, a truly human being. The Bible calls the first man God created "Adam." Accordingly, the Bible calls Jesus the "second" or "last" Adam, the real thing in flesh and blood.

Always have this in the back of your mind, now and in the coming letters. On one hand, God is teaching us through these stories: about himself, about the world, about ourselves. On the other hand, none of it is complete without reference to Jesus.

Hence, we understand Genesis best when we read it with Jesus in mind— when we read it "through" the gospel. As we continue to meditate on human nature, Adam and Eve, the image of God, sin, the Fall, and more, never let Jesus be far from your thoughts. He was never far from God's. He's everywhere in the Bible, right there in black and white or hidden in between the lines. Be on the lookout for him. He's looking back at you. He wants you to begin to learn his voice. It's his voice, after all, in the opening chapter of Genesis. The word that God speaks to bring the universe into being? It's Jesus. He's there in the beginning. He *is* the beginning. In him are all beginnings. He holds it all together; it's from him and for him and abides in him: his power, his will, his love.

Remember this, and you'll understand what's essential, even when the questions seem more plentiful than the answers. In Jesus is found every answer to every question, including the ones you haven't yet thought to ask, including the ones we'll never be able to answer this side of heaven. Keep asking. As Jesus says: "Ask, and it will be given you; seek, and you will find; knock, and it will be opened to you. For everyone who asks receives, and he who seeks finds, and to him who knocks it will be opened."

Life in Christ is one great asking, one great seeking, one great knocking. What Christianity says is: Aim your search in the direction of Christ. Not only will you find what you are looking for. Even when you don't—at least not yet—you will be happier ringing at Christ's door, over and over and over, than having any other door opened to you. No other door can offer what you are truly after. Jesus promises rest for your soul, rest from every burden and worry and anxiety. A philosopher once wrote that it would be better to be Socrates unsatisfied than a pig satisfied. That's right. In our case, it means this: better to follow Christ, without all the answers, than to follow anyone else, with all the answers in the world.

Keep asking. Keep knocking. Keep following. You *will* find him. But the secret is that we find him, or rather are found by him, *in the seeking*. He's there alongside you, in the pursuit. So start walking toward him. You'll soon realize he's been with you the whole time.

*Yours in Christ,*
*a fellow pilgrim*

## 30

*Dear future saint,*

I ended the last letter encouraging you to keep asking questions. I didn't just mean keep asking *me* questions, though you're free to do that too. I meant keep asking *Jesus* questions, all the questions you have.

This brought something to mind, a topic I would think obvious, given the nature of these letters. But I shouldn't assume it goes without saying, so I'll say it now.

"Doubt" is very popular today. Doubt is in vogue. It's often held up as a kind of ideal. The more doubting you are—about God and religion and the Bible—the more thoughtful you're supposed to be. Doubt has become a badge of spiritual maturity. I've heard more than a few ministers say that no Christian is a serious follower of Jesus until he or she has seriously doubted the truth of the gospel.

What a bunch of baloney. Don't buy into it for a second. Let me offer you an alternative perspective—albeit one that tries to retain and affirm the insights of doubt's champions.

In my experience, pro-doubters are usually after one of three things, each good in its own right. The first is the value of questions. Many young Christians grow up in a community of older believers who discourage or silence sincere questions. When the church has no time for young people's questions, you can be sure they will go elsewhere to find answers. To the extent that the word "doubts" means "questions," they are all to the good. Saint Thomas Aquinas asked thousands of them in his multivolume work called the *Summa theologiae*, written about 750 years ago. Questions are baked into the Christian cake. We ignore or suppress them in disobedience to God.

Second, folks who celebrate doubt are avowed enemies of cookie-cutter certainty, what many call "fundamentalism." Few would disagree that Christianity contains *some* answers, meaning confident claims of truth: God created the world; Jesus rose from the dead; and so on. Does Christianity, or the Bible, have an infallible answer to *every* question, though? The best form of government? The best diet? God's preferred style of dating? Or what about empirical questions that divide Christians, like the age of the earth or human origins? "Doubt" here often refers to carving out space for reasonable differences of opinion about topics that are not essential to the gospel. That's a worthy goal.

Third, the praise of doubt is in many ways an overreaction to long-standing diminishment of honest doubt among Christians. If "faith" is a virtue, then "doubt" comes to seem like a vice. The unintended effect is that ordinary believers feel extreme pressure to have *perfect* "belief"; when questions arise, or when they find themselves unsure about the Lord, instead of sharing this with others or bringing it in prayer to Christ, they hold it in, ashamed and anxious.

No one wants this. Shifting "doubt" from a vice to a virtue is an understandable response. It's not what we need, though, in two respects.

On one hand, there is already a rich tradition in the church's history of describing and responding to uncertain and fragile faith. It's called "the dark night of the soul." Another term is "spiritual dryness" or "aridity." This is when you feel, for lack of a better word, "blah" about Jesus. You don't sense his presence. His love seems distant. You're not even sure *what* you believe. You're just trying to make it through the day.

This is perfectly normal, for all believers. Great saints have suffered years, even decades, of this feeling. The church has much wisdom for those who go through it. It certainly doesn't make you a "bad" Christian. (Reminder: There are no "good" Christians. We're all "bad." That's what makes us Christians. If we were "good" already, we wouldn't need any of this.)

On the other hand, doubt and dryness may be common, but they aren't universal, and they absolutely are not required for each and every Christian. More to the point, doubt is not a landing spot. It's a way station. It's an obstacle on the path. It's real, it's hard, and it's nothing to be ashamed of. But neither is it something to desire or seek. What we're after is Christ. In this life we know him by faith. The mark of following him well is *faithfulness*. We may enter a dark night of the soul on the journey. We don't want to stay there, however. We want to come out the other side. We want to live in the light.

True, for some people maturity will come only after such an experience. But it's still maturity that's sought. The martyrs don't die for a question mark. They die for the living Christ. He will absolutely accompany me in my doubts and anxieties. His full desire, though, is to *free* me of them. That's what I want, too; what we all want, if we're honest.

So, yes, keep asking questions. Never stop. But ask questions in search of the truth. And when the Truth himself answers, be grateful. He loves us in our doubts. And by the End, when we see him face-to-face, he'll love us out of them entirely—until not one doubt remains.

*Yours in Christ,*
*a fellow pilgrim*

*Dear future saint,*

*Dominion.* Yes. Thank you for drawing my attention back to that word. Let me comment briefly on it.

Not once but twice, God grants "dominion" to humanity "over all the earth" and over its countless living creatures. There are many ways to understand this. I think the primary way is simple, so simple that it's staring us in the face every day of our lives. Human beings are in charge of this planet. It lies within our care. It is our responsibility. It is not dolphins or gorillas or dogs or octopuses that rule over the globe. It's us. Isn't it obvious?

In one sense the Bible is simply registering this reality as the fact that it is. But more than this, God is telling us that we are tasked with a job, a mission, a calling. We are to oversee, protect, preserve, and develop the good world of God's creative action. God has charged us with conservation, cultivation, and culture. We are to be makers like our Maker, lords like our Lord, governors like our Governor—with wisdom and justice like the All-Holy and Righteous One. This is what we are to do. This is part of what it means to be human.

We will see in later letters how this goes wrong. Dominion has been distorted. But distortion isn't part of God's good design. The duty is a good one, and it remains good even when we fail to live up to it.

*Yours in Christ,*
*a fellow pilgrim*

*Dear future saint,*

Genesis reads: "So God created man in his own image, in the image of God he created him; male and female he created them. And God blessed them, and God said to them, 'Be fruitful and multiply, and fill the earth and subdue it.'"

We've tackled dominion; we'll turn to God's image in the next letter. Now let's talk about sex.

As the church has read it, this passage teaches us the following:

1. God created humankind to be male and female;
2. male-and-female humankind is created in God's image;
3. male-and-female humankind is blessed by God;
4. male-and-female humankind is commanded by God to be fruitful and multiply and fill the earth.

That seems rather straightforward. So let me unpack a few key claims.

First, sexual difference is part of God's good will for human life. It is not an accident. It is not—as some have speculated—a consequence of sin or an accommodation to a problem with us. It is not a problem at all. It is a gift. And as a gift from God, it is a good to be treasured and to be grateful for.

Second, each side of human sexual difference is good. To be male is a good thing; to be female is a good thing. Neither is bad; neither is better. Each is good in itself and good in relation to the other. Both together, and only together, form what it means to be human as God made us to be.

Third, human sexual difference has at least one purpose, aim, or end: the procreation of children. Just like the other animals, human beings—in this case, male and female—mate and reproduce. This is how the human race continues. And that, too, is a good thing. Procreation, children, families, genealogies: these come from God as part of our original blessing from him.

Fourth, it follows that sex comes from God and therefore is likewise good. (So many good things to list in just a single chapter of the Bible!) Sex is nothing to be ashamed of. As with dominion, human beings have made a mess of sex. We can't deny it. But the mess comes later. Now, at this point in the story, sex is a gift from God, given for our blessing. Nor is its biological function, which we share with the animals, something to look down upon—as if it made the Lord blush. We see no evidence of this in the passage. It is a fact about us as creatures, a fact of human nature. And what is a part of our nature has its source in God, and God does not play tricks in creation; there is nothing up his sleeve. What you see is what you get. As God created it, sex is good and a part of what it means to be human.

There will be more to say about sex in future letters: where it goes wrong (due to sin), what it's really about (Christ's love for us—no surprise there), its proper context for believers (in marriage), and when it will cease (in heaven). Sex is important, but not all-important. Like every earthly good, it holds the potential to point us to God. When it points us to God, we enjoy both him and the earthly good. When it turns us away from God, we enjoy neither him nor the earthly good. It turns to dust in our hands and ashes in our mouths.

Sex is extraordinarily powerful. For this reason the church cares deeply about the sexual lives of Christians. In the power of sex lies the possibility for much good and much harm. To live wisely is to know the difference and to live out this difference with joy, gratitude, sobriety, and self-control.

*Yours in Christ,*
*a fellow pilgrim*

## 33

*Dear future saint,*

Your questions about sex will have to wait. All in due time. We still need to talk about the image of God. Genesis says humans are made "in" it, or "according" to it. What does this mean?

There are many ways of understanding this magnificent and ennobling teaching. One of the things I hope you've already noticed, but that you will continue to see in later letters, is that questions like these—theological questions about how to understand Christian teaching rooted in the Bible—do not always have one clear answer. This is a feature of Christianity, not a bug. Passages in the Bible have many meanings. Single sentences or phrases have many meanings. The problem comes only if the meanings are mutually exclusive. Often they are not. The work of Christian tradition involves cordoning off false or unhelpful answers in order to make room for all the true and life-giving ones.

Here are some of the ways Christians have understood the Bible's teaching about God's image.

Option #1: Being made in God's image is just another way of saying that we've been given dominion over the earth.

Option #2: God's image refers to something unique about human beings compared to other creatures. Usually this is called "the faculty of reason": that is, the fact that we have minds. *Rationality* is what it means to be made in God's image. (If true, this means angels are also made in God's image.) An ancient term accordingly designates us *rational animals*, because we are the only animals that possess a *rational soul*. Other candidates for the unique human characteristic, or at least signs of our rational soul, include language, consciousness, politics, and art.

Option #3: Being made in God's image refers either to some similarity between us and God or to some role he wants us to play in creation. The similarity might be rationality or freedom or morality; the function might be lordship or stewardship or priestly representation. We'll come back to this idea.

Option #4: To be made in God's image has to do, not with some characteristic we possess, but with relationship. On this view, our relationships with one another (whether as male-female or as a whole society) reflect, in some distant way, the relationships in God of Father, Son, and Holy Spirit. Or thinking vertically instead, humans belong to a unique relationship with God: alone among all the creatures of the earth, we relate to God knowingly, intentionally, and intimately. One theologian (a favorite of mine) defines the human being as *the praying animal*. What distinguishes us from other animals? We pray. Not just with words, but with ceremonies, rituals, thoughts, deeds. Our whole lives, from conception to death, are a kind of extended prayer. We are addressed by God—who, you might have realized by now, is rather chatty—and we address him in return. To exist at all is to have been spoken into being by God. To exist as a human is to talk back.

Option #5: This is the minimal option. It says plainly that we do not know what it means to be made in God's image, but we do know its implication. Its implication is that God has conferred upon human beings an inestimable and inviolable value greater than anything else on earth. "Inestimable" means it cannot be measured: we bear infinite worth. "Inviolable" means it cannot and must not be disturbed: we are not to be trifled with. We have *dignity* as creatures, and this dignity cannot be taken away from us (because it is God's gift), although, for just that reason, it is a grave evil when the attempt is made (through, for example, rape, torture, slavery, or murder).

One important implication is that a human being's value has no relationship to his or her talents, abilities, intelligence, or any other factors one is born *with* or born *into*. From conception to death, a human being is precious in the Lord's eyes, and all the absurd and evil reasons we manufacture to evaluate, denigrate, rank, ridicule, and oppress individuals and groups based on their differences—whatever they may be—are just that: absurd and evil. God abhors and rejects them. God made all and loves all. He even seems to have a soft spot for the overlooked, the unimposing, the unlucky, the losers.

Many cultures, ancient and contemporary, have it out for certain groups. The wrong color. The wrong gender. The wrong country. The wrong brain. The wrong size. The wrong timing. The church doesn't care about such things, because she knows that God doesn't either. *Every human being bears the Creator's image.* All on their own, those seven words rule out more human mischief than you can imagine.

Option #6: The image of God is Jesus Christ. In eternity, he is the perfect divine image; in time, he is the visible image, in human form, of the invisible God. The latter is true because the former is true. Once again, to see Jesus is to see God; to hear Jesus is to hear God; to know Jesus is to know God. Which means that, in some wonderfully mysterious sense, when the Bible says that humanity is made "in" or "according to" the image of God, it means that we are made in some special relation to, or on the pattern of, or in accordance with the One who *is* the image: Jesus.

This, in turn, makes sense of what the rest of the Bible says: that when we sin we turn away from God, and God's image in us is thereby distorted or broken; that when Jesus comes, it is the eternal image becoming an image-bearing creature; and that when Jesus lives a perfect life, dying and rising for our sake, he restores, elevates, and perfects his image in us. Thus the New Testament's teaching that the aim of the life of faith is to be conformed to the image of Christ. We are images of the image; we find our completion in him.

So which is it? Which of the options is the right one?

I leave it to you to decide. So far as I can tell, they all say something true. I see no reason to pick one to the exclusion of the others. But wise Christians think this or that one is especially important to emphasize. What do you say?

*Yours in Christ,*
*a fellow pilgrim*

## 34

*Dear future saint,*

Your answer jarred a thought. There is one additional and, in my view, especially illuminating way to think about humanity's status as God's image-bearers in the world.

Do you remember the three roles God gave different people in Israel? Prophet, priest, and king. The prophet brought the word of God to the people of God; the priest represented God to the people and the people to God; and the king ruled over the people in God's stead.

Now apply this to humanity in the first chapter of Genesis. Think ahead, too, to Adam and Eve in the second chapter. Do these three roles apply to them?

I think so. "King" is rather obvious: if human beings are given dominion over the whole earth, then their purpose contains a royal element. It is as though they are God's deputies or vice-regents. They are corulers, kings and queens exercising an authority derived from the one true Ruler and King.

What about "priest"? This seems apt, too. What sets humans apart is that we know God and have the capacity to mediate God to the nonrational world—a world that is no less good for not being rational. In some marvelous sense the animals and plants and trees find God in us, in our wise care of them as God's good creatures. Even the language of "image" suggests that we somehow make the invisible God visible, both to the rest of creation and to one another. The whole cosmos is a sort of temple built to the glory of the unseen God, and he has set us up as his seeable images—his "icons"—right in the midst of it. Hence the ancient view, pagan and Christian alike, that humanity is a *microcosm* of creation. We contain the whole in miniature. We are priests.

Now, what about "prophet"? I think we can make a good case, built on the first two roles, that this one applies to us as well. For one, we are the only creatures addressed *directly* by God in his act of creation. He doesn't say, "Let humans be fruitful and multiply." He looks us in the face and says, "You there—have babies." He doesn't say, "I have given *them* plants for food." He says, "Behold, I have given *you* every plant . . ." (Isn't it interesting that we aren't given animals to eat from the beginning? This hints at something important about death and violence. They're not there at the start. They come later, *after* things go wrong.)

Again in the next chapter God speaks directly to Adam, the first human individual. This tells us that in being spoken to, we are expected both to speak back to God and to *speak on behalf* of him. We are meant for a twofold movement: to hear God's word, then to turn and speak this word for the blessing of others, whether fellow human beings or fellow creatures. Human beings are prophets from the beginning.

Partly this threefold picture is just that: a picture. It's a helpful way to capture what's going on in the opening chapters of the Bible. But it's also going to come in handy later. If Jesus is the new Adam, the true human, it follows that he must fulfill whatever it is God meant from the start for our species to be and to do. And if we were meant to be prophets and priests and kings, then this is exactly what Jesus is going to be. Or put another way: If we see Jesus doing just these things *as* the second Adam, then this gives us a new window on the *first* Adam. (Even more, if these are roles meant for Adam together with Eve, and if Jesus's mother, Mary, is the second Eve, then in what way is *her* calling from God at once prophetic, priestly, and royal? Take care in your answer. What applies to Mary applies also to the church, the mystical bride of Christ and the mother of all God's children.)

The Bible can be read forward and backward. This is one of those times when reading it backward helps us to read it better forward. Like when you finish a mystery novel—upon discovering the identity of the murderer, you turn back to earlier chapters and notice all the hints lying there in plain sight. The hints of Christ are everywhere in Scripture. Knowing it's all leading to him means being on the lookout for him from the start.

*Yours in Christ,*
*a fellow pilgrim*

# five

## Sin Corrupts the Life of Creation

When Adam fell, God's son fell; because of the true union made in heaven, God's son could not leave Adam, for by Adam I understand all men. Adam fell from life to death into the valley of this wretched world, and after that into hell. God's son fell with Adam into the valley of the Virgin's womb (and she was the fairest daughter of Adam), in order to free Adam from guilt in heaven and in earth; and with his great power he fetched him out of hell.

—Julian of Norwich

**35**

*Dear future saint,*

You've waited long enough. I've been dodging and weaving, and you've been insistent. It's time.

Something goes wrong in the human story, not some ways in, but right at the start. This something is sin. Bound up with sin are weighty words like "evil," "death," "suffering," "violence," and "Satan." I told you in an earlier letter why we didn't begin there: because starting the story with sin can warp your understanding of the story. It can make you forget that God exists, sinless, from everlasting to everlasting; that God made this world, and us in it, good and very good; that God's calling of his beloved bride, Israel, is not dependent on sin. I wanted you to hear about those things in their own right, on their own apart from sin.

But we cannot avoid sin. We must not. There are many reasons why—not the least being that the Bible does not avoid it, not on a single page—but let me highlight three.

First, Christianity is *realistic* about the world. It is not optimistic; it is not sunshine and rainbows; it is not a Hallmark card or a politician's stump speech. It refuses to lie about the world. And the world, for all its goodness, is at the same time a terrible and terrifying place full of wickedness and pain and loss. I don't know your story in much detail: Have you suffered greatly? Or have you and the ones you love been spared great harm? It is difficult to do so for long. Danger, disease, death, and risk of all three lurk behind every corner, awaiting us every morning of our lives. God be praised, that isn't all there is to life. But though there is more, there is not less. Every one of us will die; every one of us will suffer; every one of us harms others in incalculable and sometimes irrevocable ways. This is the great burden of our species. The burden is the weight of sin. This is why we must talk about it.

Second, sin is not only about our experience or the experience of others. Sin is about God. Sin is a turning away from God; it is missing the mark of giving God what God is due—namely, the whole of ourselves. We aren't passively sinful. We are actively responsible for our relation to God. This relation, on our side, is a rotten mix of alienation and rejection. In other words, the problem of sin is not just who we are or what we do to ourselves and to others.

SIN CORRUPTS THE LIFE OF CREATION

87

The problem of sin is a God problem. It is a dreadful problem to have. Nor is it a problem we can solve on our own.

Third and finally, sin is about Jesus. What do I mean by this? Obviously humanity does not sin with Jesus in mind. Nor is Jesus bound to sin the way we are: he is without sin, unlike you and me. No, sin is about Jesus because Jesus comes in response to our sin. God sends Jesus, or "puts him forth" (as Saint Paul puts it in one place), for our sin-sick selves. He is, in another phrase from the Bible, an offering for sin. Put simply, he resolves the sin problem, once for all. Sin is over and done with when Jesus comes on the scene.

One of the greatest Christian teachers in history, Saint Thomas Aquinas, once wrote that, although in God's wisdom Jesus did many things to save us from our sins—teaching, suffering, dying, rising, etc.—*Jesus's conception in Mary's womb* was alone enough to merit forgiveness for all of humanity, past, present, and future. Because he is God, his mere presence as a member of the species is like a blood transfusion for a person on her deathbed: all of a sudden, the newly received antibodies start working, and the nearly dead one is sitting up, talking, and smiling again. That's us. Jesus makes us well. Jesus makes us alive.

And this is why we must talk about sin. Jesus doesn't come *only* to deal with sin. But sin is one of the reasons he comes. "The saying is sure and worthy of full acceptance, that Christ Jesus came into the world to save sinners. And I am the foremost of sinners." So says Paul. It is a "sure saying," meaning it is a reliable rule of thumb for all believers. Put it on your lips. You'll realize it involves *you*, not just others. Jesus didn't come for others only. He came for you. This is good news: he loves you so much that he came to save you! But it is also somber: you needed saving. Because you—like me, like our siblings and parents, like my children, like everyone we love, like everyone we despise, like all of humankind—are a sinner.

And you cannot save yourself.

Yours in Christ,
a fellow pilgrim

SIN CORRUPTS THE LIFE OF CREATION

## 36

*Dear future saint,*

I see you're familiar with the story of Adam and Eve in the garden of Eden. We'll get to your questions about it in a moment. The story is so potent, so compact, it's difficult for me to do it justice in summary form. What you should do is read the second, third, and fourth chapters of Genesis all in a row, then compare notes with my brief commentary.

What these chapters tell of is a primeval catastrophe at the onset of the human race. God places the first human pair, Adam and Eve, in a garden to tend and to care for it. All that surrounds them is given to them, with the exception of a single tree. They are forbidden to eat of it. A snake slithers into the scene. He approaches Eve and, initiating a conversation with her, sets question marks next to the command of God. *Did God really say . . . ?* Together with Adam, she takes the fruit and they eat it. Suddenly they realize they are naked. They are ashamed. They hide from God. Yet he knows what they have done. They have eaten from what Genesis calls the tree of the knowledge of good and evil. The serpent is cursed; so are the woman and the man. They are exiled from Eden, which also contains the tree of life. They have transgressed the divine prohibition, and they will die. God clothes them and sends them on their way.

Even in these bare outlines, you can see the contours of a great mystery. What does it all mean?

Jews and Christians have been arguing over the answer for more than two millennia. As I've written before, we need not search for *the one true meaning*. This is a story meant to generate as many meanings as there are readers honestly pursuing the truth. Echoes of this story resound in the New Testament, which is at pains to show you, the reader, that the awful disaster of Eden is somehow replayed, reenacted, redone, and undone in the coming of Jesus. This is why knowing the tiniest of details in these chapters, down to each and every word, is so helpful for reading the New Testament. Knowing the one is crucial for knowing the other. Each interprets the other, in both directions.

As for this story, there is so much to say, yet in another sense it is so simple. At the head of humanity stands a calamity of appalling magnitude. Before we even get going we fall from glorious heights to frightful depths. At home in the garden of God, dwelling there as God's royal priests, tending the temple of God's good creation, we disobey his wise command and are banished from his presence. It is as if, in the process of receiving a gift, we dropped it before it was even in our possession. It lies there, shattered, on the ground. And we cannot put it back together again.

Christians call this event, an event that includes all of us, "original sin." In coming letters I'll reflect on original sin and its implications for human life. But first we'll have to get our heads around Adam, Eve, and evolution.

Yours in Christ,
a fellow pilgrim

## 37

Dear future saint,

For most of the church's history the story of Adam and Eve was read as a description of an event that occurred in the recent past to two persons who (1) were the first human pair, (2) were brought into being by God's special creative act (i.e., apart from the usual way animals come into being), and therefore (3) were and are the parents of the entire human race, all of us tracing our common descent from these two individuals.

In the last two centuries the church has held a sustained conversation about whether this is the best way to read the story. Two things prompted this potential rereading. One is scientific evidence for the age of the universe and, therein, the age of the earth. If our best methods of dating the earth and life on it suggest that it is billions of years old, how should this inform our reading of the story of Eden?

Second is the theory of evolution. This theory holds that every living creature exists in the form that it does as the result of a process, millions or billions of years long, of small organic and biological changes that, in the aggregate, produce the relatively stable features that characterize different species and, taking a panoramic view, the extraordinary diversity of the animal and vegetable kingdoms. In less grand terms, species *evolve*, they change and develop over time; more than this, individual species evolve *into* other species through a process called natural selection. Behind every form of life that today surrounds us lie millions of years of development leading up to the present (nor is this development finished; it continues indefinitely); what we see in the natural world is not a collection of "static" life-forms, as though they all plopped onto the planet from heaven ready-made.

So much for the theory. In one form or another it is presupposed by the scientific community the world over. The question for Christians is whether it's true. And if it is true, how does it affect our reading of Genesis?

I assume that it is true. I have never encountered compelling reasons to suppose otherwise. But some Christians doubt its truth, or at least argue that parts of it are inadequate. Some believe that the Bible should be read as reporting historical events, in temporal sequence, from the beginning. On this reading God created the world in six twenty-four-hour days about six thousand years ago. The world merely *appears* to have a history longer than this in the way that Adam, created as an adult, would have appeared to have had a childhood, though he did not. Christians who propose this reading of Genesis are sometimes called "young earth creationists."

You are not going to hear me say anything snide about these fellow Christians. They are sometimes mocked in our culture as unscientific, uneducated, unenlightened—in a word, backward. Such things are not true. Read books written by them, and you will see they are full of thoughtfulness and sophistication. I know brilliant thinkers *and scientists* who belong to this group of believers. Perhaps you or your family or your church does, too. The church is a big tent, and it includes different views about Genesis and human origins.

Beneath this tent is another view, the one I want to suggest here. Though I respect Christians who think otherwise, I believe they are mistaken. The earth and the universe are billions of years old; the scientific evidence about these matters is reliable and worthy of our assent; organic life is the product of millions of years of evolutionary development.

If so, then we should read the opening chapters of Genesis as offering us a picture meant to communicate truths to us in nonhistorical form. You may use words like "myth" and "fable" so long as they do not smuggle in notions of nontruth or arbitrariness. Consequently, these early stories ought not to be read the way we read accounts (from the Bible) about Moses and David and Jesus and Saint Paul or records (from other books) about Alexander the Great and Confucius and Attila and Charlemagne. These are historical persons whose names we know who lived in locations we can place on a map on a timeline we can date with relative confidence. I suggest that we need not read the first eleven chapters of Genesis—Adam and Eve, Cain and Abel, Noah and the ark, the tower of Babel—in this way. I may be wrong. Nevertheless the church's tradition accommodates this view. It seems to make the best sense of all the evidence we have while continuing to read the Bible as the word of God to us.

The last question, then, is how to understand our first parents and their defection from God. There are many options here. Perhaps, *unlike* all other living creatures, God did not work creatively in and through the processes of evolution to produce human beings; perhaps he made Adam from the dust of the ground and Eve from his side approximately half a million years ago. That is theologically possible. It is also theologically possible that God *did* use evolutionary processes to bring the human race into existence. At some point our ancestors transitioned from "prehuman" to "human," in the form of a pair or of a small community. Perhaps this transition took the form of God infusing them with a rational soul; perhaps it took the form of language or worship or art arising spontaneously in their common life.

In any case, they discerned a word from God and they failed to keep it. Their failure was their fall. In their fall we fell all. For they passed on that

SIN CORRUPTS THE LIFE OF CREATION

failure to the rest of us. And ever since, we've been failing in ten thousand lamentable ways: as the fourth chapter of Genesis tells us, *the very first thing that occurs after the exile from Eden is murder.* Specifically, one brother slays another. The fruit of sin is fratricide. The thought should make us shudder. Sin is wretched. Whenever and however it first entered this world, it made a ruin of God's good world. We live amid these ruins; in a sense the ruins are us. We ruin and are ruined. We need help.

*Yours in Christ,*
*a fellow pilgrim*

**38**

*Dear future saint,*

Before I say more about sin, let me pause to make a connection, lest you missed it or are yourself wondering about it. I referred to God working in and through the ordinary processes of the world—in this case, evolution—to bring about the existence of a species or an individual creature. This may have raised a question: How does that work? If God doesn't (typically) create in a special or miraculous way but *through* the very biological and chemical stages of growth and development and procreation and death that we witness daily and measure scientifically, then what does it mean to say that he is nevertheless the One doing the creating?

The best way to illustrate what is happening is to think about yourself. Who made you? Well, there's one obvious answer to this question. Your parents. When you were conceived in your mother's womb, that was your beginning, a beginning we are able to date with relative confidence and to describe with scientific precision. Your mother and father made you. Their action to conceive is a complete explanation, at the biological or scientific level, of how you came to be, of where you came from, and when.

But there is another way of taking the question of who made you. If I asked the same thing of my children today, each of them would say, "God!" (The four-year old would say, "God and Jesus!") And they would be right. Because they aren't answering the question that scientists answer: Namely, what genetic materials led through what biological processes to produce this DNA and this body and this brain? They are answering the question *Who is my Creator?* And they know their father is not their Creator, nor their mother. Only God is.

What this tells us is two things. First, there are always two types of agency or operation at work in the world: one natural and one supernatural. In Saint John's Gospel, Jesus says, "My Father is always working." That's right. Behind and beneath and within and through every single event and process and cause in the world is the continuous and unceasing agency of the God and Father of Jesus our Lord. If it stopped, if he stopped, then the world's activity would stop, too. His is the condition of ours; the one enables the other.

Second, it follows that God's action is not like our action. Consider opening a door. I can open it alone or open it together with you. But if both of us

SIN CORRUPTS THE LIFE OF CREATION

do it, then the effect of the door opening is partly caused by me and partly caused by you.

This isn't how it works with God. When my action is transparent to God's—when what I do is a clear window or mirror that God works or wills *through*—then the action is simultaneously mine and God's. It is I who open the door, and it is God who opens it through me. Or, less trivially, it is I who feed the hungry person, and God who feeds her through me. The action isn't parceled out; there isn't a fraction of responsibility (so much glory to God, so much credit to me). The pie chart isn't divided up. That only happens when it's two or more creatures cooperating in the same action. But God isn't a creature. We're not at odds with each other, and he isn't nudging me out of the way with his elbow. God literally does not take up space. Just as he can be present at the same time and in the same place as me or you or others, so his *action* can be one and the same as ours: calling ours forth, empowering it from within, accompanying it throughout, drawing it to its goal.

This should help to make some sense of what a miracle is. A miracle is when God brings about an event in the world without the use of ordinary created processes. It is a natural effect without a natural cause: in the case of a miracle, the only cause is supernatural. God does the job himself, without using the world as a means, or go-between, or vehicle of his will. It happens spontaneously and without intermediaries.

Such miracles are rare but wondrous. And I hope you see why miracles are not a problem or a strange interruption of the laws of nature. *Everything that happens* in the natural world has God's loving, ongoing action beneath and within it. So the oddity in a miracle is not that God acts (as though he otherwise very rarely acts). It is that he acts "alone," apart from a medium *through* which to work. Put differently, everything in the world, even the world itself, is a divine miracle, for it is the handiwork of almighty God. Miracles are when the mask of creative conduits comes off and we see the Creator doing what he's always already doing anyway, only now without the aid or agency of us creatures.

Since God usually works in and through us—and by "us" I mean every-thing created, not just human beings—this tells us something important about God. He positively loves to include the world in his creative action. He doesn't *prefer* to act apart from us. He uses us every single day to effect countless occurrences, most of which make the world go round, all of which make life possible, some of which no doubt bless us and others unwittingly, in ways we'll only learn about in heaven.

To be sure, he uses plants and animals and other creatures differently than us. He doesn't need their permission. He doesn't need ours either, to be hon-est. But he desires it. He actively seeks the harmony of our wills with his. He wants us to want what he wants, to will what he wills, to do what he does. He wants us to say, with Jesus, "Not my will, but yours, be done."

And what we discover, when God works his will through us, is this. Far from a violation of our freedom or a coercion of our wills, we find ourselves more fully alive—happiest, freest, holiest. We are, by a great mystery, our truest and deepest selves. When we cling to our lives and our wills, we lose them. When we lose them in God, we receive them back in unlosable form.

We are not our own: in life and death we belong to the Lord. Saint James writes: "Humble yourself before the Lord and he will lift you up." He will. This is Julian's secret of being a creature. Submit yourself to the will and work of the Creator, and you will receive what he alone can give: life.

*Yours in Christ,*
*a fellow pilgrim*

## 39

*Dear future saint,*

We were talking about sin. Specifically, original sin.

Original sin refers to two things. Most basically, it refers to the first sin, the cause or source of sin's entry into the life and destiny of humankind. More broadly, it refers not to an event but to a condition, a universal condition in which every human creature shares: namely, that of being a sinner, being *sinful*. The initial moment of transgression is sometimes called the Fall, with a capital *F*. As if we "fell" from a great height. In this sense, the fact that we are all sinners, none excepted, means that we are all "fallen." Indeed, it is true to say that we live in a *fallen world*.

How to make sense of this? Let's start with humans, then work outward from there.

Think of it as a choice between two options. Are we sinners because we sin, or do we sin because we are sinners? The teaching about original sin says the second option is the right one. Sin is fundamentally a condition, not a set of actions or behaviors. It is a state we find ourselves in. In fact, it is a state we are conceived and born into. No human can help sinning.

If you doubt the truth of this statement, try to disprove it. Make it your aim to go through a day, even a single hour, without pride, self-pity, self-loathing, envy, greed, sloth, lust, gluttony, unkindness, impatience, dishonesty, contempt, or narcissism. You can't do it. These vices are in you the way aggressive cancer or a terrible virus pervades the body of a patient. They are in me, too, and in everyone you and I have ever known or loved.

The doctrine of original sin teaches that these are not merely learned behaviors. If they were, we could set up some babies supervised by especially virtuous adults on another planet and watch, with realistic hope, for them to grow up absent sin. It's true we do learn every manner of sin from society. But this isn't its ultimate origin. It's *in us*. All of us. And we can't expel it. We can't cut it out or exorcise it. We're not capable. Why? There are many reasons, but chief among them is that only someone without sin can deal with sin. Yet the very problem is that none of us is without sin. The sick can't help the sick. We need someone who is well to cure us.

You know of whom I am speaking. We're getting to him. But stay on sin for a moment.

I want to suggest that you think of two categories: capitalized Sin, in the singular, and lowercase sins, in the plural. The latter, "sins," are what you and I do every day. We tell a white lie, we permit our lust a long leash, we burn with jealousy or nurture a grudge. We steal, cheat, and murder, some of us. These are sins. Think of *Sin*, on the other hand, as a kind of power or personified force. Saint Paul calls Sin a tyrant who holds us in bondage. We are in chains; we are slaves to Sin. As Jesus says, "Everyone who commits sin is a slave to sin." The reverse is true as well: everyone who is a slave to Sin commits sins—inevitably, perpetually, constantly. Either way, we aren't capable of breaking our own chains.

Once you frame Sin in this way, you begin to move away from a very bad habit. Let's call the habit *moralizing*. It's a kind of ethical gossip (even when it happens nowhere but your own mind). Moralizing supposes we can pick ourselves up by our own bootstraps. We can *will our way* into being good. We can just try harder. If a person sins, on this view, we have every right to point and to issue blame.

Hypocrite! That's you and me. We are self-righteous hypocrites, every time we look askance at a neighbor or friend (or enemy) who stumbles. There are very few things Jesus hates more than hypocrisy. It is hatred and deceit linking arms. We fail to love our fellow human beings—a man or woman whom God loves with infinite tenderness and care—all while pretending we do not suffer from the identical condition. As if a patient on a cancer ward ridiculed her fellow patients for being ill.

No! That way lie the very flames of hell. Avoid it at every cost. I am not mincing words because Jesus does not mince words about this. The Lord came for the sick. He did not come for healthy people—none exist. There are only sick people. Some of them know the truth; some of them hide it from themselves; some of them play-act at being well. But act as though you are not in need long enough, and you'll forget it's an act. The Lord does not help those who help themselves. He helps those who cannot help themselves. Should we expect him to help those who neither ask for help nor think they need it?

*You need help.* Accept this. Don't shove it aside. Beg for it. We are beggars, and we lie if we say we are not. But the Lord is compassionate. He helps everyone who asks for it. Ask even now. He will answer.

Yours in Christ,
a fellow pilgrim

## 40

*Dear future saint,*

So passionate! Original sin strikes you as neither reasonable nor fair. It certainly is not fair. But fair compared to what?

Think of a person born with a profound disability, or a congenital disease, or a deeply felt disposition to self-destructive or evil actions. (I believe these categories cover all of us, as a matter of fact, but we'll limit our purview to such conditions as we can diagnose clinically or that people claim for themselves.) Suppose we are thinking of a man in his twenties who is an alcoholic and whose father was an alcoholic. Let's even suppose he didn't grow up in the same house as his father but nevertheless contracted from him a certain proclivity for addiction to alcohol. Now suppose this man gets drunk on the night of his twenty-fifth birthday, drives his car, and gets in an accident, killing the person in the other car.

Call our hypothetical alcoholic Will. Is Will responsible for killing the person who died? More to the point, is Will right to feel guilty for having done so? Or should we urge him to avoid what feelings of guilt he has, since (1) he was under the influence and (2) his tendency to be under the influence is something he inherited?

The Christian tradition holds that Will is morally responsible for the death of the other person. He is guilty. It follows that he is right to feel this guilt, deep in his soul. His guilt should not bring him to despair. It should not grip him in the hot furnace of self-hatred and debilitating shame. But to have killed an innocent human being is a grave matter. It is a moral evil. It is sin. Guilt is a rational, psychologically apt, and morally right response.

Is Will's culpability for this homicide mitigated to some degree by the fact that he was drunk and therefore did not consciously intend to take human life? Yes. Is it further mitigated by the fact that his drunkenness is intimately related to his genetic makeup, which he did not choose but was born with? It is reasonable to think so. Does this entail the further proposition that Will is not morally responsible for the loss of human life? No. Does it further entail that he is not responsible for getting drunk, now or in the future? No, it does not. And because he is responsible, it is just for him to suffer consequences for his actions.

The same goes for sins in general and for original sin. Let me leave off hypotheticals and speak for myself. I have long been predisposed to a mixture of vanity and self-loathing. I want to be, and thus I want to believe that I am, better than others; but when I am awakened from this fantasy, I feel crushed by the weight of the truth. I cannot look away from it, and it has the power to send me into a depressive spiral. I feel myself drawn toward the abyss. I wonder—emotionally, not rationally—whether my life has value, whether it is worth living. I withdraw into myself and punish others who draw near to me; I disbelieve anything they say to persuade me that I am wrong—that is, that I have value, that I have worth, that I am loved.

It does not matter where or why or from whom I inherited this predisposition, and I doubt we could ever truly chase down those answers anyway. What matters is that the experience is real, that it is mine, and that I am responsible for it. I cannot assign blame to others. The problem lies within. This doesn't mean self-blame or self-hatred. Quite the opposite. It means, on one hand, owning up to the truth, taking responsibility, saying, "I admit it. I have a problem. I can't point a finger at anyone else. I confess. I want to do better. I want to be better. I need help." But it also means, on the other hand, *that now I am in a position to receive the help I need*. I cannot be helped so long as I am self-deceived. I must accept the truth and live in it—no ifs, ands, or buts.

A psychological illustration is fitting, I think, because at this moment in time, in our culture, we struggle to know how to speak of such things. If a person is not a fully self-possessed rational agent, we sometimes talk as if whatever she feels or does or experiences cannot be a matter of personal responsibility—cannot, in Christian language, be a matter of sin. But it can. What we suffer is part of who we are. What we inherit is part of who we are. They are inextricable. We are entangled creatures, and the power truly to disentangle lies in God alone.

Mental health is a real thing. We cannot wish away illness in the mind any more than we can wish away illness in the body. And sometimes medicine is an important part of the solution. The only point I want to make here is that, contrary to your first impression, original sin is not an obstacle here but an aid. It *helps* to make sense of our moral, emotional, and psychological experience, not to mention our laws and social norms. A boy who grows up in an abusive household is not thereby sanctioned to be an abuser as an adult. His history may help to *explain* certain tendencies and temptations he experiences; the former sets the latter in an important context. But it does not excuse it. And such a man's first step toward unlearning what he learned as a child is admitting his problem, taking responsibility for himself, and seeking help.

Go attend a local meeting of Alcoholics Anonymous. You'll see this dynamic with your own eyes. The church is the same. It is the local chapter of a universal community. Call it Sinners Anonymous. Each week I stand up and say, "Hi, I'm Brad. I'm a sinner. I need help. And only a higher power can give me the help I need—though I admit I also need y'all to help me on the way."

As you well know, Christians know the name of that higher power. It's Jesus. He is the help we need. He is where we're going. He is the way to where we're going. His people, sisters and brothers in Christ, are fellow sinners on the way. They are Jesus's uncountable hands and feet and eyes and ears, his friends guiding your steps along the path, one by one. When you fall, and you will, you can't get up alone. He will pick you up, through them.

This is the Christian life, dear friend. It is a fragile and vulnerable thing, but beautiful for just that reason.

*Yours in Christ,*
*a fellow pilgrim*

*Dear future saint,*

So, you and I are sinners. *Is the good news bad news after all?* Your question is pointed. It doesn't just sound like bad news. It is bad news! In a sense it's unfair, too.

Does this mean God is unjust to hold us accountable for our sins? No, as we saw in the last letter. But there's a deeper reason why.

The reason is simple. We do not learn that we are sinners in the abstract. We learn that we are sinners *when we hear the good news about Jesus.* We are told: "Happy day! You are forgiven because of Jesus!" We say: "Oh, how wonderful. Wait. Forgiven of what?" Answer: "Your sins!" Us: "What are sins?" And then it's off to the races, explaining the thing that's already been taken care of by God's mercy and grace.

Do you see? God doesn't reveal to us just how damnably wicked we all are. He draws near to us in love and, having already provided the cure, informs us that we are sick, whether we suspected it or not. Would you blame a doctor for saying, "Here's the medicine to fix your terminal disease," when you didn't know until that moment that you were ill? Of course not! The fact is that you *are* sick, but this news is contained in the larger, extraordinary news that your sickness is treatable, indeed has already been treated.

This is why I waited so long in these letters to talk about sin. The world is awash in sin. There's no denying it. But God and God's goodness and the truth about both are not soaked in sin. Sin, like creation, is *contingent*. Sin does not come from God. And he has already provided the remedy. We can foresee the possibility—no, the reality—of a world free from sin. That's heaven. Here on earth, we see the purest glimpse of it in Jesus and in his announcement about God's kingdom. This is what makes the good news he brings so very good.

Let's put some of this together. Seven or perhaps eight points in total.

First, creation is *good* but, as we have seen, creation is *fallen*. The goodness remains and the fallenness remains, and so long as this world endures they are intermixed and inseparable. Nothing you see in this world is wholly bad or wholly good. Inasmuch as it is God's creature, it is good; inasmuch as it is fallen or sinful, it is bad. The same is true of you. You are God's handiwork, and that makes you good. You are also fallen, and that makes you sinful. You are right to want to be rid of sin; you are right to desire divine chemotherapy for the cancer of sin. The hard medicine God offers is the blood of Jesus. It may hurt. But it will heal you.

Second, when we refer to "nature," we must be careful what we mean. "Human nature" is not sinful. It is colonized and corrupted by sin, but human nature in itself is God's good creation. Sin is an invader. It is a foreign contaminant. It doesn't belong. And one day it will be gone for good. Meanwhile, we must remember that our nature is not meant to be sinful, and sin is not a necessary or acceptable part of ourselves and our experiences, actions, and feelings.

Third, sin is parasitic. What do I mean by this? I mean that sin is not a *something*. Remember that God creates only what is good. Sin is not good. Therefore God didn't create it. It's not a "thing" like an atom or an animal or an angel or even a number. One helpful way to think about it is that sin is the *absence* of something. We are meant for a fullness of goodness that sin keeps us from. Sin is the lack of this fullness. In this sense it really is a kind of negative or negation, a parasite or cancer that eats away at what we are meant for, what we are meant to be and to do.

Fourth, sin is not imperfection or limitation. I spoke in an earlier letter about *finitude*: to be created is to be dependent, needy, limited. This just means we're not God. That's not a bad thing. Only God is supposed to be God. God is perfect, moreover, but God *alone* is perfect. To be imperfect is to be fallible, and this is how we are made. We aren't created to know everything, to be everything, to never fail or fall short or err. The problem is when we do so *in response to God's command*; in other words, when we fail to love God with our whole selves and our neighbor as ourselves. This failure is sin. Other kinds of limitation and imperfection are as natural as having two eyes, two ears, and a mouth.

Fifth, sin is democratizing. Because original sin includes the whole species, beginning to end and top to bottom, *everyone is in the same position*. Everyone is a sinner. No one gets to lord it over others from the high horse of no-sin or less-sin. We're all stuck in the same muck. It's quicksand. The more we resist—the more we act as though we aren't in it like everyone else—the faster we sink. There is a sort of radical equality in sinfulness. We're all in the same boat. This boat is called "Need" and on its side is written in huge, sprawling letters, "S.O.S. HELP!" No need to jump out. Help is on the way. The ship won't sink before rescue arrives.

Sixth, the human condition of sin is a matter of the will. The will is that part of ourselves that decides, deliberates, chooses, does this or that. To say that we are sinful is to say that our will is *disordered*. What does this mean? Imagine your heart as a kind of compass. The needle of your heart wants to point to true north. God made us to work this way, when we are running exactly as we should: for our hearts, our will, to point toward God. Being sinful, having a disordered will, means your compass is out of whack. It's constantly spinning. Or it points at things other than God: at money, at sex, at success, fame, or safety. If we were *well-ordered*, our deepest desire would always be for God. But because we are disordered, we seem to want anything and everything *but* God. And the one thing other things cannot do for us is make us happy. Treated like gods, they make us miserable.

Seventh, then, what makes sin so awful is that it separates us from God. It pulls us like a magnet to God's creation *as if* the creation were the Creator. We are made to love and know God the way we might love and know a spouse. But instead we run after other lovers. We are one with them when we should be one with him. This is why the Bible makes much of the metaphor of adultery to describe our sinful ways. It is also why it describes God as jealous. *He wants us, and he wants us for himself alone.* Having made us, he knows that only he can satisfy us. But we want to be satisfied by trinkets and gadgets and other minor goods. We fear and resist the real thing whenever we see it. We can't help ourselves.

Eighth and last, sin is about idolatry. This is what I have been describing the whole time. Idolatry is worshiping something that is not God. And because only God is God—"Hear, O Israel, the LORD our God, the LORD is one"—if you worship anything else but the Lord, you're worshiping an idol. By "idol," don't think of a small statue you believe to be divine. Think of what you give yourself to. Think of what you devote yourself to. Think of what you most deeply love. A parent, a significant other, a job, a hobby, an idea: if that's what your compass needle points to, then that's what you worship. It's your idol. God's amazing work of salvation in Jesus is his loving rescue of us from our helpless idolatry. To be saved, to be freed from sin, is no longer to worship idols, but to worship God alone, the one true and living God.

Sinlessness, in a word, is knowing Jesus, the Sinless One. To love and worship him is to be on the road to freedom from sin and therefore freedom from idolatry. The process begins here below. It will be completed at his return. But first we die. For death is bound up with sin.

Yet the theme persists, the great relentless drumbeat of God's work in the world: out of nothing, he creates; out of death, he brings life.

*Yours in Christ,*
*a fellow pilgrim*

SIN CORRUPTS THE LIFE OF CREATION

*six*

# Death Opposes the Life of Creation

Imagine a number of men in chains, all under sentence of death, some of whom are each day butchered in the sight of the others; those remaining see their own condition in that of their fellows, and looking at each other with grief and despair await their turn. This is an image of the human condition.

—Blaise Pascal

## 42

*Dear future saint,*

Death is a terrible thing. Our culture has spent a long time and a good deal of money and ingenuity in the attempt to make us all forget about death, or at least to whitewash how dreadful it is. But Christianity is not denialist about death. It looks death straight in the face and sees it for what it is: the enemy of God.

Death is the opposite of life. Therefore it is the opposite of God. The reign of death on earth makes life on earth a living hell for many people. Pain, suffering, loss, violence, accidents, injuries, viruses, bacteria, cancer, diseases, tornadoes, hurricanes, hunger, starvation, malnourishment—death, death, death, death. Saint Augustine once remarked that because our lives are so defined by death, it is less that we live before dying than that we endure one long living death.

Perhaps you have suffered the loss of loved ones, or know those who have. It is a truth we can bear only for the briefest of moments: everyone we know, everyone we love, everyone who has ever lived, including ourselves, will one day die. Even if we all lived healthy, happy, fulfilled lives till old age, we would each still die. But we know that most of us do not have that blessing. Babies die in the womb. Infants die. Children die. Every age and class and race of human beings die every damn day. It is intolerable. It is frightening. It cannot be contemplated for long before looking away, thinking of something else, sedating one's mind or emotions with some numbing alternative: TV, the Internet, junk food, alcohol, kitsch.

It is so hard to allow ourselves to admit that the world we live in is ruled by a power bent on our destruction, and this power has an unbroken track record. Its record is 100 percent success. It kills us all.

This is not how God created the world to be. Death, like sin, is not part of God's good design. Death, like sin, is an intruder. Saint Paul goes so far as to call death the final enemy of God's kingdom. The last one to be defeated. But it must be defeated. Or else we would still suffer under its tyrannical rule.

In another letter, which he sent to the Christian community in the city of Rome a little under three decades after the crucifixion of Jesus, Paul writes that death is a product of sin. Meaning: sin comes first, then death follows. Death enters God's good creation when sin does. Sin is like a doorway, and death—or rather Death, capitalized—walks right through into God's world of teeming and bustling and overflowing Life. Just as Paul describes Sin as a kind

DEATH OPPOSES THE LIFE OF CREATION

of larger-than-life tyrant holding us sinners in its sway, so he describes Death. Death is the ultimate evil master from whose clutches we need deliverance. We are subject to Death. We are slaves of Death. We are bound to Death, hand and foot. We need liberation. We need a Liberator.

Sometimes the Christian story is told in such a way that the big problem Jesus resolves is Sin. And that's true. It is a perfectly good telling of the gospel.

But sometimes it is told, and I think Paul tells it this way, such that the big problem is not Sin but Death. It is Death that Jesus comes to do battle with. And do battle he does. The great victory, then, is not so much the cross of Jesus as his resurrection from the dead. Jesus dies—*but Jesus comes out the other side*. Jesus lives! He is alive! And being alive, he lives no longer in the shadow of Death. It has no power over him. So he will never die again. Never. He put Death to death. Now it's Jesus who is in charge of human affairs, not Death.

In the book of Revelation we see Jesus, risen in shining glory, and he's holding something in his hands. The author falls down at his feet, as though dead. But here is what Jesus says:

> Fear not:
> I am the First and the Last and the Living One;
> I died, and behold I am alive forevermore,
> and I have the keys of Death and Hades.

Do you see? Sometimes I think this sentence may be the greatest, most important, most profound verse in the whole Bible.

Jesus is alive. He went all the way down, and he came back up. But he didn't return empty-handed. He holds in his hands the keys—the power—of Life and Death, heaven and hell. Death no longer has the power to lock us up for good. We aren't fated to be stuck in hell forever. Jesus unlocked the gates. The keys are in his hands. He's in charge now. And he means to unleash Life where once there was Death. He is spreading it everywhere he goes. He's announcing freedom and Life *everywhere*, to *everyone*. Life, Life, Life, Life. And more Life. Life abundant. Life forevermore. Life eternal. Life for all. Life for good. Life with God.

Death is defeated. Life has triumphed. What else is there to do but fall before him, face to the ground, and worship?

*Yours in Christ,*
*a fellow pilgrim*

DEATH OPPOSES THE LIFE OF CREATION

## 43

*Dear future saint,*

I spy two major questions in your letter, amid all the others. One concerns why people continue to die—why Death appears still to be in charge—even though Jesus rose from the dead. We'll return to this question in a later letter. Another question, or set of questions, surrounds human origins and the Fall. What does it mean to say that Death, or death, entered the world with sin? Did no one die before Adam and Eve? What about animals? Are humans naturally immortal?

You just won't let me off the hook, will you?

There *is* a way of avoiding these questions, though you know by now that it's not the route I endorse. If you assert that God created the world some six thousand years ago in a six-day period, then you are not faced with questions about either animal or human death prior to the Fall, because the Fall follows immediately upon the creation of the world. This is what most Christians believed until the last two hundred years, and many Christians continue to believe it today. Nevertheless, as I wrote previously, it does not seem to fit the best cosmological, archaeological, biological, genetic, and other scientific evidence available to us about the age of the universe, the age of the earth, and the prehistory of organic life on this planet.

What then should we say?

The best answer, in my view, runs in two directions. One concerns angels and one concerns humans.

As you will recall, the picture in Genesis is not of Adam and Eve alone. Not only are there other animals, there is a talking serpent: the tempter. The church has long understood this character to be Satan, also called the Devil. Now who is that?

Banish from your mind the popular image of horns and a forked tail. All the more so if the image that comes to mind is not of wickedness but of a happy-go-lucky maker of mischief, akin to Loki among the Norse gods.

According to Christian teaching, Satan is one among many angels who, like our first parents, "fell" from a right relationship with God. This angelic fall came before our creation, for it is generally supposed that the angels were created first, perhaps even "before" the creation of this universe. (Time language is tricky here; we do not know how angels relate to our experience of time.)

But unlike us, for whom the Fall means that every human being is stuck in the common condition of sin, angels do not all fall together: there are angels who remain faithful to God and angels who do not. The first category of angels continue to serve God in love, obedience, and worship. The second category, better called demons or devils, no longer serve God but actively oppose him and his purposes in every respect.

This is just what we see in Eden. Satan bends the truth ever so slightly in order to lead the minds of Eve and Adam astray from the express command of God.

Now think globally, even cosmically. We have already seen that "sin and death" are really Sin and Death. They are personified powers that act as nefarious forces in our lives, doing us harm and holding us in bondage. What this shows is that Sin and Death have consequences for God's creation far beyond human life and experience. Sin and Death touch every nook and cranny of creation. This makes sense, both because a good thing once tainted remains tainted throughout (a single drop of red dye in a glass of clear water will change its color all over) and because human beings are the crown or microcosm of creation. What happens to us affects the rest of the good world God has made.

Keep thinking big. One way of understanding why the serpent is already in the garden is that the fall of the angels *affects creation at the source, from the beginning*. In other words, creation is fallen even before we humans get on the scene. Through angelic activity in the world, sin is already abroad in it. And thus, because sin is already in the world, death has already walked through that sad door and infected the life of the world—again, even before we arrive. This is why death and all that comes with it are a feature of organic and biological life from the moment it appears on earth. It's why death is paramount in the scientific record of every sort of earthly life of which we have evidence.

Is this the only way to explain death before humans? No. Perhaps uppercase Death is a different phenomenon than lowercase death, and God created the world from the beginning to feature the organic cycle of life and death in plants and animals, and this is a sort of brute fact baked into the nature of things. That could be true. Christians differ on this point. But my two cents is that an angelic fall makes the most sense of the evidence in conjunction with scriptural teaching.

What we must not do is let our decision sanitize our view of Death. You always know you have made an error in Christian theology when you make Death *merely* part of the natural order, *merely* an unavoidable aspect of the way of things. Death is the last enemy of the Lord Christ. Whatever else we say, we must say that.

Yours in Christ,
a fellow pilgrim

## 44

*Dear future saint,*

Once more on evolution, since it's clearly of interest to you. Let me put a bow on it. Then another bow or two on that bow. Then Jesus.

Suppose, with me, that God draws along the evolutionary process and at a certain point (say some 400,000 years ago) he brings into being a bona fide human being, one we would recognize, bearing the image of God and infused with a rational soul. Suppose, too, that the world in which this creature awakens is one marked by perpetual and uninterrupted death. What do we say about the human, then?

The church teaches that, while our soul is immortal, we humans as a species are not naturally immortal beings. We are mortal. By nature we will not live forever. Apart from some special grace, left to our own devices, we would die.

I think the best way to make sense of Genesis, the New Testament, and the scientific evidence is that whenever God made the first human beings, he provided, or rather made available, the very grace that would enable them to be kept from death. In the story of Eden this is called the tree of life. And after Adam and Eve sin, they are exiled from the garden *so that* they will not eat from this tree.

I take this to mean that, had we not sinned, God would have given us this extraordinary gift, a gift that goes beyond our nature, the gift of immortality or eternal life. But because we sinned, we lost this gift. Which is to say, we lost *the receiving of it*, since we never actually possessed it in the first place. Lacking this gift, entrapped and captured by Sin, we became subject to Death. No longer in the safe confines and loving protection of God our Creator, no longer in happy fellowship with him, we entered the world enslaved to Sin and Death, oppressed by them as dictators oppress their subjects in totalitarian countries.

This, in brief, is the sorry estate of the human race "east of Eden." Banished from the presence of God, we cannot help but sin, suffering our estrangement through every manner of folly and wickedness. We worship idols; we fashion weapons of war; we hate our neighbor; we kill our brother; we envy our sister; we disobey our parents; we steal what is not ours; we want what is not good; we reject what would bless us; we are proud, contemptuous, greedy, lustful, petty, dishonest, distrusting, untrustworthy, violent, impious, debaucherous, gluttonous, lazy, ungrateful—and more.

In a word, we are unhappy.

One philosopher summed up the human condition by saying the life of man is "solitary, poor, nasty, brutish, and short." Even with all the affluence and medicine and entertainment and creature comforts of the Western upper middle class, our unhappiness is unabated. We will not, as theologian Stanley Hauerwas puts it, make it out of life alive. Sin and Death appear unchecked and untamed.

This is the world we have made, the world of Sin, Death, and the Devil. This is the state into which God's good creation has been plunged headlong. This is the world every human being has ever known, the world every human will ever know. This is the fallen world.

And it is this world, not some other, that God loves. For what does Jesus say? "God so loved the world that he gave his only Son, that whoever believes in him should not perish but have eternal life. For God sent the Son into the world, not to condemn the world, but that the world might be saved through him." To grasp the significance of these verses, you must understand what is meant by "the world." Now you know.

Yours in Christ,
a fellow pilgrim

## 45

*Dear future saint,*

We are very close now. Soon we will turn to Jesus, face-to-face as it were. But first I want to draw together a complete picture about creation, original sin, and the Fall.

I have long thought that nothing—I repeat: nothing—makes so much sense of the world as we experience it as this combination of Christian doctrines. On one hand, the doctrine of creation makes sense of why we see so much beauty and depth and richness and glory in the world around us. It is well ordered. It is harmonious. It speaks to us. We spy peace in surprising corners. We grasp a providence at work, a knowing and loving and liberal hand that is generous in bounty and care. And we see it in ourselves as well. What is more precious than a newborn child? Who is happier than an expectant mother? Could you ever be convinced that the value of a single human life is anything but priceless? How many times have you walked outside, looked at the sky, the trees, and the grass; heard birdsong or a dog's bark; glimpsed a family walking by; felt the sun on your skin or the wind at your back; and thought, *This is good. Life is good. Whomever or whatever or wherever this comes from, THANK YOU.* Every culture from every period in history offers testimony to this experience. It is undeniable.

And yet. There is another hand. This hand is everything we spoke of in the last few letters. Pain, suffering, loss, danger, illness, evil, death. These, too, are undeniable. Nor are they just the hard parts of an otherwise good life. They make nonsense out of it. They make the happy speech of the cosmos pure gibberish. Martin Luther, the Protestant reformer, said that if all we had to go on was our experience of the world, we would conclude either that there is no God or, if there is a God, that he must be evil. His fellow reformer John Calvin agreed: "Although God is still pleased in many ways to manifest his paternal favor toward us, we cannot, from a mere survey of the world, infer that he is a Father."

This is a harsh teaching, but it resonates. There is so much horror in the world. It is incalculable. It is unfathomable. The Russian writer Fyodor Dostoevsky says as much in his novel *The Brothers Karamazov.* (This is a magnificent work of Christian wisdom, by the way. Read it.) One of his characters wonders aloud whether all the goodness and pleasure of the world is worth it if even a single child must suffer for it to be possible. I have four children. I must tell you, it is a hard question to answer. It may well be unanswerable. I do not know, myself, how to compare the suffering of a child with the beauty of this world. I am very tempted to say that it is not worth it—by which I mean that I do not know how to say it could be worth it, even if it is. A child's suffering is a horrendous thing.

*And yet*. We do live in this world, and we do see greatness and goodness in it. I, for one, am grateful to be alive, though I know all the evil that threatens me and all the evils that may befall me and my loved ones at any moment. I want to live. I love to live. I want to live in this very world, the one with all its evils and dangers and risks. And I am grateful to God from the bottom of my heart for making me alive and placing me in this world, me and everyone I know and love, including my children—my children who not only may but will suffer. And not only suffer but die.

Why do I feel this way? Why do so many of us feel this way?

The doctrine of creation and the doctrine of original sin—not to mention the doctrine of salvation, which we have not yet discussed in full—are the answer. The world is good but fallen. The world is God's but also the Devil's. The world is beautiful but also rotten. The world is life but also death.

Together, these make it all make sense. Nothing else comes close. Without them, I honestly wouldn't know what to think. I've studied the alternatives. They just don't fit together. The pieces are a jumble; the numbers don't add up. Look for yourself. See if they make sense to you. The technical term here is "explanatory power." What account of the world has the power to explain the whole and all its parts, including the most difficult ones?

I think the answer is the church's account. It's the true one. Not because it explains it all away. It remains a mystery. But it functions like a lens, or glasses, that bring into focus what once was blurry or obscure.

Not to mention that creation and original sin, as I alluded to a moment ago, are not the whole story. The third element is salvation. We aren't stuck in this state forever. We aren't left to our own devices. We aren't abandoned as orphans. We aren't exiled indefinitely.

The Lord is coming. He comes, I say, he comes to save the earth. Let us go out to meet him.

*Yours in Christ,*
*a fellow pilgrim*

## 46

*Dear future saint,*

Blaise Pascal was a brilliant Christian thinker and writer, born around four hundred years ago, who also happened to be a scientific and mathematical genius. He wrote an enormous collection of what he called *pensées*, which is French for "thoughts" or "reflections." Here is one especially powerful passage from his writing, on the same theme as the last letter. He is able to capture what I was gesturing at far better than I could:

> Man's greatness and wretchedness are so evident that the true religion must necessarily teach us that there is in man some great principle of greatness and some great principle of wretchedness.
>
> It must also account for such amazing contradictions.
>
> To make man happy it must show him that a God exists whom we are bound to love; that our true bliss is to be in him, and our sole ill to be cut off from him. It must acknowledge that we are full of darkness which prevents us from knowing and loving him, and so, with our duty obliging us to love God and our [sinfulness] leading us astray, we are full of unrighteousness. It must account to us for the way in which we thus go against God and our own good. It must teach us the cure for our helplessness and the meaning of obtaining this cure. Let us examine all the religions of the world on that point and let us see whether any but the Christian religion meets it.
>
> Do the philosophers, who offer us nothing else for our good but the good that is within us? Have they found the cure for our ills? Is it curing man's presumption to set him up as God's equal? . . .
>
> What religion, then, will teach us how to cure pride and [sinfulness]? What religion, in short, will teach us our true good, our duties, the weaknesses which lead us astray, the cause of these weaknesses, the treatment that can cure them, and the means of obtaining such treatment? All the other religions have failed to do so. Let us see what the wisdom of God will do.

As Pascal writes more succinctly elsewhere: "God alone is man's true good," yet it is "not only impossible but useless to know God without Christ." In sum:

Knowing God without knowing our own wretchedness makes for pride.

Knowing our own wretchedness without knowing God makes for despair.

Knowing Jesus Christ strikes the balance because he shows us both God and our own wretchedness.

*Yours in Christ,*
*a fellow pilgrim*

# *seven*

# *God Becomes a Human Being*

The Only Begotten Word, even though he was God and born from God by nature, he it was who became man. He did not disdain the poverty of human nature. As God he wished to make that flesh which was held in the grip of sin and death evidently superior to sin and death. He made it his own, and so he is said to have undergone a birth like ours, while all the while remaining what he was. The same one was at once God and man. He was God in an appearance like ours, and the Lord in the form of a slave. This is what we mean when we say that he became flesh, and for the same reasons we affirm that the holy virgin is the Mother of God.

—Saint Cyril of Alexandria

*Dear future saint,*

At long last, we come to Christ. Yet he has never been far. Now, though, the veil begins to be removed. We see clearly the face that has been staring back at us the whole time.

I began, many letters ago, by saying that the first thing to know about Jesus is that he was (and is) a Jew. Which meant we had to turn to the Jews in order to understand Jesus. But the Jewish Scriptures themselves, which tell us of God's covenant people, point us all the way back to the beginning. Having traced out those lines, we now jump back into history, into Israel, into wars and empires and pagan occupiers of the Holy Land. We find ourselves in Nazareth, sitting in the quiet with a young girl. She is studying the Scriptures of her people. And then something miraculous happens.

An angel from God named Gabriel appears to Mary and announces to her the most startling news. She will conceive and give birth to a boy. His name will be Jesus—*Yeshua*, or Joshua, which means "the Lord saves"—and he will be the Son of God and of David both. In other words, he will be king: king over Israel, king of heaven and earth.

*But how?* Mary asks. *I know not man.* What she means is that, though she is engaged and thus as good as married, she is a virgin. Virgins are not often mothers.

It is a sensible reply. The angel's answer is simple: The power of God will work a wonder in her womb, a wonder that is at once without precedent (have you ever met a virgin mother? a child without a human father?) and the fulfillment of Israel's long history. That history is full of barren wombs, promised sons, and joyful celebrations of God's unexpected gift of life.

Now we see the logical, or rather theological, culmination of that happy line of unlikely mothers.

God Almighty, the faithful God of Abraham, is beginning his long-awaited and extraordinary work of delivering Israel from her suffering, of drawing near in presence and love, of approaching David's royal throne once for all to rule his people with justice and compassion.

God has sent his Son. To a young, unknown virgin. In faraway backwater Galilee. Without fanfare or warning.

GOD BECOMES A HUMAN BEING

At this moment—called "the Annunciation"—human cells begin to multiply and cluster in the womb of Mary. These cells are the cells of God's own Son. They are his flesh. The Son of God has a human beginning in the secret mystery of Mary's body, hidden from sight and from any knowledge save hers.

For when Gabriel told Mary what would happen, that God would work a miracle in her own body, this is what she said: "Behold, I am the handmaid of the Lord; let it be to me according to your word."

These words are the beginning of the gospel. It all comes down to Mary. The Lord entrusts her with the salvation of the world. And she says yes.

Her faith is a resounding echo and reiteration of her father Abraham's faith. Her faith is the fruit and the root of her Son's faithfulness. In her faith our own has its source and pattern. Look to Mary, and you will see exactly what it means to be a Christian—even a saint.

*Yours in Christ,*
*a fellow pilgrim*

## 48

*Dear future saint,*

Speaking of saints, Mary is a good excuse to say a little more about them. I wrote to you early on about what a saint is, what sainthood and sanctity are, and why I address you as someone called and created for holiness.

Sainthood is not only future. It's also past. What I mean is that the practice of remembering actual saints is a part of striving toward holiness ourselves. This is why it's worth learning who the saints *are*. They're not decoration. Just as Israel's story is your family history, so is the church's. It's been two millennia since the time of the apostles. Your heroes and models, the names and lives you know by heart, shouldn't be limited to the Bible. Heaven is populated by far more souls than those mentioned in Scripture.

This explains the church's stubborn repetition of the same title before so many names. It's a way of both honoring and claiming Jesus's disciples for himself. They belong to him first of all. They are defined by him and by their devotion to him. They are alive, even now, because of him, since to be alive at all, following death in this world, is to be "in" Christ. To be in Christ, beyond this life, is to be in heaven. Why? In Saint Paul's words: heaven is "where Christ is."

So Augustine is not only Augustine but *Saint* Augustine, just as his mother is *Saint* Monica and his teacher *Saint* Ambrose and his fellow church fathers *Saint* Gregory and *Saint* Cyril and *Saint* Maximus and the rest.

The same goes for biblical characters and authors. Paul is an apostle, but he is also a saint; likewise for Priscilla and Aquila, Elizabeth and Peter, James and John. (Church custom is divided about whether to call saints in the Old Testament "Saint X." Sometimes you will encounter "Saint Elijah" or "Saint David" in Christian writing or prayer, but more common is just "Elijah" and "David." Out of deference to tradition and to thorny questions about Christianity and Judaism, I opt for the latter practice.)

This way of speaking is more than semantics. It clarifies, in daily speech, and especially in the language of devotion and worship, that these people aren't merely historical or literary characters but women and men made holy by God's grace. They are vessels of divine power and instruments of his peace.

More, it reminds us that the history of salvation, indeed the history of God's people, is *ongoing*. It is not yet finished. The holiness that captured Elijah and Ruth and Phoebe and Barnabas continues to snare sinners down through the centuries: Perpetua and Cyprian, Athanasius and Macrina, Bernard and Catherine, Thomas and Teresa, Oscar Romero and Maria Skobtsova—and so many more. Among that "many more" could be you, too.

The church uses visual aids to tell this history of holiness. They're called *icons*. "Icon" is the name for Christian images. These images are made in a very particular way. They depict scenes or persons from the Bible or church history. They do not portray God in himself, which is both impossible and against God's own command. Instead they portray Jesus, who is God in the flesh. Because he is fully human—because he is the invisible image of God made visible for us—images of Christ are permitted. Not to be worshiped like an idol; to remind us, rather, of the mystery of our faith. And to draw together in our minds the whole single story, from Adam and Abraham to the present, in which all of us, without exception, are included; in which God, without ceasing, is at work.

One result is that some of us are drawn to certain saints more than others. As G. K. Chesterton once put it, to see Christ in the life of Saint Francis is to realize not just that Francis is like Christ but that Christ is like Francis. "Christ plays in ten thousand places," writes the poet Gerard Manley Hopkins:

> Lovely in limbs, and lovely in eyes not his
> To the Father through the features of men's faces.

Each of us is a little Christ, in C. S. Lewis's phrase. I see Christ in you, even now, as I hope you see Christ in me. We see Christ in the saints, because in them his victory is complete. Looking to them—as they say, with Paul, "Imitate me as I imitate Christ"—we see the Lord; in seeing him, we are conformed to his image, as they already have been.

In this way we shall all be made perfect, and Christ shall be all in all of us, and all shall be well.

*Yours in Christ,*
*a fellow pilgrim*

## 49

*Dear future saint,*

A few letters ago I meditated on the opening chapter of Saint Luke's Gospel, with a glance or two in the direction of Saint Matthew's Gospel. A "Gospel," capitalized, is the name for one of the four start-to-finish stories of Jesus in the Bible; together they open the New Testament.

The way each one begins tells us something about that Gospel's perspective. And each of them does have a perspective. It is as though four people in your life—say, your mother, brother, spouse, and best friend—were put in separate rooms and asked to write a detailed account of your story, who you are and what you've done with your life. Would the stories be identical? Not at all. Would each of them be true? Yes, and all the more so for being different from one another. They would give a stranger not one but many angles on your identity, your deep character known differently by different people.

This is what the four Gospels do. Hence their name. For "the" gospel is nothing but the good news about Jesus, and the Gospels tell us about Jesus, beginning to end.

Luke opens with Saint Elizabeth, a relative of the Virgin Mary, and her own experience of barrenness before a surprising pregnancy. Her son is Saint John, or "John the Baptist," who later prepares the way for Jesus. After Elizabeth comes the Annunciation to Mary in the story I recounted previously.

Matthew opens with a genealogy, meaning a record of the family tree leading from Abraham, through David, to Jesus. Then he tells the story of Jesus's miraculous conception, only this time from the perspective of Saint Joseph, to whom Mary was betrothed.

Saint Mark opens with Jesus, already a grown man of around thirty years old, approaching his relative John to be baptized in the Jordan River. It is this magnificent royal moment—in which a voice from heaven announces to onlookers that Jesus is God's Son while God's Spirit descends upon him in the form of a dove—that Mark uses to begin Jesus's public ministry, and therefore his story. He won't let you forget who Jesus is: God's Son and Israel's king.

Saint John (not the Baptist) opens still differently. The Fourth Gospel doesn't begin in time. It begins in eternity. It opens with the exact same words as Genesis: "In the beginning . . ." But before John describes, or rather redescribes, the event of creation, he needs to tell you who the actors are. For God appears not to be alone—though we know that God is one, and only God is Creator. John writes:

> In the beginning was the Word, and the Word was with God, and the Word was God. He was in the beginning with God; all things were made through him, and without him was not anything made that was made. In him was life, and the life was the light of men. The light shines in the darkness, and the darkness has not overcome it.

Just who or what is this Word? Answer:

> And the Word became flesh and dwelt among us, full of grace and truth; we have beheld his glory, glory as of the only Son from the Father.... And from his fullness have we all received, grace upon grace. For the law was given through Moses; grace and truth came through Jesus Christ. No one has ever seen God; the only Son, who is in the bosom of the Father, he has made him known.

The Word is Jesus; Jesus is the Word. Jesus is the Word made flesh. Which is to say, since the Word is not only with God but is God, Jesus is God in the flesh.

These words—*God in the flesh*—form the unsurpassable mystery of Christian faith. The reality they name is called the "incarnation." This word comes from the Latin for "flesh." It means, literally, "enfleshing." In Jesus God was enfleshed: God himself put on flesh and bone, skin and hair, a body like yours and mine. When the angel came to Mary and she consented to the Lord's announcement, he himself, the living Word from all eternity, began to gestate in her womb. He was a clump of cells. He was a fetus. His was a human life: vulnerable, silent, unseen, the Author and Creator undergoing, somehow, the process of an unborn child's development, step by step, day by day.

Words fail. God was a baby. God was born. God had a mother—God has a mother. God, the newborn, looked into his mother's eyes with the same universal look of need, hunger, love, and desire that every newborn has. And she looked back.

In light of this mystery, Christians later gave a special title to Mary: "Theotokos." It means *God-bearer*. Applied to Mary, it honors her as the human being who bore the one true God in her womb. Sometimes the title is rendered *Mother of God*. If Jesus is God (which he is) and Mary is Jesus's mother (which she is), then it follows that Mary is God's mother. Not God's *creator*, mind you, any more than your mother created you or mine created me. Mary, strictly speaking, is the mother of *God in the flesh*, since that's who and what Jesus is. Thus the church's title for her. She is Theotokos.

Words, as I say, fail. They fail absolutely. But the truth is still there, staring back at us like the newborn Jesus—Creator and creature, Maker of Mary and yet made within her. In a poem by W. H. Auden, the angel Gabriel says to Mary:

> . . . child, it lies
> Within your power of choosing to
> Conceive the Child who chooses you.

This is the reach of God's love, the scope of his solidarity with us. He becomes one of us in every respect. His vulnerability and need are ours. He is us. He shares our lot. Why?

So that we might share his.

*Yours in Christ,*
*a fellow pilgrim*

**50**

*Dear future saint,*

Being a Christian is about Christ, knowing and loving and following him. Hence my talking about him from the beginning. The centrality of Christ also means we could camp out here, in the Gospels, for the rest of time. But neither you nor I want that.

So how can we make sure to talk about the most important things concerning Jesus without my writing, and you being forced to read, thousands upon thousands of letters? As Saint John remarks on the last page of his Gospel: if someone wrote down everything Jesus did and said, the world wouldn't have enough libraries to contain all the books that would be written.

Here's what I propose. Read the following. We'll use it as a template for our reflections on the life and career of Jesus. Then we'll use it as a touchstone and measure for what we say about him in letters to come.

> I believe in one Lord, Jesus Christ,
> the only Son of God,
> eternally begotten of the Father,
> God from God, Light from Light,
> true God from true God,
> begotten, not made,
> of one Being with the Father.
> Through him all things were made.
>
> For us and for our salvation
>     he came down from heaven:
> by the power of the Holy Spirit
>     he became incarnate from the Virgin Mary,
>     and was made man.
>
> For our sake he was crucified under Pontius Pilate;
>     he suffered death and was buried.
>     On the third day he rose again
>         in accordance with the Scriptures;

he ascended into heaven
and is seated at the right hand of the Father.

He will come again in glory to judge the living and the dead,
and his kingdom will have no end.

This comes from the middle section of the Nicene Creed, what is called the "second article." The first article we already discussed in previous letters regarding God as Creator. The third will come later, when we turn to the Holy Spirit.

The second article is the beating heart of the Creed, because it is a snapshot—in as few words as possible—of the mystery of our salvation in Christ. Jesus is God made man for us. He came to earth, was born of a virgin, suffered and died on a cross, rose from the dead, ascended to heaven, and will return once and for all as King and Lord and Judge and Savior. This is Christian faith. This is Christian hope. This is what makes you Christian. The name and life and work of Jesus Christ.

Remember: Although the coming of Jesus is new, the God who comes in Jesus is not. He is the God of Israel, the Creator God, the God we have been getting to know in all our previous letters. Jesus reveals this God with utter perfection, radiant beauty, and compelling clarity. But he is not some other God. We are not meeting him for the first time, at least not if we have been paying attention to the history and Scriptures of Israel.

Yet Jesus is God's Son: a human being, a descendant of Abraham, one of the sons of Israel. How can he be both Abraham's Lord and Abraham's child? How can he address God as "Father" while himself saying, "Before Abraham was, I am"? What mystery is here revealed, or hidden? Can we even capture it with human words?

We can't capture it, that's for sure. But we can attempt to find the least inadequate words for it. In the next few letters I'll make that my goal. I am sure to fail. In my failure, though, don't loosen your grasp on the crux of the matter: Jesus Christ, friend of sinners, suffering servant, your God and mine—come to save us all.

Yours in Christ,
a fellow pilgrim

## 51

*Dear future saint,*

I've quoted from the Nicene Creed. I've explained what "Theotokos" means. I've mentioned saints and icons. But I've somehow neglected to talk about church councils.

In the first eight hundred years of the church, major controversies occasionally arose. Conflict is not unusual in the church. In fact, as theologian John Webster writes, conflict over how to interpret Scripture is a primary way "in which God keeps the church in the truth." The fruit of such conflict, by the guidance of God's Spirit, is often greater clarity about the gospel: what it entails and how to live it.

In response to these controversies in the early church, Christian leaders called bishops would gather together in the hundreds in a single place. They would discuss the matter; listen to competing views; read and reread Scripture; pray; then issue a decision. These decisions were meant to be broadly defined statements that drew clear boundaries for orthodox faith. ("Orthodoxy" means *right belief*.) Their goal was to eliminate obvious errors and invite all Christians to sign on the dotted line, so to speak.

The topics they addressed were not insignificant. The first council met in the city of Nicaea, in modern-day Turkey, about three hundred years after Jesus's crucifixion. The second met about half a century later in Constantinople (modern-day Istanbul). Together they rejected any and all denials of either Jesus's or the Spirit's divinity by issuing what the church calls the Nicene Creed (begun at the first council and revised at the second).

The third and fourth councils met in Ephesus and Chalcedon, respectively, in the following century. They confirmed that Jesus was fully human, soul and body, though without sin; that given his full divinity, Mary is rightly called Theotokos; and that Jesus possesses two "natures," human and divine, while being a single person.

The fifth and sixth councils met over the coming two centuries, mostly hashing out unfinished business about the nature of the incarnation. The seventh council met just before the year 800, again in Nicaea, confirming for the church that icons of Christ and the saints were not forbidden but welcomed as edifying and beneficial for all the faithful.

These seven councils are often called "great" or "ecumenical" councils, because they are the common inheritance of all Christians everywhere in the world. Their proper function is to unite us in the one faith of the apostles, recorded in the Bible and handed on to us by the church fathers. When we recite the Creed or defer to the decisions they made in council, our trust is not in them but in the Holy Spirit, who, Christ promised, would lead the church into all truth. As he said, he would not leave us orphans. His Spirit remains. The councils are eloquent testimony to his living presence among us, a presence that ensures that the gates of hell will never prevail against his people.

*Yours in Christ,*
*a fellow pilgrim*

## 52

*Dear future saint,*

Your guess is on the money. I figured you'd know. It's time for us to talk about the Trinity.

First things first. No, it's not a bad math equation. The mystery of the triune God is not about how one plus one plus one equals one.

I am not, God forbid, going to *explain* the Trinity. That's impossible. What I'm going to do instead is say a little about why the early church saw the *doctrine* of the Trinity as both biblical and essential to the truth of the gospel.

The doctrine of the Trinity is, for all its potential to intimidate, rather straightforward. God is one being in three persons. Put differently, God exists eternally in and as three persons: the Father, the Son, and the Holy Spirit. Each is God. All are God. All are one God.

Yet the Father is not the Son, nor is the Son the Spirit, nor still is the Spirit the Father. They are distinct from one another, though their unity is complete. In their lasting difference, they are one God. Always have been, always will be.

The God of Israel is the Holy Trinity, from everlasting to everlasting.

When you pray to God, therefore, you are praying to the Trinity. When you refer to the Creator, you are referring to the Trinity. When you worship on Sunday morning or say that the Lord is present, it is the Trinity being worshiped, the Trinity who is present.

The Trinity is God; God is the Trinity.

This is why the church worships Jesus and prays to the Spirit. If either were not God, or something less than God, we would be worshiping or praying to an idol. The church obeys the Lord's commandment to worship him and him alone. When she worships Father, Son, and Spirit, she is keeping the command, not transgressing it.

Now, why is this important? How is it related to Scripture and to the gospel that Scripture proclaims?

First, the Trinity matters because God matters. If God is triune, and you want to know God, then you want to know the Trinity. Who God is matters in and of itself.

Second, while the doctrine of the Trinity is not laid out verbatim in the Bible, the Bible does teach the Trinity. How? By teaching that God is one and that God is Father, Son, and Holy Spirit. In other words, by telling the story of Israel, Jesus, and the church, Scripture *unfolds the identity of the Lord God*. The church's name for this identity is "Trinity." It's her one-word catchall to show that she has read the *whole* story, has listened to *all* the witnesses of Scripture. In fidelity to the complete testimony of God's word, she confesses faith in God the Father, God the Son, and God the Spirit.

Third, apart from the doctrine of the Trinity, the gospel falls apart. If Son and Spirit are not God together with the Father, the gospel is no good news at all. Why?

Because the gospel is the good news of "Immanuel," a title taken from the prophet Isaiah and applied by Saint Matthew to the child Christ. It means *God with us*. It is Jesus's own name. The good news is that Jesus is God with us.

It would not be the same news, it would not be good, if Jesus were *almost-*God with us, or *nearly-*God with us, or *two-steps-removed-from-*God with us. Jesus is either God or not. There are no grades to the Lord's divinity. You're either all-God or not-God. We creatures are not-God, full stop. Jesus is a creature. But he is also the Creator. If he were not, he'd just be an ordinary creature like you and me. How could he save us if that were true?

This is what the early church saw so clearly, led by pastors and teachers like Origen, Saint Irenaeus, Saint Athanasius, Saint Basil the Great, Saint Gregory of Nazianzus, Saint Gregory of Nyssa, and Saint Cyril of Alexandria (among many others). If God alone is our Savior, yet Jesus saves us, either Jesus is not our Savior or Jesus is God in the flesh. Likewise, if God alone is holy, yet the Spirit of Christ sanctifies us, either we have not truly been made holy, or the Spirit is himself fully God.

As Basil remarks in one of the earliest writings we have on the Holy Spirit: How could we be cleansed of our sins by being baptized into the name of Father, Son, and Spirit—as Jesus commanded—unless this is the very Name of God? I cannot be baptized for the remission of my sins in the name of Jim or Jane, no matter their moral character. Only the Creator can make creatures whole.

It turns out, then, that Father, Son, and Spirit are the one divine Creator. They were there at the beginning, as Genesis shows us they were, if only we have eyes to see.

> In the beginning *God* created . . .
> . . . and the *Spirit* of God was moving . . .
> And God *said* . . .

There they are, acting as one. God the Father creates a universe from nothing by speaking his mighty Word, breathing it out by the power of his Spirit. Recall the psalm I quoted in my fifth letter to you:

> By the word of the LORD the heavens were made,
> and all their host by the breath of his mouth.

And the opening of Saint John's Gospel:

> In the beginning was the Word, and the Word was with God, and the Word was God. He was in the beginning with God; all things were made through him, and without him was not anything made that was made.

In the phrase of one scholar, Jesus the Word is both God's *self* and God's *fellow*. In the phrase of another, Jesus is God's "second self." God's life is a perfect communion of these two—Speaker and Spoken, Father and Son, God and Image—in the unity of their common Spirit or Breath. To know God is to enter this infinite circle of giving and receiving, going and returning, naming and glorifying, working and resting. The gospel is the good news that this God has turned his face toward us, has drawn near in the calling of a people and the birth of a child.

Jesus is God with us. Because of him, God will always be with us. More: Because of him, we will always be with God.

*Yours in Christ,*
*a fellow pilgrim*

## 53

*Dear future saint,*

I thought I was done with the Trinity, but you want more. Specifically, you want to know whether this doctrine is *practical*, or just an idea.

"Just an idea" is not itself an idea I want to endorse. As I've already said, who God is matters, whether or not it turns out to be "practical."

Furthermore, if the truth of the gospel depends on the truth of the Trinity, then I'd say that's pretty practical.

Finally, practices like public worship and reading the Bible rely on this doctrine. Without it, they are only so many vague words and empty forms. They don't hold together. The Trinity is the bond that unites them in truth.

In one sense, then, the doctrine is already practical enough. In another sense, it is a mistake to try to make everything practical. Is the beauty of the beloved "practical" to a lover? Is it there "for" something? Or is its value precisely its "uselessness," its "just there"-ness, its "good in itself"-ness? This is what the lover loves, what transfixes him. The beauty is there to behold, to pursue, to be adored, perhaps. But it is just *there*. It's not for "use." The same holds for the beauty of the triune Lord.

Having said that, let me show you one way to "practice" the Trinity.

In the Gospel of Saint Matthew, in what is called the Sermon on the Mount, Jesus teaches his disciples how to pray. "Pray then like this," he says:

> Our Father who art in heaven,
> Hallowed be thy name.
> Thy kingdom come,
> Thy will be done,
>     On earth as it is in heaven.
> Give us this day our daily bread;
> And forgive us our trespasses,
>     As we forgive those who trespass against us.
> And lead us not into temptation
>     But deliver us from the evil one.
>     For thine is the kingdom
>     And the power and the glory,
>     Forever and ever: Amen.

GOD BECOMES A HUMAN BEING

Some call this the Lord's Prayer; others, the Our Father. It is prayed daily by millions of believers and recited every Sunday in worship by most Christians. I cannot unearth all its many treasures. I want to single out one all-important thing.

Jesus invites you, his disciple, to address the God of Abraham as Father, in fact as "our" Father. It's easy to guess who the "our" is there: the people of God. But *is* God your Father? Jesus regularly refers to him as "my" Father. Is calling God "Father" the same as calling him "Creator"? Is he *everyone's* Father? If so, why does it matter that Jesus calls him Father?

The doctrine of the Trinity teaches us that Jesus is the eternal Son of God in human form. From all eternity, he is the Son of the Father, both of whom are fully divine. To be precise, he is the *one, only, unique* Son of the Father. There is no one else in the Godhead except the Father of whom Jesus is the Son and the Spirit in whose love they are united.

The upshot: No, God is *not* your Father just because he is your Creator. "Father" and "Creator" are not synonyms. By nature, God is Father only to his Son Jesus. If God is your Father, it is because he becomes—has become, may become, will become—your Father. How?

Through Jesus. And the Our Father is one way it comes about.

Jesus invites you, his follower, to stand in his place. Standing there, filled with his Spirit, you call on God the way Jesus does: *Abba*, which is Aramaic for "Father." The Spirit of Jesus is the Spirit of Sonship—the Spirit of adoption—and when you are baptized, what happened to Jesus at his baptism happens to you. The Spirit of God descends upon you, and a voice from heaven declares that you are his beloved child.

All this is contained in the opening two words of the Lord's Prayer, simple as they may seem. Pray them, and you are "practicing" the Trinity, because you are not just praying *to* but *in* the Trinity. Through your words the Spirit of God's Son cries aloud to the Father of Jesus—and he hears you, calling you by name in turn. Try it now. See what happens.

*Yours in Christ,*
*a fellow pilgrim*

## eight

# God Offers Himself for the World

In the cross is salvation, in the cross is life, in the cross is protection from enemies, in the cross is infusion of heavenly sweetness, in the cross is strength of mind, in the cross is joy of spirit, in the cross is highest virtue, in the cross is perfect holiness. There is no salvation of soul nor hope of everlasting life but in the cross. Take up your cross, therefore, and follow Jesus, and you shall enter eternal life.

—Thomas à Kempis

## 54

*Dear future saint,*

You see, the thing to do instead of reading me is to read the Gospels, all four of them. I would recommend Saint Mark first, followed by Saint Matthew, Saint John, and Saint Luke—then Acts, which is Luke's sequel to his own Gospel: the second volume in a two-volume story. Any order is fine, though. (If you couldn't do all of them, I'd suggest Luke-Acts in one fell swoop.) But you need depth and texture and detail, not mere summary, certainly not by me.

Nevertheless, I want to lay out, in a few brief paragraphs, the course of Christ's life and ministry, death and resurrection. Then in subsequent letters I'll comment on a few crucial elements as I see them. As I've said before and will surely say again, we could remain here forever. But we have other things to talk about, and limited time. Happily, we've never *not* been talking about Jesus in these letters. And I won't stop talking about him even as we leave the thirty years he spent on earth.

As for those thirty years.

His divine life begins in eternity—in truth, it is without beginning or end—but his human life begins in the womb of Mary. (Because she was a virgin and, in her song of praise for having conceived Jesus, prophesied that all future generations would call her blessed, she is called by the tradition not only Saint Mary but the Blessed Virgin. I will from time to time also use that title, out of respect for the Lord's holy mother.)

We know next to nothing about Jesus's childhood. His first three decades of life are almost entirely hidden from us. He was raised in Nazareth the son of a carpenter. Nazareth is in Galilee, which is north along the Jordan River, to the west of the Sea of Galilee. Think of it as a kind of country backwater, compared to southern Israel, where Jerusalem is located, to the west of the Dead Sea. Put differently, Nazareth of Galilee is far from the halls and palaces of power.

At the same time, Galilee also spanned the juncture of numerous local cultures and international cities; Jesus would have grown up seeing Roman soldiers and hearing Greek and other languages spoken, in addition to his native Aramaic. We may take for granted that he grew up making regular pilgrimages to Jerusalem—just under one hundred miles from Nazareth—for major festivals like Passover.

Jesus enters the public eye when he is baptized in the Jordan by Saint John, a wild prophet who preached the imminent arrival of God's kingdom. This moment begins his ministry. His ministry consists of traveling from town to town teaching in synagogues, gathering followers, healing the sick, and casting out evil spirits from those possessed by them. Saint Peter sums it up this way, proclaiming

"the word which [God] sent to Israel, preaching good news of peace by Jesus Christ (he is Lord of all), the word which was proclaimed throughout all Judea, beginning from Galilee after the baptism which John preached: how God anointed Jesus of Nazareth with the Holy Spirit and with power; how he went about doing good and healing all that were oppressed by the devil, for God was with him. And we [apostles] are witnesses to all that he did both in the country of the Jews and in Jerusalem."

The message of Jesus was simple. In his own words:

"The time is fulfilled
and the kingdom of God is at hand.
Repent, and believe in the good news."

"Repent" means *turn*, a kind of total collective revolution. As if you were walking down the street, saw protesters marching the other way, and joined them.

Jesus isn't talking to anyone or everyone. He's talking to his fellow Jews. He is a prophet—more than a prophet, but not less—sent to God's people. The kingdom of Israel's God is drawing near, so Israel had better prepare.

What is God's kingdom? The word can also be translated *rule* or *reign*. The advance of God's kingdom is the spread of his rule, his domain, his dominion or empire. It is where his will is done, not resisted; his commands obeyed, not flouted; his grace and healing received, not rejected. God is king, regardless of our wishes or actions, but his king*dom* is fully present only where all things are right—all wrongs made right. Hence our petition in the Lord's Prayer:

Thy kingdom come,
Thy will be done,
On earth as it is in heaven.

The signs of the kingdom's nearness are present in Jesus's words and deeds alike. When he speaks, he speaks with authority. His word is like God's (because it is God's): the demons flee from it; the winds and the waters obey it; illness heeds its command; even the dead rise in response to it. Nothing but a simple word from Jesus's lips is necessary for a man's sins to be forgiven. He touches blind eyes, and they see; he steps out onto water, and it holds his weight; a mob tries to seize and kill him, but he walks right through them. A woman bleeding for twelve years grabs but the hem of his cloak and is immediately healed.

This rabbi not only teaches with authority. His very being exudes power.

He is a rabbi, though. A teacher of the Jewish Scriptures. He argues with fellow teachers of the Law of Moses. He interprets it differently than they do. Almost as though he knows its inner secrets. Almost as though he is its final arbiter—the way an author is.

The conflicts escalate. The symbolism of his mission and message is difficult to escape. The twelve followers he appoints stand for the twelve tribes of Jacob: this Jesus is forming—reforming and re-forming—a renewed Israel, an Israel within Israel. Standing at the center is himself.

Who does he think he is?

Peter knows: Jesus is "the Messiah, the Son of the living God." He is anointed with God's own Spirit, beloved as God's own Son. He is the rightful king of Israel. He is the Christ.

The city of Jerusalem welcomes him as such. They cry out in ecstasy at the Son of David, riding into the Holy City on a humble donkey. This is the Chosen One, the Deliverer, the Liberator, the Rescuer. As in the exodus from Egypt, God will use Jesus to save Israel from Roman bondage. Not just another David, he is another Moses. Hosannah in the highest!

Five days later, Jesus's lifeless corpse hangs from a tree, just outside Jerusalem's walls. On a hill for visitors to notice on their way into the city. The message is clear: *This is what happens to Jewish rebels. Know the power of Rome; behold the might of Caesar.*

Above his head is nailed a piece of wood with a small slogan written in Aramaic, Greek, and Latin for all to see. It is bitterly ironic—a final mocking humiliation for Jesus, his disciples, and the entire Jewish people:

JESUS OF NAZARETH, THE KING OF THE JEWS.

*Yours in Christ,*
*a fellow pilgrim*

*Dear future saint,*

I understand why you would find my last letter so dour, even despairing. That's part of the point, though not the whole point. I wanted you to see at least three things.

First, how simple the movement is from Jesus's baptism to his arrest and execution in Jerusalem. It's a straight line. The basic story there is not in dispute among historians.

Second, this story is simultaneously "religious" and "political." It concerns a man who spoke on God's behalf and died a rebel's death, sentenced for sedition against the emperor. The imperial governor, Pilate, made this clear with Jesus's crown of thorns and the title above his head. *Here's where would-be Jewish kings end up; tread carefully.*

Third, the climax of Jesus's earthly career was swift, brutal, surprising, shameful, frightening, and dispiriting. You can understand why his followers abandoned him—all but a few women and one especially devoted friend. None of them saw the cross coming. What they expected was victory over the Romans and Jesus's enthronement as king of Israel. Not this.

So they scattered. Another failed messiah. Death is the end of every story, including this one. "We had hoped," one follower lamented, "that he was the one to redeem Israel." Apparently not.

What then? Had God forsaken his people? Could he? When would he act? *Wouldn't* he act?

Similar questions had arisen some centuries earlier, in the life of the prophet Ezekiel. The Lord took him to a valley of dry bones. In the paraphrase of theologian Robert Jenson, the Lord asked Ezekiel: *"Can these bones live? These bones that are the whole of my people? Can the death of my people be reversed?"*

Jenson goes on: "Christians are those who believe Jesus' Resurrection was the Lord's answer to his own question."

*Yours in Christ,*
*a fellow pilgrim*

GOD OFFERS HIMSELF FOR THE WORLD

*Dear future saint,*

I realize how hard it is to *feel* the weight of Jesus's death when the two things anybody knows about Jesus is that he died on a cross and, supposedly, rose on the third day. We can't unlearn that knowledge. But we can widen the frame.

What do I mean? Just this. Nobody knew Jesus was going to "die on the cross for our sins." Nobody thought *anyone* was going to do that. There, at the cross, Saint Mary of Nazareth and Saint Mary Magdalene and the other women are simply grieving what appears to be senseless violence and unspeakable loss. It's called "Good Friday" because *we* understand, in retrospect, what God accomplished that day on our behalf. In the moment, though, the friends of Jesus are distraught, disjointed, and scattered.

It is into *this* moment, *this* darkness, *this* sorrow that the power of God erupts in all its shocking glory.

God raises Jesus from the dead.

You and I may not be surprised, but *they* were surprised. So surprised they couldn't believe it at first. So surprised they dismissed the women's reports as wishful thinking. So surprised they huddled together behind a locked door, scared of being found out by the authorities. So surprised they *went back to Galilee to take up fishing again.*

These are not men prepared for resurrection. They can scarcely believe it when Jesus is standing right in front of them.

The good news of Jesus is founded here, at an empty tomb. No empty tomb, no gospel. Everything else unfolds from this point, Day One of the new thing God is doing in the world.

The empty tomb is like a crater where a meteor crashed. This stone from heaven carries an unknown virus. Jesus is Patient Zero. From him, it begins to spread to others.

Only this is a good infection (to use the metaphor of C. S. Lewis). You *want* this virus. It's the Death-killer. The Sin-cleanser. The Devil-defeater. Its name is Resurrection, Eternal Life, Holy Spirit. Jesus is the host. Draw close to him, and you'll catch it too.

After the third day, it starts to catch like wildfire. It's been spreading ever since.

*Yours in Christ,*
*a fellow pilgrim*

## 57

*Dear future saint,*

As you say, God's resurrection of Jesus cannot be the same as Jesus's raising of his friend Lazarus. Saint Lazarus's rise, though a miracle, is in truth a kind of deferred death. It's a resuscitation. Lazarus died a second time, as did others Jesus brought back to life.

I understand, though, why you find it difficult to put into words what *makes* Jesus's rise different. Theologians have had the same difficulty for millennia. Let me do my best to report their best attempts.

The first thing to say is that Jesus was really dead. He wasn't asleep. His body was a corpse. He didn't pass out for a while. He wasn't clinging to life inside the tomb. He was dead the way any and all deceased human beings are dead. As his life was truly human, so was his death.

Nor is the life to which he returns merely a natural human life—though he remains the human being he is, as the God he always was. The God-man died, the God-man rose again.

The life, then, that bursts forth on Easter morning is not an increase in degree in the life Jesus had before, the life he shared with us. It is a difference in kind. It is a new and unprecedented life: indestructible, invulnerable, impassible. It is *eternal* life. But "eternal" doesn't mean "duration without end." It means *God's* sort of life. It's a qualitative claim, not quantitative. The risen Jesus doesn't have your and my kind of human life, only more of it, even the most of it. His new life transcends the old way of things. It brings about an entirely new order.

Think of it this way. God's coming world will be free of pain, injury, illness, suffering, loss, and death. God will wipe away every tear from our eyes, and Death will be no more.

When Jesus rises from the dead, *God's world invades ours*. It erupts like a detonation; it irrupts like a military offensive. Jesus tells us to pray that the Father's will be done on earth as it is in heaven. The empty tomb is the Spirit's resounding Yes. As Saint Paul writes, "all the promises of God find their Yes in Christ. That is why we utter the Amen through him, to the glory of God."

God raises Jesus in the body. I won't ask whether you know why, because I'm confident by this point you do. After all, who made the human body? God. What did he call it? Good. Were we meant to be souls alone, rid of our bodies like a burden, a prison even? Of course not. A human being is body and soul. When Jesus dies, his soul is separated from his body; this is what makes the latter a corpse. Of necessity his resurrection is the reunion of his soul with his body—only now transformed, transfigured, suffused with light and life and immortality: never to die again.

For this reason the church calls Easter Sunday both the first and the eighth day: the first, because it is the Lord's Day, when God created the world; the eighth, because it is the start of a whole new dawn, the Resurrection Day of the new creation.

God is coming—God has come—to rescue and restore, to renew and renovate, to redeem and reconcile his beloved but fallen creation. He is making all things new. Starting here, starting now, in the silence and darkness of an unmarked tomb, in a garden outside Jerusalem.

"Why do you seek the Living One among the dead? He is not here; he is risen." Thus the angels spoke to the women who came to the tomb. They preached the good news then, as the women did to the apostles, as the apostles did to the Jews, as the Jews did to the nations.

Praise the Lord!

*Yours in Christ,*
*a fellow pilgrim*

*Dear future saint,*

You write, with not a little impatience: *So how does Jesus save us?* That's the whole ball game, isn't it?

When I teach my students the "atonement"—the theological term for what Jesus does to save us—I give them six distinct categories, and *each* of them contains five "theories." All told, that comes out to thirty different ways of understanding how Jesus saves us. And there are plenty I leave out.

There is no single master theory. But this is not to say that the question, or the answers we give, are unimportant. It's just that we can get stuck when we think of them like the Ring in Middle-earth: *One theory to rule them all . . .*

Let me give you a few important approaches.

Start with the incarnation. In a previous letter I used the analogy of a blood transfusion. The church fathers *loved* this sort of image. God became human, that humans might become gods. What God is by nature we become by grace. God took upon himself all that we are and suffer, that we might receive in ourselves all that he is and enjoys.

On this view, the incarnation is a beautiful exchange. And it is the incarnation itself that accomplishes the exchange. *Becoming human* is what God does to save us, to make us his own, to raise us up to himself. The divine life—the breath and blood of God himself!—enters us from the outside, just as our own life—full of sin and death—enters his. Because he is God, all that ails us is extinguished in him. Because his life and blood and breath are divine, when they enter us they do not kill us but heal us. More, they elevate us to a higher life than we have by nature, for they are supernatural in source and power.

By nature we are children of Adam and Eve. By grace we are children of God the Father, sisters and brothers of Jesus through the gift of his Spirit. This is how he saves us.

Now think about what ails us in particular: our threefold bondage to Sin, Death, and the Devil. The story of the Gospels is Jesus's cosmic conflict with these forces and his eventual triumph over them in his passion.

"Passion" means *suffering*. Jesus suffered for us. Why?

Jesus, we know, is God in the flesh. He is as fully human as he is fully divine, like us in every way except one. He is not a sinner. He is sinless.

What the apostles realized, after the fact, was that the suffering and death of Jesus were *sacrificial*. He was offering himself, his own perfect life, for the sins of the world. Our sins, Sin itself, was placed on his shoulders. He carried it to Calvary, where it was nailed to the cross, in him and through him. "For our sake," Saint Paul writes, God "made him to be sin who knew no sin." And unlike the sacrifices of birds and goats, the sacrifice of Jesus is once for all. For Jesus, we know, is at once a sinless man and the holy God. God offers *himself* as an atoning sacrifice for Sin. Nothing greater could be sacrificed; nothing else could cover our sins. Once done, nothing more is required. "It is finished," Jesus says.

Our sins die with Jesus; Sin itself is crucified and buried. Its power to enslave is at an end. We need no longer live under its tyranny. As the old hymn proclaims:

> What can wash away my sin?
> Nothing but the blood of Jesus.
> What can make me whole again?
> Nothing but the blood of Jesus.
> Nothing can for sin atone:
> nothing but the blood of Jesus.
> Naught of good that I have done:
> nothing but the blood of Jesus.

Jesus sheds his blood for our sake and is buried in a tomb. Yet he does not stay there. Sin does remain there, a lifeless corpse. But not Jesus. He is the victor. On the third day he rises to life forevermore.

Here is the saving work of God in Christ over Death. Death dominates us because it is inevitable and, except for Jesus, undefeated. Its track record, as I wrote previously, is 100 percent. Humanity is death-ridden, death-haunted, death-bound. It even comes for Jesus.

But just as Jesus "stands for" us in our sins, *representing* us in our place, so his death stands for ours too. Death is the fruit of sin. Jesus never sinned. He need not die. His death is chosen.

As Jesus says: "For this reason the Father loves me, because I lay down my life, that I may take it again. No one takes it from me, but I lay it down of my own accord. I have power to lay it down, and I have power to take it again." The death of Jesus is not forced or coerced. He is God and Lord. His death is for us and only for us, because and only because he loves us.

In his resurrection Jesus conquers Death once for all. "For we know," Paul writes, "that Christ being raised from the dead will never die again; death no longer has dominion over him. The death he died he died to sin, once for all, but the life he lives he lives to God." And how does this life reach out and touch us? Through baptism:

Do you not know that all of us who have been baptized into Christ Jesus were baptized into his death? We were buried therefore with him by baptism into death, so that as Christ was raised from the dead by the glory of the Father, we too might walk in newness of life. For if we have been united with him in a death like his, we shall certainly be united with him in a resurrection like his. We know that our old self was crucified with him so that the sinful body might be destroyed, and we might no longer be enslaved to sin. For he who has died is freed from sin. But if we have died with Christ, we believe that we shall also live with him.

Notice how inseparably Paul interweaves baptism, union with Christ, crucifixion, resurrection, Sin, and Death. (This is what makes him such a master theologian.) When we are one with Christ, what happened to him happens to *us*. Baptism is like a glue, and it binds us to Jesus forever. His death becomes our death; his freedom, our freedom; his life, our life. If Death no longer has dominion over him, and you and I are "in Christ" (as Paul likes to say), then neither does Death have dominion over us. He has smashed our chains and broken down the prison doors. As Paul writes elsewhere:

> The Father has delivered us from the dominion of darkness and transferred us to the kingdom of his beloved Son, in whom we have redemption, the forgiveness of sins.

It should be obvious how this relates to Satan. Here is how Saint John puts it:

> He who commits sin is of the devil; for the devil has sinned from the beginning. The reason the Son of God appeared was to destroy the works of the devil.

The works of the Devil are Sin and Death. To destroy the one is to destroy the others. The Gospels are nothing less than the story of God himself joining battle against this ancient enemy and all his servants. As the book of Hebrews describes it:

> Since therefore the children share in flesh and blood, he himself likewise partook of the same nature, that through death he might destroy him who has the power of death, that is, the devil, and deliver all those who through fear of death were subject to lifelong bondage. . . . Therefore he had to be made like his brethren in every respect, so that he might become a merciful and faithful high priest in the service of God, to make expiation for the

sins of the people. For because he himself has suffered and been tempted, he is able to help those who are tempted.

I cannot improve on that. But here is one more excerpt, this time from the book of Revelation:

Then I saw an angel coming down from heaven, holding in his hand the key of the bottomless pit and a great chain. And he seized the dragon, that ancient serpent, who is the Devil and Satan, and bound him for a thousand years, and threw him into the pit, and shut it and sealed it over him, that he should deceive the nations no more.

This is not quite the end for Satan, but it is a fitting image for it. Here is *the* end:

And the devil who had deceived them was thrown into the lake of fire. . . . Then Death and Hades were thrown into the lake of fire. This is the second death, the lake of fire.

Sin is dead, Death is dead, the place of the dead is dead. The Devil himself is handed over to the second death along with them. Remember John's vision of Jesus I wrote about in an earlier letter:

"Fear not, I am the first and the last, and the living one;
I died, and behold I am alive forevermore,
and I have the keys of Death and Hades."

John goes on to describe Jesus, glorious in heaven, as "the Lamb who was slain," seated on the throne with God. This comes in the fifth chapter of Revelation, and you should go read all of it. Its summit is a chorus of praise from creatures already in heaven; they cry out in worship to Jesus:

"Worthy are you
to take the scroll and to open its seals,
for you were slain
and by your blood did ransom humankind for God
from every tribe and tongue and people and nation,
and have made them a kingdom
and priests to our God,
and they shall reign on earth."

The passage concludes:

Then I looked, and I heard around the throne and the living creatures and the elders the voice of many angels, numbering myriads of myriads and thousands of thousands, saying with a loud voice, "Worthy is the Lamb who was slain, to receive power and wealth and wisdom and might and honor and glory and blessing!"

And I heard every creature in heaven and on earth and under the earth and in the sea, and all therein, saying, "To him who sits upon the throne and to the Lamb be blessing and honor and glory and might forever and ever!" And the four living creatures said, "Amen!" and the elders fell down and worshiped.

There is nothing else to do. With them we say Amen and fall down and worship the Lamb, our Savior.

*Yours in Christ,*
*a fellow pilgrim*

*Dear future saint,*

I let the last letter run rather long. Fitting, given our topic. But let this one be short. It is a poem by John Donne, one of his Holy Sonnets. It tells the gospel in fourteen lines:

> Death, be not proud, though some have called thee
> Mighty and dreadful, for thou art not so;
> For those whom thou think'st thou dost overthrow
> Die not, poor Death, nor yet canst thou kill me.
> From rest and sleep, which but thy pictures be,
> Much pleasure; then from thee much more must flow,
> And soonest our best men with thee do go,
> Rest of their bones, and soul's delivery.
> Thou art slave to fate, chance, kings, and desperate men,
> And dost with poison, war, and sickness dwell,
> And poppy or charms can make us sleep as well
> And better than thy stroke; why swell'st thou then?
> One short sleep past, we wake eternally
> And death shall be no more; Death, thou shalt die.

*Yours in Christ,*
*a fellow pilgrim*

GOD OFFERS HIMSELF FOR THE WORLD

*Dear future saint,*

I apologize, but I can't grant your request. We must turn soon to what happened *after* Jesus's death and resurrection. So I can't fill out the rest of the thirty theories (or subtheories).

What I can do is say a little more.

Jesus is a truly human being, we have said, but he is not Human Being in General. He is not generic. He is Mary's child. He is the seed of Abraham and of David. He is a Jew.

Remember the roles or offices in Israel, for which a man was anointed with oil: priest, prophet, and king. We have already seen how, in his own unique way, Jesus filled and fulfilled each of these.

Anointed with the Spirit, he spoke God's word to God's people and worked among them signs and wonders—like a prophet.

Anointed with the Spirit, he offered to God the sacrifice of his own blameless life for the sins of God's people, at once the offering and the offerer—like a priest.

Anointed with the Spirit, he announced God's kingdom and embodied it wherever he went, doing justice in accordance with God's holy law with a special affection for the widow, the orphan, the marginal, the poor—like a king.

To be clear, my use of "like" here is to show you correspondence, not to suggest Jesus may be *compared* to such roles. He *is* king of Israel. He *is* priest. He *is* prophet. Just as the Law and the prophets find their consummation in Christ, for they bear witness to him and were always destined for him, so Israel's threefold office was always about him, because it was made for him. Moses and Aaron, Melchizedek and Samuel, David and Elijah, Solomon and Isaiah—these men are *types* and *figures* who anticipate the coming of the true and final priest, prophet, and king. They are living signs who point to him, in all their frailties and imperfections.

Knowing this, we read their lives and see in them glimpses of the Coming One, just as we read the Gospels and see echoes and reiterations of them.

This is how God "writes" the plot of salvation history. The Author of Scripture knows the end all along, an End with a Name. We read well when we read the story knowing the end, rather than pretending we don't.

During his earthly career, Jesus taught (as I've quoted already before) that salvation comes from the Jews. Indeed, in terms of Jesus's own ministry, he is a Jew sent to the Jews by the God of the Jews. What gentiles Jesus encounters on earth are mostly accidents of circumstance; certainly they are peripheral to his central mission. We will turn to the gentiles in later letters, and how they come to be included in the salvation Jesus accomplishes. My point here is that, while Jesus works this salvation as a human being, he does so as a *Jewish* human being. As he said not once but twice, "I was sent only to the lost sheep of the house of Israel."

Saint Irenaeus describes this mission with a special term: "recapitulation." Jesus *recapitulates* not just humanity's relation to God but Israel's history with her Lord. He relives or reenacts or redramatizes key scenes from Israel's life.

Like Moses, he must be rescued from a genocidal tyrant willing to slaughter newborn children.

Like Israel, he comes out of Egypt.

Like Israel, he passes through the waters before a time of testing in the wilderness.

Like Moses, he goes up the mountain and delivers instruction from God to his people.

Like Samuel, he is born to a faithful mother whose conception is a miraculous gift from the Lord.

Like David, he is a king in exile, walking the highways and byways of the land, pursued and persecuted with his band of followers.

Like Elijah and Elisha, he wanders the land doing good, healing the sick, and proclaiming the word of the Lord to a harried and hurting people.

Like Solomon, he administers justice, dispenses wisdom, and honors the Lord's true temple (namely, his body).

Like Adam, he is tempted in a garden to transgress the express will and command of God.

Like Israel, he is the servant of the Lord, suffering mockery and anguish and punishment at the hands of the gentiles for the sins of the people—in fact, for the gentiles themselves.

Here's a dead end to avoid: It is not that Jesus is the light of the world, *unlike Israel*. Rather, it is that Jesus *is* Israel, and *as* Israel he is the world's light. Jesus is a microcosm not just of creation or humanity but of Israel herself. He sums up Israel in himself, accepting her election and vocation as his own. What is hers becomes his: both the curse and the blessing. Likewise, what is his becomes hers: obedience, righteousness, holiness, reconciliation. A beautiful exchange once again, one that does not erase or reject Israel but honors and blesses her.

As Mary sings:

> "He has helped his servant Israel,
> in remembrance of his mercy,
> as he spoke to our fathers,
> to Abraham and to his seed forever."

And as Zechariah, the father of Saint John the Baptist, sings:

> "Blessed be the Lord God of Israel,
> for he has visited and redeemed his people,
> and has raised up a horn of salvation for us
> in the house of his servant David,
> as he spoke by the mouth of his holy prophets from of old,
> that we should be saved."

In the final chapter of the book of Acts, Saint Paul has made his way to Rome, albeit as a prisoner bound for Caesar. Once he arrives in the city, the Jews come to see him and to hear his case about Jesus. He tells them: "I have asked to see you and speak with you, since it is because of the hope of Israel that I am bound with this chain."

Jesus is the hope of the world. But he is the hope of the world only because he is first the hope of Israel.

*Yours in Christ,*
*a fellow pilgrim*

*nine*

# God Pours Himself into His People

Were the Spirit not to be worshiped, how could he deify me through baptism? If he is to be worshiped, why not adored? And if to be adored, how can he fail to be God? One links with the other, a truly golden chain of salvation. From the Spirit comes our rebirth, from rebirth comes a new creating, from new creating a recognition of the worth of him who effected it.

—Saint Gregory of Nazianzus

# 61

*Dear future saint,*

No, I have not forgotten the Creed. We have not left Jesus behind. Next in the sequence comes this confession:

> he ascended into heaven
> and is seated at the right hand of the Father.

The ascension of Jesus is all-important. It is the hinge on which the whole story turns. It is typically overlooked, or at best underemphasized, in retellings of the gospel. We often hear of the "life, death, burial, and resurrection" of Jesus. If anything falls out, it's the ascension.

It's easy to see why. It seems an anticlimax. Jesus rises triumphant from the grave. . . . He appears to his apostles. . . . Sin is forgiven. . . . Death is defeated. . . . Jerusalem is right there for the taking . . .

And Jesus disappears.

That's how it seems, at least. But there's more going on than a divine vanishing act. Here's how the story reads:

> So when they had come together [following forty days of the risen Jesus appearing to the apostles], they asked him, "Lord, will you at this time restore the kingdom to Israel?"
>
> He said to them, "It is not for you to know times or seasons which the Father has fixed by his own authority. But you shall receive power when the Holy Spirit has come upon you; and you shall be my witnesses in Jerusalem and in all Judea and Samaria and to the end of the earth."
>
> And when he had said this, as they were looking on, he was lifted up, and a cloud took him out of their sight.
>
> And while they were gazing into heaven as he went, behold, two men stood by them in white robes, and said, "Men of Galilee, why do you stand looking into heaven? This Jesus, who was taken up from you into heaven, will come in the same way as you saw him go into heaven."

That's it. This is not a bad moment to learn that the Bible often tells stories of extraordinary significance in as few words as possible, with as little detail as possible. This is a *snapshot*. The snapshot gives us the point. It doesn't give us everything.

So what are we to make of this scene?

Think of it this way. If Jesus had *not* ascended to heaven, what would have happened? And with what implications?

I'll tell you. If Jesus had remained on earth, he would have brought God's kingdom in full, just as he promised (just as we believe he will, one day). In other words, he would have wrapped up the scroll of history. Heaven and earth would be one. God would be all in all. The Lord would reign; every knee would bow and every tongue confess; his glory would cover the new creation as the waters cover the fallen world today.

That's not a bad vision. It would have been beautiful, just as it will be beautiful when he does it upon his return from heaven in our future.

So why didn't he? And why is this good news for you and me?

Here's why: *Because you and I wouldn't have been there to enjoy it.*

What Jesus's ascension does is open up time, within ongoing history, for more women and men to follow him. For more people to *join Jesus*, to receive the gift of salvation, to be delivered from Sin and Evil and Death, to be liberated from bondage to the Devil and all his works. To expand the rolls of heaven. To swell the ranks of God's people. To grow the body of Christ.

God did not bring about *the* end, then and there, because he wanted *you* to be a chapter in his story. Jesus is waiting to return because he simply cannot help himself from creating, and calling, and saving, and sending more and more and more and more *yous*—and *hims* and *hers* and countless others. He's not taking his sweet time. He's not passive or inactive. He's not *absent*.

He's busy. He's conquering Satan's territory, one inch at a time. *Glory, glory, hallelujah! His truth is marching on.*

*Yours in Christ,
a fellow pilgrim*

## 62

*Dear future saint,*

The church has a word for what I described in the last letter: "mission." I've used this term in its ordinary sense a bunch of times so far, but it has a technical meaning for Christians. It comes from the Latin *missio*, for "sending." The church is a *sent* people. As we saw, Jesus calls his apostles to be *witnesses*, a word I explained in one of my first letters. In truth Jesus calls all his followers to be martyrs: testifying to the Way of Jesus by their lives and, if necessary, by their deaths.

Here is a parallel passage. The snapshot of the ascension comes from Saint Luke, at the beginning of Acts. This one comes from the final three verses of Saint Matthew's Gospel. Jesus is risen from the dead, gathered with his disciples on a high mountain in Galilee. Here is what he says:

> "All authority in heaven and on earth
> has been given to me.
> Go therefore
> and make disciples of all nations,
> baptizing them in the name
> of the Father and of the Son and of the Holy Spirit,
> teaching them to observe
> all that I have commanded you;
> and behold, I am with you always,
> to the close of the age."

The church calls this the Great Commission. The whole life of Jesus's followers stands forever under this one word: "Go." We are a going people, constantly on the move.

Not that each believer is a "foreign" missionary, sent elsewhere than her home—though plenty are. The idea, rather, is that *the entire community* is sent by God to the particular place of its residence to be a witness to Christ. And when curious onlookers draw near, the community should invite them to become fellow disciples of Christ.

How? By baptizing them (in the name of the Holy Trinity) and teaching them (to live holy lives as Jesus commanded).

This is the church's mission.

We see the beginning of this mission in the book of Acts, which narrates the first three decades of the church's life, her struggles, conflicts, sufferings, decisions, and expansion. It tracks the work of the apostles from about AD 30 to 60, particularly Saint Peter and Saint James *in* Jerusalem and Saint Paul and Saint Barnabas *beyond* Jerusalem.

Tradition says that Luke, a doctor and coworker of Paul's, wrote Acts. Sometimes he reports on events he was not present for; sometimes he gives you the play-by-play of what he saw with his own eyes (he signals this when he says "we" rather than "they"). If it was in fact Luke, then the action stops, presumably, in "real time"; he finishes the unfinished story because he's living it, and the next chapter hasn't been written yet. This would mean he wrote it in the early 60s, not knowing the fate of Peter or Paul or James or Jerusalem.

Nothing much rides on this—perhaps it was written later, by someone else—but it's helpful for your imagination as a reader.

In any case, I want to draw your attention to two things of massive importance in Luke's telling, because they are no less important for Christian life and faith today.

First, while the traditional name for the book is the Acts of the Apostles, believers have long substituted an alternative title: the Acts of the Holy Spirit. For the protagonist of the story is not human beings but God. Others have coined the title "the Gospel of the Spirit—according to Luke," as a kind of pair to "the Gospel of Jesus—according to Luke." If volume 1 is about the good news, so is volume 2. Each refracts the one gospel by a distinct person of the Trinity and his particular mission from heaven. Jesus came to live and die and rise. The Spirit came to indwell and abide and empower. The Spirit's coming, in this sense, is every bit as important and every bit "good news" as the coming of Jesus.

In truth, the coming of the Spirit *is* the coming of Jesus, only in a different way. For the Spirit is the Spirit of Jesus, sent from heaven by the ascended Lord. When the Spirit works, it is Jesus working *by* the Spirit, just as when Jesus worked on earth, it was the Father working through him. Whenever and wherever One works, All are working in him and by him and through him. The works of the Trinity are united and undivided.

Second, then, the story of Acts shows us that Jesus is not dormant in heaven while we remain on earth awaiting his return. Luke opens Acts by referring to his first volume, where he "dealt with all that Jesus began to do and teach." What a lovely way to put it. Jesus *began* doing and teaching in Nazareth. But he did not cease acting or speaking after his resurrection and ascension. His work entered a new mode. Now he acts *from heaven* through his Spirit's presence *on earth*. It's the same Jesus, though, doing the very same thing—now distributed among thousands upon thousands (eventually, millions upon millions and, later, *billions*) of believers, filled by his own Spirit.

And the reason Luke's story is unfinished is because *the* story is unfinished. The Spirit didn't cease working in the first century. Nor did Jesus. Both are alive and well, doing the will of the Father on earth as it is in heaven, even now, even in you and me.

This is the good news of the Holy Spirit. This is the good news of Pentecost.

*Yours in Christ,*
*a fellow pilgrim*

**63**

*Dear future saint,*

*What's Pentecost?* I'm glad you asked.

Pentecost (or Shavuot) is an annual Jewish festival that comes fifty days after Passover. Passover is the high point of the Jewish calendar. It celebrates the exodus of Israel from Egypt. Pentecost and Passover, together with a third festival (called Sukkot or Booths), are the three annual celebrations that call for pilgrimage to Jerusalem, as commanded of Israel in the Law of Moses.

Jesus appeared to his followers for a period of about forty days after his resurrection. Before he ascended to heaven, he instructed them to remain in Jerusalem and "to wait for the promise of the Father." The promise in question was the gift of the Holy Spirit from heaven. Ten days after he ascended, at Pentecost, the Spirit descended on the apostles in a miraculous manner. Jews were gathered in Jerusalem from their dispersion among the nations, and when the Spirit fell on the apostles—looking like tongues of fire—they began speaking "in tongues." The crowd of listeners understood what the apostles were saying in their own "tongues," meaning in their own languages, even though the apostles were Galileans who did not speak dozens of languages.

This is the event of Pentecost. It is sometimes called the birth of the church.

Pentecost is God's own Babel, or rather his anti-Babel. Whereas God, long ago, confused the tongues of men attempting to mount a ladder to heaven, here Jesus builds a ladder from heaven to earth, and by his Spirit makes his people understand one another, even across barriers of regional, cultural, and linguistic difference. We catch a glimpse here of one of the Spirit's primary works: unifying human beings who are divided by difference. In doing so, he does not abolish difference but unites *in* difference. Division was never part of the divine plan. Difference was.

Here is the beginning of the third article, or section, of the Creed:

> I believe in the Holy Spirit, the Lord, the giver of life,
> who proceeds from the Father.
> With the Father and the Son he is worshiped and glorified.
> He has spoken through the Prophets.

GOD POURS HIMSELF INTO HIS PEOPLE

The Spirit is no mere creature, nor even a mighty angel. The Spirit is God. The Spirit had been present throughout Israel's history, but only occasionally or in specific persons' lives. Now he comes to *all for all time*. The prophet Joel's phrase is "all flesh": women and men, young and old, slave and free—anyone and everyone who calls on the name of the Lord, who (as Saint Peter commands them) repents and is "baptized . . . in the name of Jesus Christ for the forgiveness of [their] sins; and [they] shall receive the gift of the Holy Spirit."

Where the Spirit descends, there is power. There are signs and wonders. The Spirit is God's own presence, moving into the neighborhood of one's heart and mind and body—one's life. The Spirit comes for good. He *abides*. He equips and empowers for the work and will of God. He cleanses from sin and sanctifies. He applies what Jesus accomplished on the cross and in the empty tomb to *you in particular*. Wherever the Spirit is present, there is Jesus, too.

The Spirit is alive and out of our control. "He blows where he wills," Jesus says. He also says this: "I tell you the truth: it is to your advantage that I go away, for if I do not go away, the Paraclete will not come to you; but if I go, I will send him to you." The Paraclete is the Spirit; the Greek word means advocate, counselor, or comforter. It is one of his many names (another is "Gift").

What I want you to see in Jesus's words is the stupefying claim that it is *better for Jesus to go away*, and what makes it better is the coming of his Spirit. The presence of the Spirit in one's life is so good, so sweet, so precious, that it not only makes Jesus's "absence" tolerable. It makes it desirable.

Now, we know that Jesus is not truly absent. Granted, he is not present in the body. But he is present to us *from* heaven *by* his Spirit. When children say that Jesus lives in their heart, they are not wrong. Jesus lives in their heart because his Spirit resides there, a "seal" (in Saint Paul's words) until the day when Jesus *is* present in the body: visible, tangible, before our very eyes. On that day he will complete his work in us, and the presence of the Spirit in us is a kind of deposit until then. A seed, hidden in secret, until the proper time for the bloom to burst forth in all its glory.

Adam was a gardener. Jesus, risen from the grave, was mistaken for a gardener, buried in a garden tomb as he was. But Saint Mary wasn't wrong when she took him for one. He is a gardener. He tends and keeps us, waters and prunes us, shines his light on us—from womb to tomb and beyond.

*Yours in Christ,*
*a fellow pilgrim*

## 64

*Dear future saint,*

Before I answer your latest question, a final word or two about the ascension and the Spirit.

Jesus ascends to send the Spirit. Jesus ascends to initiate the mission. Jesus ascends to expand the reach of his presence—to be present not just in Galilee or Jerusalem but to any and all who put their faith in him. To the whole world.

He ascends, too, *to be glorified*. His ascension is his exaltation. God the Father brings his beloved Son to sit at his right hand, as Lord and King of the cosmos. Hence the courage of the martyrs. No matter who sits on an earthly throne, we Christians know who sits on the heavenly throne. It is he alone whom we have to love—and to fear. Mere human rulers can hurt the body, but nothing more. They cannot touch the soul. If we do not deny him when threatened, if we do not forsake him when facing death, he will neither deny nor forsake us before the Father. He will vouch for us. He will keep us. He will raise us to himself, in heaven.

Jesus ascends, finally, to continue his work as priest. We have seen how he rules as king: He presides from on high over the affairs of human history, in his wise and inscrutable providence. He speaks from heaven by his Spirit through his holy word and among his people; in this he continues to act as prophet. What then does he do as priest?

He intercedes for us. This is the testimony of Hebrews:

> [Israel's] former priests were many in number, because they were prevented by death from continuing in office; but Jesus holds his priesthood permanently, because he continues forever. Consequently he is able for all time to save those who draw near to God through him, since he always lives to make intercession for them.
>
> For it was fitting that we should have such a high priest, holy, blameless, unstained, separated from sinners, exalted above the heavens. He has no need, like those high priests, to offer sacrifices daily, first for his own sins and then for those of the people; he did this once for all when he offered up himself. Indeed, the law appoints men in their weakness as high priests, but the word of the oath, which came later than the law, appoints a Son who has been made perfect forever.

In sum, "we have such a high priest, one who is seated at the right hand of the throne of the majesty in heaven, a minister in the sanctuary and the true tabernacle which is set up not by man but by the Lord."

The idea is that the tabernacle, or temple, on earth is but a copy or image of the heavenly tabernacle-temple. Christ offered himself on earth for our sins, but *he takes his blood into heaven* and there applies it, for our sake, within God's heavenly temple. He represents or stands in for us, interposing and interceding for us, on our behalf. Because he is human, he may stand in our stead; because he is divine, his offering is perfect and holy and acceptable. It need never be repeated. It is once for all.

In this way Jesus's work continues. He is King and Prophet and Priest, not only once, but always, even now, in heaven, for you and for me. This is what he lives to do.

Now to your question. You want to know about the Spirit. You want to know whether the signs and wonders in the Bible, the miraculous works and events in Israel and the church, persist into the present or whether they came to an end sometime in the distant past.

I won't belabor the point or defer an answer. Yes, they continue. There is no expiration date on God's mighty works. Throughout the history of God's people, from Pentecost to the present day, followers of Christ have reported both witnessing and experiencing the Spirit's power, a power that surpasses the ordinary workings of "nature." The only word for such power is "*super*natural."

The sick are made well. The future is foretold. Dreams and visions abound. Demons are cast out. Tongues are spoken.

There are some Christians who doubt this. They suppose such things happened to kickstart the church, but then died out with the apostles. Perhaps they are right. I doubt it. There is no good reason from Scripture to believe they are. And the testimony of the church down through the centuries is that the Spirit has never ceased working in these ways.

To be clear, "these ways" are not *ordinary*. This is what makes them extraordinary. We do not expect, much less demand, that God work miracles each and every day. Or rather, we learn to see that God *does* work daily miracles, but not of the spectacular variety.

Every day the Spirit reconciles enemies, and mends broken hearts, and forgives sinners, and imparts courage, and brings Life where once only Death reigned. Every day the Spirit grows in the fertile soil of believers' souls his own special fruit: love, joy, peace, patience, kindness, goodness, faith, gentleness, and self-control. Such virtues are not natural to fallen women and men. Without the Spirit—prior to baptism, apart from faith—we are sunk in our own flesh. We are impatient, unkind, faithless, joyless, loveless, unfree, brutal, and bound to constant total war: against others and within ourselves and with God most of all. Christ alone, by his Spirit, delivers us from these and all other maladies. "Now the Lord is the Spirit," writes Saint Paul, "and where the Spirit of the Lord is, there is freedom."

As he writes elsewhere: "For freedom Christ has set us free; stand fast therefore, and do not submit again to a yoke of slavery." This is the Spirit's primary work: freedom. Freedom from the flesh, from Sin and Satan and Death. How could God himself indwell a person also filled with such things? As Paul says again—a theologian of the Spirit *because* a theologian of the resurrected Lord—"no one speaking by the Spirit of God ever says 'Jesus be cursed!' and no one can say 'Jesus is Lord' except by the Holy Spirit." The Spirit of the living God casts out all other spirits, evil or otherwise. We live by the Spirit's freedom or not at all.

So yes: the Spirit is alive, at work in the world, moving and active and everywhere all at once. We should not, must not, quench his fiery power. Let us not be surprised when he takes our breath away. Let us welcome it.

But neither assume it nor demand it. Expect the ordinary. For the supernatural ordinary is extraordinary indeed, and beyond all that we could ask or imagine.

*Yours in Christ,*
*a fellow pilgrim*

GOD POURS HIMSELF INTO HIS PEOPLE

## 65

*Dear future saint,*

Pentecost was a new moment in the history of God's people. Abraham's God drew near to Abraham's children, becoming a child of flesh and blood just like them. He suffered and died and rose for their sins, conquering Death as he had promised centuries prior by the mouth of the prophet Isaiah:

> On this mountain the LORD of hosts
> will make for all peoples a feast of fat things,
> a feast of wine on the lees,
> of fat things full of marrow,
> of wine on the lees well refined.
> And he will destroy on this mountain
> the covering that is cast over all peoples,
> the veil that is spread over all nations.
> He will swallow up death forever,
> and the Lord GOD will wipe away tears from all faces,
> and the reproach of his people
> he will take away from all the earth;
> for the LORD has spoken.

In pouring out the Spirit of the Messiah upon Jews from every nation and language, Israel's God continues to fulfill his promises: that he would be their God, and they, his people. That he would *dwell in their midst* forever. Once he journeyed with them in a tent, the tabernacle. Now he dwells from within them. No more is a man-made temple necessary. The temple is now the people, or rather the people are now the temple. The people, filled with the Spirit who is God himself, is where God dwells on earth. Each believer is a kind of micro-temple, a chapel in the great cathedral of God's presence. And just as Christ was the fulfillment of the temple—he spoke of his own body as God's true and final temple—so God's people, a temple of his Spirit, are now called the body of Christ.

Here, in short, is the church: the people of God centered on Jesus, defined by him, filled with him from tip to toe: his Spirit, his word, his cross, his resurrection. They are God's covenant people, because they keep the new Passover feast (the Lord's Supper) in honor of the new covenant the Lord made on Good Friday, a covenant ratified in Christ's blood and sealed by his rising on Easter Sunday. And just as the covenant of Passover marked the people's salvation from Egypt by the waters of the Red Sea, so the new covenant of the new Passover celebrates the same people's salvation from Sin and Death by the waters of baptism. The promised land to which we now journey through the wilderness of this world is God's own kingdom, which is coming soon with Jesus's return. We enter it when we pass through the waters of the Jordan in death. He will bring us all to the holy mount, to Zion, when he comes in his glory and raises the dead to everlasting life.

This, I say, is the faith and hope of Christ's church. But how does it relate to Israel? And how does it relate to gentiles?

Israel first. There are things here to avoid saying. That's the easy part. What exactly to say instead is harder and more delicate.

We must not say that the Jews *were* God's people and now (Christian) gentiles *are* God's people. That involves a callous, in fact disastrous, revision of God's story, his own word, his very heart. Recall that God loves Abraham and all his children, and he chose them for no reason other than this love. This love, moreover, is the one sure foundation of his love for you and me. How could we trust God's love if he rejected the people who were his first love?

As Saint Paul puts it: "I ask, then, has God rejected his people? By no means! I myself am an Israelite, a descendant of Abraham, a member of the tribe of Benjamin. *God has not rejected his people whom he foreknew.*"

So that's out of the question.

Nor can we say that the Jews rejected Jesus. That's a bit of silliness posing as a thoughtful position—although its silliness has not kept it from underwriting centuries of anti-Jewish and even anti-Semitic preaching, teaching, and behavior on the part of otherwise "devout" Christians.

"The Jews" were not and are not a monolith. Every one of Jesus's disciples was a Jew. Every one of the Twelve was a Jew. The women standing at the cross were Jews. The men in the Upper Room were Jews. The women and men who received the Spirit at Pentecost were Jews. Those first baptized into Christ were Jews. The disciples who carried the gospel to Judea and Samaria and Ethiopia—to Jews far and wide in the diaspora, in every direction on the compass—were Jews to a person. Jewish apostles and deacons, Jewish evangelists and missionaries took the Jewish gospel of the Jewish Messiah of the Jewish God first to fellow Jews, around the Mediterranean Sea, then to non-Jews. But reread the book of Acts. Every single leader of the church, every baptized and Jesus-following teacher or elder named in the entire story, is a Jew.

Hence the absurdity of supposing "the Jews" rejected Jesus but "the gentiles" accepted him. Many Jews accepted him, as did many gentiles. Many Jews did not, just as many gentiles did not.

Finally, although most believers the world over and in the centuries since the apostles have been gentiles (there are a lot of us in the world!), there have always been Jewish followers of Jesus. I've known plenty, as I'm sure you have and will.

Okay then. We see what Paul means when he says that "as regards election [the Jews] are beloved for the sake of their fathers. For the gifts and the call of God are irrevocable." God doesn't do takebacks. His heart is set from all eternity on Abraham's children "according to the flesh" (that's Paul's phrase— it means *biological descendants*). This is where we have to begin, along with Jesus's own teaching:

> "Think not that I have come to abolish the law and the prophets; I have come not to abolish them but to fulfil them. For truly, I say to you, till heaven and earth pass away, not an iota, not a dot, will pass from the law until all is accomplished."

The Law itself bears witness to Jesus. For Jesus is the aim and inner rationale of the Law, its ultimate source and final end, from the beginning. More than a few writers have suggested that we should paraphrase Saint John's line that "the Word became flesh" by saying *the Torah became flesh*. Not a bad way to understand it. When we look at Jesus, we see the Law as God always intended it. His own life interprets Torah perfectly. Both the letter and the Spirit of the Law are fulfilled and revealed in him. If you want to understand Moses, just look to Jesus.

In this way Jesus didn't so much displace Torah as the center of Israel's life as reveal what it *means* for Torah to lie at the center. For Torah is about Jesus—full stop. Torah is a throne, and on it the slain Lamb is seated as David's Son. The king of Israel is king of Torah, for he is God and man in one: the Good Shepherd who alone is fit to rule his people.

This truth is the sure ground for the church's confident proclamation of the new covenant in Christ's blood, as it is for her own status as Christ's body and the Spirit's temple, for her calling as God's people, bought by his Son. The mystery of the gospel concerns him. But he is never alone. He is the head of his body. The mystery of the gospel, therefore, concerns the church, too. She is an inner part of the mystery kept hidden for ages but now unveiled in these final days, a mystery that means our redemption.

*Yours in Christ,*
*a fellow pilgrim*

## 66

*Dear future saint,*

I want to say more about the "mystery" of Christ's body. Here is Saint Paul:

> For this reason I, Paul, a prisoner for Christ Jesus on behalf of you gen-
> tiles—assuming that you have heard of the stewardship of God's grace
> that was given to me for you, how the mystery was made known to me by
> revelation. . . . When you read this you can perceive my insight into the
> mystery of Christ, which was not made known . . . in other generations as
> it has now been revealed to his holy apostles and prophets by the Spirit;
> *that is,* how the gentiles are fellow heirs, members of the same body, and
> partakers of the promise in Christ Jesus through the gospel.

"Mystery" here does not mean a complex subject very difficult to understand.
It means a plan or purpose or design that once was kept under wraps but now
stands unveiled for all to see. This mystery, Paul writes, is God's inclusion of
the gentiles in the promise and people of Christ.

*Remember,* he writes further, you gentiles in the flesh were at one time
"separated from Christ, alienated from the commonwealth of Israel, and
strangers to the covenants of promise, having no hope and without God in
the world." To be born a gentile, according to the Bible, is to be born apart
from the family of God, because a gentile is not a part of the family of Abraham. To be in this condition is, in Paul's words, to be hopeless and godless
*by definition.*

"But now," he proclaims, "in Christ Jesus you who once were far off
have been brought near in the blood of Christ. For he is our peace, who has
made us both one, and has broken down the dividing wall of hostility." To
accomplish this

> [Jesus] came and preached peace to you who were far off and peace to
> those who were near; for through him we both have access in one Spirit to
> the Father. So then you are no longer strangers and sojourners, but you are
> fellow citizens with the saints and members of the household of God, built
> upon the foundation of the apostles and prophets, Christ Jesus himself
> being the cornerstone, in whom the whole structure is joined together

and grows into a holy temple in the Lord; in whom you also are built into it for a dwelling place of God in the Spirit.

This—one people from two, a single family of Jews and gentiles, in a word: *the church*—is "the plan of the mystery hidden for ages in God who created all things." But if you think back, the mystery wasn't completely invisible. If you go back to Abraham, you'll see the plan was hiding in plain sight.

Recall: the calling and promise to Abraham was not only that his family would be blessed. It was that *all the families of the earth* would be blessed *through his family*. "They" would find blessing "in him," meaning in Abraham and his children.

So here is the question. How does this happen?

What you need to do is read chapters 10 through 15 in the book of Acts, together with Ephesians, Romans, and Galatians, capped by Hebrews and Revelation. Since I can't capture their contents in only a few paragraphs, know that what I write is inadequate (always, but now more than ever). I'll try to limit my explanation to a handful of major points.

First, the apostles did *not* realize the gospel was meant for gentiles. At first they assumed it was just for fellow Jews. Jesus, after all, was the hope of Israel. He was her Messiah. Why would gentiles care?

Second, the apostles continued to keep the Law. This was a no-brainer. They may have had disagreements with other Jewish groups over how to observe Torah, and especially over how Jesus fit within Torah. But Torah was a given. It certainly was not a problem.

Third, the initial event of gentiles coming to faith was a clear and wondrous work of the Holy Spirit. Jesus poured out his Spirit on a gentile named Cornelius and his whole household—a man who already honored the God of the Jews and venerated their Scriptures—in a manner neither Saint Peter nor his fellow apostles in Jerusalem could deny. It involved dreams and visions and angels and tongues. In astonishment at what he was seeing, Peter asked aloud, "Can anyone forbid water for baptizing these people who have received the Holy Spirit just as we have?"

*God* joins gentiles to Christ. This is no human effort.

Fourth, the question was never whether gentiles could join Jews in the church, as fellow disciples of Jesus. The question was whether, in doing so, they ought to convert to Judaism—that is, become Jews, and thereby keep the Law of Moses, as all Jews must. Such conversion happened in Jesus and Peter's time, as it continues to happen today. The apostles and elders gathered in Jerusalem to discern God's will on the matter. Circumcision was the key symbolic ritual here, since circumcision was commanded by God of all male members of Abraham's family; and along with circumcision, the rest of Moses's commands and statutes followed.

After much heated discussion, the Jerusalem council gives a decisive answer: *no*. While Torah remains mandatory for Jews, it does not apply in the same way to gentiles. Put differently, gentiles may join God's covenant people, through baptism and faith in Jesus, *without* thereby becoming Jews in the process. Jews will remain Jews and gentiles will remain gentiles, together in one household, so that with one voice they might give glory to the one God and Father of all.

But how can gentiles join God's family without circumcision or Torah? How can they be children of Abraham without becoming children of Abraham?

This is the insight the Lord granted Saint Paul; it's why Jesus appointed him apostle to the gentiles.

For the biblical rule remains in effect. One *cannot* belong to God *without* belonging to his people; one cannot be a child of God without also being a child of Abraham. Yet how can one join a family without being born into it?

I spoiled this answer in an early letter, so you know it by now, and have surely guessed it during this long buildup. The answer is adoption. By faith in Christ, through baptism that unites us to his death and resurrection, gentiles are adopted into the family of Abraham *and thereby* into the family of God. We gain Abraham as father *and therefore* God as Father.

Some of us are born children of Abraham; none of us, except Jesus, is by nature a son or daughter of God. Jews are not baptized in order to become Abraham's children; only gentiles are. Both are baptized, however, in order to become God's children: this is a gift of grace, beyond nature. No one is *born* a child of God. "But to all who received him, who believed in his name, he gave power to become children of God; who were born, not of blood nor of the will of the flesh nor of the will of man, but of God."

This is why Jesus came: to make us his sisters and brothers. To give us what is his by nature: the imperishable status of God's own beloved children.

The church consists of Jews by birth and gentiles by birth who, through the gift of Christ's Spirit in baptism, belong by faith to God as his sons and daughters. This is divine grace in action. The gift is unconditioned by anything we are or ask or do; it follows no good deed or upright character or criterion we have met. The Lord simply grants us this status, "for nothing" but love.

To join the church is to gain this status; to be baptized is to join the church and Christ simultaneously. For the church is Christ's body and bride. In the words of Saint Cyprian, a person "cannot have God as his Father who does not have the Church as his Mother." In this role the church "watches over us for God, she seals her sons, to whom she has given birth, for the kingdom."

Salvation is there, in Christ's church, because *he* is there. Salvation is there, too, because there is no salvation apart from Abraham's covenant family. This is the meaning of Cyprian's claim that "there is no salvation outside the

Church," since "there is no baptism outside the Church." By God's unexpected and marvelous work, he has opened up his ancient family to the nations. Any and all may enter, through Christ. United to him, the seed of Abraham, you join God's chosen people. You become a child of Abraham. In him you will be blessed, as God promised so long ago. Abraham believed the promise of God. For this reason he is the father of faith and thus of the faithful.

He is your father, too, if you put your faith in the same promise, the promise of Christ. Like Abraham, you will not be disappointed.

*Yours in Christ,*
*a fellow pilgrim*

*ten*

# God Gives Life to His People

I accept the bait from the fishhook and welcome you, coming in with a bad intention, but being saved by a good hope. Perhaps you did not know where you were coming, or what attraction was catching you. You have come into the nets of the Church. Be caught! Stop fleeing! For is not Jesus catching you, not that you might die, but that in dying you might be made alive?

—Saint Cyril of Jerusalem

## 67

*Dear future saint,*

You'll notice that these letters aren't finished. The book isn't done yet. There's more to say. Why?

Because God's people aren't finished. The story of Christ in the world, the story the Spirit is telling, isn't done yet. You and I are in the middle of this story. The final chapter won't come until Christ does. So there's more, much more, to say.

Having meandered my way to this point, I finally have some sense of the overall journey we've made. Let me recap the itinerary so far before giving you a sense of how we'll begin to approach the end.

We started with martyrdom: the call to discipleship as a call to follow Christ, through Death, into Life. Turning to Christ, we turned to his people, the Jews. We traced the trajectory of Israel from Abraham to exile. Then we moved backward all the way to creation from nothing; from there, to human beings; and thence to the Fall: Satan, Sin, and Death, and the bondage of all of God's good creation to that unholy trinity.

Then, lost in the exile from Eden and the exile from the promised land, we joined Mary in shocked delight at the Annunciation: God became one of us—"God with us," *Immanuel*—in the womb of a young Galilean girl. He took our nature upon himself, and with it our burdens, the sorry weight of Sin and Death and the terror of our enemy, the Devil. All this he extinguished by his power and exhausted with his mercy and grace. By his death and resurrection he reconciled us to himself. More, he *gave* us himself, through the gift of his Spirit. He opened up the doors of Israel to the gentiles, through the gate of adoption in Christ:

> "Very truly, I tell you, I am the gate for the sheep. All who came before me are thieves and bandits, but the sheep did not listen to them. I am the gate. Whoever enters by me will be saved and will come in and go out and find pasture. The thief comes only to steal and kill and destroy. I came that they may have life and have it abundantly.
>
> "I am the good shepherd. The good shepherd lays down his life for the sheep. . . . I know my own, and my own know me, just as the Father knows me, and I know the Father. And I lay down my life for the sheep.

I have other sheep that do not belong to this fold. I must bring them also, and they will listen to my voice. So there will be one flock, one shepherd."

Jesus is the one shepherd of the one flock of the church. He is the one head of his one body. For

there is one body and one Spirit, just as you were called to the one hope of your calling, one Lord, one faith, one baptism, one God and Father of all, who is above all and through all and in all.

This is the testimony of Scripture; this is the word of the Lord, the good news of Jesus. So what more is there to say?

Very early in our correspondence, I said I wanted to tell you *what Christianity is, what Christians believe, and what it means to live as a Christian*. I think I've given you a good sense of the first and the second, but only a partial glimpse of the third. So in the coming letters I want to describe the shape of the Christian life, which as you now know is the shape of life in and as God's people, the church. Christian life is church life. Discipleship is ethics is worship is mission is service is evangelism is sacraments is preaching is martyrdom. It's all convertible. It's all one and the same thing, considered from different angles.

Let's look at those angles together. Before the end, we'll turn to *the* end. Which, as I hope you will not tire of me repeating, is nothing but Christ himself. In the words of Saint Augustine, Christ is both our end and our way to the end:

The truth itself, God, God's Son, assuming humanity without destroying His divinity, established and founded this faith, that there might be a way for man to man's God through a God-man. For this is the Mediator between God and men, the man Christ Jesus. For it is as man that He is the Mediator and the Way. Now the only way that is infallibly secured against all mistakes is when the very same person is at once God and man: God our end, man our way.

*Yours in Christ,*
*a fellow pilgrim*

**68**

*Dear future saint,*

You have written before about "being" or "becoming" a "good person." It surely seems odd to you, then, that I have waited so long to describe the virtues of Christian living.

The first thing to say is that I *haven't* waited this whole time. I've been describing the Christian life all along. But you're right that I haven't turned my gaze to the topic itself just yet.

The second thing to say is why this is the right order. Why, I mean, I've been directing your gaze *away* from yourself and your behavior all this time. This is no accident. It points to the essence of what it means to be a Christian.

Christianity is "eccentric" and "ecstatic." It teaches that our center lies outside ourselves. We follow *Jesus*, place our trust in *him*, set our hope on *him*, crown *him* with our highest love. Christianity goes desperately wrong when we are constantly looking within ourselves, whether for "real" faith or "good" works or "right" motivation or "sincere" feelings. It's worked its magic on us, instead, when we are self-forgetful, looking to Christ alone in everything.

Have you ever gotten lost in a novel, a movie, a concert, a dinner with friends? So lost that hours went by without your noticing? And when you "came to," realizing what had happened, you weren't upset or frustrated but awestruck at the spell the experience cast over you?

That's the kind of self-forgetfulness I have in mind. Christ is so beautiful, so captivating, so rapturous that we can't look away. It doesn't even occur to us to look to ourselves, to think of ourselves. He is the newborn child in a mother's arms, the bride at the end of the aisle, the newly crowned king at his coronation. *We lose ourselves in him.* And in losing ourselves in him—as he taught—we find ourselves at last.

*Yours in Christ,*
*a fellow pilgrim*

## 69

*Dear future saint,*

I'm not quite done on this theme.

It isn't just that Christian faith looks beyond itself in the living of it. It's that *everything precious* in the Christian life is a gift from outside us. Christianity is not the story of me and my well-intended attempts to be a good person. Christianity is the story of God rescuing me from the pit of hell—from Sin and Death, from depression and despair, from poverty and anguish, from suffering and loss, from Satan himself.

Not every religion is a "salvation" religion; not every faith or philosophy sees humankind in desperate need and proposes a solution to our plight. But this is precisely what Christianity is and does.

This, too, is why there is an important balance to strike in describing the Christian life. The Christian life is about God in Christ, reconciling the world to himself. To the extent that it is about me, it is about a *wretch* (in the words of "Amazing Grace") in dire straits and unable to do anything to save himself. This wretch *is saved* by the Creator of the universe. Note how passive that is! My story consists not in what I've done but in *what Another has done for me.*

Furthermore, Christianity isn't just a salvation religion. It's a divinization religion. That's a theological term for what God does for us *once* he's restored us to our original condition of innocence before him. He doesn't leave us there. He raises us up to live with himself. This is where adoption enters in. We don't remain mere natural children of earth. We become adopted children of heaven. We call on God as Father, not just Maker. We call on Jesus as Brother, not just Redeemer. We find the Spirit within us, not just in heaven or in creation.

Wise teachers in Eastern Christianity have long used the word "divinization" or "deification" to describe God's *additional* work of granting us a share in his own heavenly life and happiness. It is as though we become gods, even as we remain the human creatures we are.

And note, once again, that this gift has nothing to do with our efforts or accomplishments! We don't earn or work our way into heaven. That's the way of Babel. Instead, we receive heaven as a gift, which is the way of Pentecost.

The Christian life is "pentecostal" in just this sense. God enters us, sets up shop in the midst of our hearts and bodies, and all we have to do is receive the gift in gratitude, by letting it run its course in every nook and cranny of our lives.

*Yours in Christ,*
*a fellow pilgrim*

## 70

*Dear future saint,*

I see. This is all rather a rosy picture. I appear to be leaving out the hard bits. On one side, the cross. On the other, the labor of following Jesus, in this life, *toward* the cross.

Well said. Saint Paul once wrote to newly baptized gentile believers with these instructions:

> Work out your own salvation
> with fear and trembling;
> for God is at work in you,
> both to will and to work
> for his good pleasure.

Salvation is something we hash out over a lifetime, wrestling with others, with ourselves, with God. Yet God is at work in our work, willing our willing, drawing us to himself in gentle but sovereign grace. As Saint Augustine prayed to God, "Grant what you command, and command what you will."

Meaning: *What you want, Lord, make known to me; and having made it known to me, make it possible by your power: for I can do nothing apart from you.*

There is a moving story in Saint Matthew's Gospel that illustrates this point. Jesus enters Capernaum, a town familiar to him, and a gentile soldier called a centurion comes to him, "beseeching him and saying, 'Lord, my servant is lying paralyzed at home, in terrible distress.'"

> And [Jesus] said to him, "I will come and heal him." But the centurion answered him, "Lord, I am not worthy to have you come under my roof; but only say the word, and my servant will be healed. For I am a man under authority, with soldiers under me; and I say to one, 'Go,' and he goes, and to another, 'Come,' and he comes, and to my slave, 'Do this,' and he does it."
>
> When Jesus heard him, he marveled, and said to those who followed him, "Truly, I say to you, not even in Israel have I found such faith." . . . And to the centurion Jesus said, "Go; be it done for you as you have believed." And the servant was healed at that very moment.

*But only say the word.* This is Christian prayer. This is Christian faith in the power of God's word, the living word of the living Lord Jesus. Christian life begins and ends with the power of Jesus's voice. His voice alone can raise the dead to life, for it is one and the same voice that spoke the heavens and the earth into existence at the beginning of all things.

Yet only dead things need to be recalled to life. You brought my attention to the cross, in two respects. You were right to do so. Let me say something about that.

Christian life is not only pentecostal. It is baptismal as well. We rise from the waters of baptism into the new life of Pentecost. But first we die. Our old self, the flesh of Sin and bondage, is buried with Christ. Drowned, even. As the poet Franz Wright opens his poem titled "Baptism":

> That insane asshole is dead
> I drowned him
> and he's not coming back. Look
> he has a new life
> a new name
> now
> which no one knows except
> the one who gave it.

Theologians call this dynamic "mortification and vivification." These words come from the Latin for *being put to death* and *being made alive*. God drowns us in the floodwaters of baptism, then breathes the new life of his own Spirit into our lungs as we rise.

In Jesus's words, "unless a person is reborn from above, he cannot see the kingdom of God." How can this happen? Jesus again: "unless a person is born of water and the Spirit, he cannot enter the kingdom of God. That which is born of the flesh is flesh, and that which is born of the Spirit is spirit." And finally: "It is the Spirit that gives life, the flesh is of no avail; the words that I have spoken to you are Spirit and life."

So yes: Being a Christian involves not just Pentecost but the passion, not just resurrection but crucifixion, not just Easter Sunday but Good Friday. In each pair, the first comes, but only after—by and through—the second.

Consider Paul's words:

> So then, sisters and brothers, we are debtors, not to the flesh, to live according to the flesh—for if you live according to the flesh you will die, but if by the Spirit you put to death the deeds of the body you will live.
>
> For all who are led by the Spirit of God are children of God. For you did not receive the spirit of slavery to fall back into fear, but you have re-

ceived the Spirit of adoption. When we cry, "Abba! Father!" it is the Spirit himself bearing witness with our spirit that we are children of God, and if children, then heirs, heirs of God and fellow heirs with Christ, provided we suffer with him in order that we may also be glorified with him.

Sometimes the Bible rhymes with magnificent eloquence. This is one of those places.

I trust you see why I thought of this passage. That last line is proof of your point: *provided we suffer with him in order that we may also be glorified with him.* The glory comes later. First comes the suffering.

There is a famous English translation of a line by German theologian Dietrich Bonhoeffer, who died in a Nazi concentration camp. It reads: "When Christ calls a man, he bids him come and die." As I have quoted before, this is Jesus's own teaching:

> "If anyone would come after me,
> let him deny himself
> and take up his cross
> and follow me.
> For whoever would save his life will lose it;
> and whoever loses his life
> for my sake and the gospel's
> will save it."

We must die—therefore, we must be killed—before we embark on the Christian life. And the Christian life itself is a cross-bearing journey. The cross, as it were, imprints itself on the whole shape of our lives. The cross defines the church; when she is faithful, she is cruciform.

*Yours in Christ,*
*a fellow pilgrim*

71

*Dear future saint,*

The cross is a way of life. For Christians, it is *the* Way. The only Way. The rest of what I have to share with you is for the most part one reflection or another about how the cross of Christ takes its stand in our lives, how it shapes, guides, governs, and directs us in the Way we should go.

This centrality is reflected in a simple practice: the sign of the cross. Perhaps you already do this, or know Christians who do it. Perhaps it's foreign or strange to you. It's easy to grasp and just as easy to practice. I commend it to you.

Here is what you do: Touch your forehead, your chest, then each shoulder. Some Christians use their right hand and go up, down, left, right. Others use their left hand and go up, down, right, left. It largely depends on what part of the world you're in. Either way works.

Typically, as you cross yourself, you say: "In the name of the Father [*forehead*], the Son [*chest*], and the Holy [*shoulder*] Spirit [*shoulder*]." You do it before and after prayer; or before a meal; or at the name of the Trinity; or at certain points in public worship; or in the presence of the Lord's Supper.

Why do this? Because some actions speak louder than words. When I kiss my wife, must I enunciate "I love you" in order to communicate it? Not at all. The kiss does that for me. If a mother has tears rolling down her eyes as she drops off her firstborn at college, must her daughter ask, "Mom, what do your tears mean?"

In the same way, we mark ourselves by Christ's cross, day after day, as a sign that we belong to him; that the Way of his cross defines our lives; that apart from his cross our lives are lost. We don't neglect words, but our actions are eloquent in themselves. Like saluting a general, kneeling before a queen, or pledging allegiance to a flag. Our whole body speaks. It's legible to anyone, including ourselves, without our saying a single audible word.

The cross shapes Christian life in an even more pronounced way than this. I'm talking about "ascetic" practices. The word comes from *ascesis*, Greek for "exercise" or "training." The Bible compares following Christ to being a pilgrim on a journey, a soldier in an army, an athlete in competition. In this case, it wants you to imagine being Christian as a lifelong regimen of intense preparation, as if you were training for a marathon. Except that your rigorous daily exercise is not (only) physical. It's spiritual, moral, mental, and emotional. You are subjecting your body and soul to a self-mastery surpassing any professional athlete's. When trial and temptations come—when Sin and Death, the Enemy and his demons attack—you will be ready, equipped by God's own Spirit of power.

More than anything, ascesis happens through prayer. Prayer is the crucible of the spiritual life. In the fires of prayer God, like a blacksmith, hammers you into shape: the shape of Jesus.

In addition, ascesis incorporates a range of practices that involve "abstention," meaning the temporary giving up of some good or regular thing in your life. Most common is "fasting": not eating (perhaps not drinking, too) for some stretch of time—a single meal, a full day, three days, a whole week. You can also "fast" or "abstain" from other things: sleep, sex, alcohol, tobacco, caffeine, meat, shopping, TV, the Internet. Christians can fast whenever it seems wise to do so, but they always fast during the season of Advent (the four weeks leading up to Christmas) and the season of Lent (the forty days leading up to Easter), in imitation of Jesus's own period of fasting.

Why fast? And what does it do?

First, we fast because Israel, Jesus, and the church all fast in the Bible. It is modeled for us and commanded of us. To fast is to obey God's will for us.

Second, we fast because it deprives us, for a time, of some earthly good that is not our highest good. God alone is our true and ultimate good. He generously gives us earthly goods, but our flesh too often forgets that they are not God. We look to their pleasures—food, fame, sex, sports, entertainment, and the like—to satisfy us, when we should know better: only God can do that. Like Jesus, we remember that we live not by bread and water but by God's most holy word.

Third, we fast in order to learn self-discipline. Who's in charge, me or my stomach? Sometimes it's hard to tell. Or consider sexual desire. If my body wants something (or someone), am I free to tell it no? Or must I always say yes? If I can't say no, then I'm a slave to my own desire. The Christian East has a relevant proverb here: "Gluttony is the mother of adultery." If you can't control your appetite for food, how could you ever expect to control your appetite for sex? Fasting trains us how to "go without," so that our passions are not the masters of us, but we the masters of them.

Fourth and finally, fasting is a practice of solidarity. Some people don't give up food because they don't have food to give up in the first place. They're just hungry. When you fast, then, not only should you pray for those in need of sustenance. You should find a way to give it to them. Donate the money you would have spent on lunch. Or spend your lunch hour serving in a food pantry or soup kitchen. Feed the hungry. That's what Jesus did.

"If you carry the cross willingly, it will carry and lead you," writes Thomas à Kempis. "The whole life of Christ was a cross and a martyrdom." What then should you do? "Drink the chalice of the Lord with affection if you wish to be His friend." Discipleship is not about worldly prosperity; that is not how Christ rewards his friends. "Realize that you must lead a dying life; the more a man dies to himself, the more he begins to live unto God."

The crown of life is first a crown of thorns. If you would follow Christ to the empty tomb, you must tarry first at Calvary.

*Yours in Christ,*
*a fellow pilgrim*

## 72

*Dear future saint,*

The aim and end of human life is friendship with Christ. I pray this for my children, my godchildren, my nephews and niece every morning: that by God's grace they would be lifelong friends of Jesus. Whatever else God does for them, whatever else he gives them or protects them from or permits to happen to them, friendship with the Lord is the one thing, the sole petition, I plead with God to answer. It is what Jesus calls "the one thing needful." Saint Martha is busy with chores, even the crucial tasks of hospitality. But Saint Mary is at Jesus's feet, learning, listening, feeding. "Mary has chosen the better part," Jesus says. It "will not be taken away from her."

As it happens, Mary of Bethany is a model of the Christian life. We see her at least three times in the Gospels. This first time she is hosting Jesus in the home she shares with her sister. The second time is when her brother, Saint Lazarus, whom she and Martha appear to care for in their home, dies. As Jesus approaches the town, she does not go out to him at first (Martha does: always so wonderfully direct and unintimidated, qualities Jesus does not admonish her for). But eventually she rises from her grief to greet him:

> Then Mary, when she came where Jesus was and saw him, *fell at his feet,* saying to him, "Lord, if you had been here, my brother would not have died." When Jesus saw her weeping, and the Jews who came with her also weeping, he was deeply moved in spirit and troubled; and he said, "Where have you laid him?" They said to him, "Lord, come and see." Jesus wept. So the Jews said, "See how he loved him!"

This comes in the eleventh chapter of Saint John's Gospel. I have never succeeded in reading the story without crying myself.

In the next chapter, Mary appears once more. Hosting Jesus in her home again, she "took a pound of costly ointment of pure nard and anointed the feet of Jesus and wiped his feet with her hair; and the house was filled with the fragrance of the ointment." Though Judas rebukes her for the extravagance of the gesture—couldn't the money have been given to the poor?—Jesus defends her. For he knows she is anointing him for his impending death.

Do you see? Where is Mary of Bethany always found? Nowhere but at the feet of Jesus: learning as a disciple, anointing as a believer, begging as a supplicant. She is where we must be. Her place is ours. Christian life is Marian life, modeled on the many Marys of the gospel.

What we want, as believers, what this life of faith is pointed toward in every respect, is intimacy with Christ. We want to be one with him: he in us and we in him, he in the Father and his Spirit in us. The Christian life begets this union in baptism, nourishes it with the Lord's own body and blood, and grows it into depth and maturity across a lifetime of discipleship, surrounded by sisters and brothers likewise following Jesus to the cross.

Earlier I gave you a word for this process: "sanctification." Across the whole of our lives, Christ by his Spirit makes us holy. Which is to say, he makes us holier and holier, as we draw nearer and nearer to him.

We draw closer to Christ, we feed on him and learn at his feet, in two main ways. In the worshiping life of his church; and in our daily lives of devotion and discipleship "outside" the assembly of God's people, "in the world" (but not of it). The former we'll call "liturgical," the latter "ethical." Both are components of following Jesus. Neither the Bible nor Christian tradition sees them as divided, much less opposed. They are two sides of the same coin.

We'll touch on one before turning to the other.

*Yours in Christ,*
*a fellow pilgrim*

## 73

*Dear future saint,*

Human beings are made to worship. Every man and woman on earth worships something. The only question is what.

Our worship—our highest love—is rarely private, hidden in our hearts. It bursts forth in song and dance, ritual and custom, speech and action. Our *lives* reveal our loves. Take a look at my life, and you'll see pretty quickly what I worship.

Saint Paul once wrote a letter to some recent converts in a city called Thessalonica, fresh newborns in Christ who were not Jews but gentiles. He spoke with pride of how they had "turned to God from idols, to serve a living and true God, and to wait for his Son from heaven, whom he raised from the dead."

I have been giving you models and types of the shape of Christian life: pentecostal, baptismal, Marian, and so on. Here is another. To be a Christian is to share in one great turning, one long *conversion*, from the idols of this world to the true and living God, revealed in his Son, Jesus. This happens decisively in baptism, from which the great confession of faith in Christ resounds. But it characterizes the rest of your life, too. Daily life in Christ is daily dying to self. This dying is a death to our idols.

John Calvin called the human heart a perpetual factory of idols. He was right. There might as well be an assembly line running out of your chest, and off it drops a new idol every day of the week, and twice on Sunday.

This is our fallenness at work. We were made to worship God, not idols. The fix for our idolatry is not avoidance of worship but right worship. God gives us this in Christ.

I told you, very early, to be sure that you were worshiping with a local body of believers. This is why. Worship makes us human. Worshiping Christ makes us divine. We cannot be Christians apart from worship any more than we can be Christians apart from the church.

The traditional word for communal Christian worship is "liturgy." From the beginning, baptized believers have gathered together on Sunday morning—"the Lord's Day," recall, since he rose the morning after the Sabbath—in order to worship God the Father in the name of Jesus by the power of his Spirit. This worship contains certain essential elements and follows a certain order. It is *ritualistic* in the sense that it involves habits meant for repetition; it forms a kind of script we perform as a community.

Banish from your mind any hint that rituals or habits or similar things are bad or to be avoided. Far from it. In every area of our lives they are both unavoidable and desirable. God, knowing our nature, gives us the right rituals, filled with good habits, all of which are conduits of life and channels of his saving grace.

We gather in the name of Jesus. A pastor, representing Jesus, invokes his presence among us by his Spirit. We pray. We sing. We encourage and edify one another. We confess our sins. We confess our faith. We hear the word of the Lord read from each Testament, Old and New. We hear the gospel proclaimed in a sermon or homily. We feed on Christ in the Supper of Holy Communion, also called the Eucharist. The pastor blesses, commissions, and sends us out into the world in the name of Christ, to love and serve the Lord and our neighbors as ourselves.

We do this, week in, week out, each and every Sunday morning. And when I say "we" do this, I mean the Spirit does it *in us*, through Jesus, to the glory of the Father. We give all honor and glory and praise to God, who alone is worthy, but all the while it is God inspiring and indwelling our worship. The liturgy is a divine work before it is a human work. Because it is divine, it is also human. For the liturgy is when we enter, ever so briefly and tantalizingly, into the circle of infinite love and mutual glorification that is the eternal life of Father, Son, and Holy Spirit.

Worship, at its heart, is a glimpse or taste of heaven. The Spirit raises us up to the heavenly throne room and there, with the angels and elders and all the host of creation, we fall down before the Lord God Almighty. *To him who sits on the throne, and to the Lamb, be praise and honor and glory and power forever and ever!*

God purifies and sanctifies us through the repetition of this worship, over and over and over again. God conforms us to the image of his Son over the weeks and years and decades. The liturgy is where and when and how this happens. It is not the only place. But it is the first and lasting one. There is, Christians believe, an eternal liturgy in heaven. We will join it one day. Earthly worship is preparation. It's practice, so we'll be ready when the Day comes.

*Yours in Christ,*
*a fellow pilgrim*

## 74

*Dear future saint,*

Christian liturgy is *sacramental*. I've mentioned this word once or twice so far, but I've not yet defined it. You may be familiar with it, but many Christians are not, though the sacraments lie at the heart of living faith.

"Sacrament" comes from the Latin word *sacramentum*, which is a translation of the Greek word *mysterion*. Very early in the church believers began calling baptism and Eucharist the "mysteries" of Christian life and faith. The word stuck. For anyone in western Europe or connected to the church that took root there, "sacrament" became a borrowed word from Latin that pretty much everyone came to use, whatever their native tongue.

A sacrament is a symbolic practice of Christian worship, a practice instituted by Jesus himself for the communication of the gospel and of the grace he offers us through it. Sacraments are symbols, which means they "say" something in and of themselves, the way a kiss or a hug or a handshake or tears "say" something. They are not merely symbols, however. God acts in them, with them, by them, through them. They mediate his action. They impart his grace. They are conduits, channels, instruments.

Think of a check, a piece of mail, a straw. A check isn't money, but it's the means by which you deposit money in the bank. The mail is *how* you receive the handwritten letter from your mother; it's the means or middleman. A straw isn't the water inside the cup, but it's the way the water gets to your parched mouth.

Each of these is a medium, a means, a vehicle. God works *through* them. The words of the Bible are human words written by mortals, yet they *mediate God's word to us*. In the same way, the waters of baptism and the elements of Communion *mediate God's grace to us*. Not because God needs them to, but because God wants them to. He set it up this way. He's no enemy of matter. In the phrase of C. S. Lewis: "[God] likes matter. He invented it." Throughout Scripture God uses simple elements like oil, water, bread, and wine—not to mention dirt, spit, and other things—as carriers and vehicles of his power.

Saint Paul calls us "earthen vessels" or "jars of clay": we carry around the treasure of Christ in ordinary mortal bodies, made from the dust of the earth, "to show that the transcendent power belongs to God and not to us." Jesus himself once answered Paul's prayers for deliverance from some terrible pain with this reply: "My grace is sufficient for you, for my power is made perfect in weakness." Paul concluded: "I will all the more gladly boast of my weaknesses, that the power of Christ may rest upon me. For the sake of Christ, then, I am content with weaknesses, insults, hardships, persecutions, and calamities; for when I am weak, then I am strong."

The sacraments are clay jars that contain and communicate what is more precious than life itself: Christ. They are weak because he is strong. They are mundane because he is mighty. They are ordinary because he is extraordinary.

The Lord delights to honor and lift up the meek. He opposes the proud but gives grace to the humble. He does just this in the sacraments. First in the sense of using simple earthly elements to share his grace with us, and second in the sense of giving us visible, tangible helps and aids in the pilgrimage of faith. We cannot see the Lord, but we can see bread and wine. We cannot join him on the cross, but we can join him in the waters. We cannot hear his voice with immediacy, but we can hear his word spoken by the apostles and prophets.

He draws near to us in ways we can understand, in accordance with our senses, our limits, our needs. The sacraments are gifts from a humble God. We receive in faith now what we will soon see in the clear light of day.

*Yours in Christ,*
*a fellow pilgrim*

## 75

*Dear future saint,*

I wish I could give you what you want: a full-blown theology of the sacraments! Not to mention of the Bible. Alas, an impossible request for a series of letters drawing near to its close.

Let me say a brief word about each. To be clear, the pressing task is not to read my words or even others' words but simply to *do* these things. Be baptized. Take Communion. Listen to Scripture. But best to do so with some understanding. Here's a nudge in that direction.

1. *I confess one baptism for the forgiveness of sins.* This sentence comes from the Nicene Creed. Its inclusion should tell you something about the importance of baptism.

Baptism is the formal, public beginning of our life in Christ. Baptism is what it looks like: a bath. Instead of washing dirt from our bodies, it washes sin from our souls. In baptism we join Christ on the cross; united to him there, we rise with him from the empty tomb. The same Spirit that filled him on Easter morning fills us as we rise from the waters. As the church fathers liked to say, in being baptized by Saint John, Jesus did not receive sanctification, for he had no sins to be forgiven. Rather, he sanctified the waters for all time, so that they would purge us of our sins by his power and grace.

Baptism is your entrance into the body of Christ. Through it, God adds you to his church. The Spirit that indwells the church now indwells you. For the Spirit of Jesus is the Spirit not only of resurrection but of Sonship. Baptism is therefore your adoption ceremony. You're in family court, and when the gavel comes down—when the water touches your skin in the name of Father, Son, and Spirit—you are *in*. You are part of the household. For good. Like the younger brother in the parable of the prodigal son, you are free to run away. But you will always be a child of the Father. And if you ever return, skulking or ashamed, he will burst out of the house at a dead sprint to clasp you in the arms of his love.

This is why we are baptized only once. There is no such thing as "rebaptism." You can take a thousand more baths in your life, you can make them as spiritual as you like, but the first one always takes. No repeats necessary. God doesn't have to *readopt* you; you don't have to make sure you "feel" it the second or seventh time. The pledge of baptism is as sure as God's gospel word: you can stake your life on it.

Baptism is a second birth ("from above," in Jesus's words, "by water and Spirit"), and so baptism has always been linked in one way or another to birth and new life. What to do about actual newborn babies, then? Most Christians, past and present, whether Catholic, Orthodox, or Protestant, have baptized them. In the last few hundred years, a minority of Christians have practiced waiting until the candidate for baptism is capable of professing faith on his or her own. This is a reasonable and well-intended position—it's the one I was raised with—and it may be familiar to you as well. Given its popularity in our time and our part of the world, I'd like to lay out the main reasons why it has never carried the day. In other words, I want to explain why baptizing infants developed into the predominant practice of Christian history and church tradition, up through the present day.

First, baptism is the successor to circumcision. Abraham's children do not wait until they're a certain age before becoming or joining God's people. They are chosen and claimed by God, through his people, from birth. This is fitting because it expresses God's prior decision and gracious initiative. The same goes for baptism in the church.

Second, personal understanding or maturity is hard to measure. Signing up for lifelong discipleship to Jesus is a more serious matter than getting married, drinking alcohol, or serving in the military. Yet communities that do not baptize babies are willing to baptize children and teenagers too young to marry or enlist or have a beer. If they are too young for the latter, are they not too young for the former? And if not too young, then why not nudge the appropriate age for baptism from nine to six or from seven to four? Some congregations have done just this. At that point, though, why not go all the way to infancy?

Third, the historic church has never been especially interested in "personal choice" or "individual freedom." Speaking for myself, I don't pray that my children "choose" Jesus. I pray that Jesus chooses them: converts them, confronts them, befriends them, elects them. I want Jesus to make himself so dear, so known, so wonderful to my children that it's no choice at all.

This is why I, like all Christians, raise my children in the church. They pray to Jesus and worship him and read the Bible from their earliest days onward. If you want to call it brainwashing, fine: we brainwash our kids to love Jesus. This only sounds scandalous because we don't think about all the *other* ways everyone brainwashes their kids: to be kind, to tell the truth, to honor elders, to stay in their beds, to eat their vegetables, to play outside, to help their siblings, to do their homework. Childhood is nothing but education in what the child never chose for herself, because by definition she had no choice to make.

The choice Christian parents make for their children is to give them Christ—indeed, to give them *to* Christ. Tradition says: Do this by baptizing them.

2. The Eucharist (which means "thanksgiving") is the sacred meal instituted by Jesus on the night before his death, what tradition calls Maundy Thursday. As we call that the Last Supper, so we call this the Lord's Supper. Its other name is Communion. After celebrating Passover with his disciples, this is what happened:

> Jesus took bread, and blessed, and broke it, and gave it to the disciples and said, "Take, eat; this is my body." And he took a cup, and when he had given thanks he gave it to them, saying, "Drink of it, all of you; for this is my blood of the covenant, which is poured out for many for the forgiveness of sins. I tell you I shall not drink again of this fruit of the vine until that day when I drink it new with you in my Father's kingdom."

So says Saint Matthew. Here is how Saint Paul describes it:

> The Lord Jesus on the night when he was betrayed took bread, and when he had given thanks, he broke it, and said, "This is my body which is for you. Do this in remembrance of me." In the same way also the cup, after supper, saying, "This cup is the new covenant in my blood. Do this, as often as you drink it, in remembrance of me." For as often as you eat this bread and drink the cup, you proclaim the Lord's death until he comes.

In the Gospel of Saint John, finally, Jesus tells the crowds that he is "the bread of life." This begins a remarkable discourse in which Jesus compares himself to the manna with which God fed the Israelites in the desert; it concludes with reference to believers feeding on Christ in the Eucharist:

> "I am the bread of life. Your fathers ate the manna in the wilderness, and they died. This is the bread which comes down from heaven, that a man may eat of it and not die. I am the living bread which came down from heaven; if anyone eats of this bread, he will live forever; and the bread which I shall give for the life of the world is my flesh." ...
>
> "Unless you eat the flesh of the Son of Man and drink his blood, you have no life in you; he who eats my flesh and drinks my blood has eternal life, and I will raise him up at the last day. For my flesh is food indeed, and my blood is drink indeed.
>
> "He who eats my flesh and drinks my blood abides in me, and I in him. As the living Father sent me, and I live because of the Father, so he who eats me will live because of me. This is the bread which came down

from heaven, not such as the fathers ate and died; he who eats this bread will live forever."

I will let the word of Jesus and of his apostles do all the explaining here. In the Eucharist we commune with the Lord because he is really and truly present in the meal. He feeds us with himself, for his body is true food and his blood is true drink. We need not shy away from this teaching. The Eucharist is both the source and the summit of our faith. As Paul exhorts us: Let us keep the feast!

3. The Bible is the word of the living God to and for his people, the church. The prophets and apostles are the embassy of God's powerful speech from heaven. The Spirit who inspired their words is the same Spirit who fills our hearts to receive their words as his own, here and now, in the present tense.

In an early letter I laid out the composition of the Old Testament. For its part, the New Testament is made up of the four Gospels, the book of Acts, many letters from various apostles, and the book of Revelation (the record of a vision given to Saint John "the Seer," a prophet and preacher who was not "the Baptist" and may also not have been the author of the Fourth Gospel; John was a popular name at that time!). These texts were composed in the decades following the resurrection of Jesus. They quickly spread around the Roman Empire, being copied by hand and circulating from one Christian community to another.

The Old Testament was already a given for believers, and the writings of the apostles and their delegates, as authorities and eyewitnesses to Jesus, quickly came to be seen as a peer to Israel's sacred Scriptures. Both were read aloud when Christians gathered together for worship. (Remember: Almost no one was literate at this time. And for most of the church's history, in fact. Knowing and loving Scripture was primarily an *oral* phenomenon, heard with the ears, not read with the eyes.) After a few centuries, the church's sense of which books "counted" as Scripture and which did not reached a basic consensus. The name for this official list of scriptural books is "canon." The word also means *ruler* or *measure*, in the sense that this collection and it alone rules and measures the faithfulness of the church's faith and practice.

Considered as a single entity, the Bible is not "a sacrament." But the logic is the same. The words of the Bible mediate the word of Jesus to his beloved bride. When we hear it read aloud in the liturgy, we are hearing our Savior speak to us. This is why we respond the way we do: "The word of the Lord. Thanks be to God!"

God's word is the lifeblood of God's people. By its power the worlds were made; by its power Jesus rose from the dead; by its power your sins are forgiven. Nothing compares. It slays and makes alive. It sets the captive free. As the Lord himself says, by the mouth of Isaiah the prophet:

As the rain and the snow come down from heaven,
    and return not thither but water the earth,
making it bring forth and sprout,
    giving seed to the sower and bread to the eater,
so shall my word be that goes forth from my mouth;
    it shall not return to me empty,
but it shall accomplish that which I purpose,
    and prosper in the thing for which I sent it.

If you read the book of Acts, as well as Paul's first letter to the Thessalonians, you will see what the phrase "the word of the Lord" means. It's one and the same as the gospel. The word of the *Lord* is the word about *Jesus*—because Jesus is the Lord. God's word, then, is always, in one way or another, about Jesus and the good news of God's work in him for us. This is one of the many reasons why Christians are right to look for Jesus, to seek to learn about him, in every verse and book of the Bible. It was written by him and about him and for him, through his servants.

In the middle of his Gospel, John quotes a passage from Isaiah and then makes the following statement: "Isaiah said this because he saw his glory and spoke of him." The "him" there is Jesus. Isaiah saw *Jesus's* glory and thus spoke of him, in advance of his advent. As Jesus says, "If you believed Moses, you would believe me, for he wrote of me." And later: "Your father Abraham rejoiced that he was to see my day; he saw it and was glad."

Whether Old Testament or New, the Bible is Holy Scripture for the church. It is God's living word, till kingdom come. It is nourishment for our ears—a verbal bread—just as the Eucharist is nourishment for our mouths—a visible word. In both, Christ proclaims his gospel: to the church and, through her, to the world. In both, we are fed as we await his return: manna in the wilderness, on our long march to the promised land.

*Yours in Christ,*
*a fellow pilgrim*

## eleven

## God Makes His People Holy

It was because God made us for incorruption that he condemned the transgressors of his saving commandment to the corruption of death, but in his compassion he condescended to his servants and having become like us delivered us from corruption by his own passion. He made a fountain of remission gush out from his holy and immaculate side, on the one hand water for rebirth and cleaning from sin and corruption, and on the other blood as a drink productive of eternal life, and gave us commandments to be born again through water and Spirit with the Spirit coming upon the water through entreaty and invocation. For because human beings are twofold, consisting of soul and body, he also gave us a twofold cleansing, through water and Spirit, the Spirit renewing in us what is in "the image and likeness," and the water purifying the body of sin through the grace of the Spirit and delivering it from corruption, the water fulfilling the image of death, and the Spirit providing the pledge of life.

—Saint John of Damascus

## 76

*Dear future saint,*

Sanctification happens both within the church and without. It begins within—in the womb of baptism, if you will—but never stays there. The world Christians live in is the world God loves. They live in it *having been sent to it* by Christ. His Spirit drives them on into the wilderness. What awaits them is temptation and trial, but not only these. What awaits them is women and men who bear God's image, who are in desperate need (whether they know it or not). In this sense they are potential sisters and brothers in Christ. Each of them is a person, in Saint Paul's words, "for whom Christ died."

This is the prism through which we believers see the world. Not according to the flesh, but according to Christ's Spirit, who gives us eyes to see.

God keeps making us holy, above all as we meet and love and welcome the stranger.

The pattern for our life in the world, therefore, is Jesus himself. "Christ also suffered for you, leaving you an example, that you should follow in his steps." That's Saint Peter. He knew from personal experience.

Saint Thomas Aquinas said this: "All of Christ's action is our instruction." No detail in the life of Jesus is irrelevant to our lives as followers of Jesus. It is a pattern or paradigm for all we are and do. This pattern is exemplified in the cross. Here is how Paul puts it:

> Do nothing from selfishness or conceit, but in humility count others better than yourselves. Let each of you look not only to his own interests, but also to the interests of others. Have this mind among yourselves, which is yours in Christ Jesus,
>
> > who, though he was in the form of God,
> > > did not count equality with God
> > > a thing to be grasped,
> > but emptied himself,
> > > taking the form of a slave,
> > > being born in the likeness of men.
> > And being found in human form
> > > he humbled himself

GOD MAKES HIS PEOPLE HOLY

and became obedient unto death,
    even death on a cross.
Therefore God has highly exalted him
    and bestowed on him the name
    which is above every name,
that at the name of Jesus
    every knee should bow,
    in heaven and on earth and under the earth,
    and every tongue confess
that Jesus Christ is Lord,
    to the glory of God the Father.

This call to imitate the Messiah's suffering servanthood goes back to Jesus. Here's what he taught his disciples at a crucial juncture, when they had (once again) mistaken his mission for worldly glory rather than the triumph of the cross:

> "You know that among the gentiles those whom they recognize as their rulers lord it over them, and their great ones are tyrants over them. But it is not so among you; instead, whoever wishes to become great among you must be your servant, and whoever wishes to be first among you must be slave of all. For the Son of Man came not to be served but to serve and to give his life a ransom for many."

The Christian life is intimacy with Christ, as I have said. This intimacy goes all the way down and all the way up. It is an intimacy of suffering, of service, of sacrifice. The Christian life is *Christ's own life* manifest in ordinary sinners. The Spirit of Christ wells up in our lives and bursts forth in words and deeds of *imitatio Christi*: the imitation of Christ.

We are, as Paul says, "always carrying in the body the death of Jesus, so that the life of Jesus may also be manifested in our bodies. For while we live we are always being given up to death for Jesus' sake, so that the life of Jesus may be manifested in our mortal flesh."

But, he concludes,

> We do not lose heart. Though our outer nature is wasting away, our inner nature is being renewed every day. For this slight momentary affliction is preparing for us an eternal weight of glory beyond all comparison, because we look not to the things that are seen but to the things that are unseen; for the things that are seen are transient, but the things that are unseen are eternal.

*Yours in Christ,
a fellow pilgrim*

**77**

*Dear future saint,*

We're circling around to matters you raised many letters ago. *What are Christian morals? How do we know? How should we live?*

There are two primary places to go in Scripture for basic teaching regarding the moral life: the Ten Commandments and the Sermon on the Mount. The first is found in the Law of Moses (in two places, in fact). The second is the very first (and longest) set of teachings by Jesus in the Gospels, as reported by Saint Matthew.

The Sermon is sometimes interpreted as Jesus revising or correcting Moses. This is inaccurate. Far from amending, much less criticizing, the Torah, Jesus in the Sermon is extending, deepening, and enriching it. He is showing us the soul of the Torah. He is moving the Law from the outside in. He wants to write it on our hearts, through the Spirit.

Here is an abbreviated form of the Ten Commandments (sometimes called the Ten Words, or Decalogue):

1. Worship the one true God alone.
2. Honor God by avoiding idols and all images of God.
3. Keep the name of the Lord holy; do not misuse it.
4. Observe the Sabbath: rest on the seventh day.
5. Honor your father and mother.
6. Do not murder.
7. Do not commit adultery.
8. Do not steal.
9. Do not lie.
10. Do not covet.

It's easy enough to see that these brief commands carve out space for human life to flourish. A community beset by deceit, theft, infidelity, and violence will not last long. Likewise a community filled with idolatry, blasphemy, slavery, and ruptured families. Notice how freeing, even life-giving, are *negative* commands, or prohibitions. They don't tell you exactly what to do. They just make clear what to avoid.

It's common to hear people bemoan such things as an indefinite list of

GOD MAKES HIS PEOPLE HOLY

203

"thou shalt nots." What's to bemoan? These are the guardrails of life itself. It's not burdensome to avoid murder. It's good for you—and for others. Commands, even divine commands, are not quite the gospel on their own. But as one theologian puts it, they are the gospel clothed in an imperative. Put differently, they prescribe the form of life *in which* the gospel is discovered and expressed.

You will not find life, much less God's life, in a community that rejects the Ten Commandments. Only in a community that honors and obeys these commands will true life—true justice and holiness—be possible.

Jesus once was asked about the greatest of all the commands found in Moses. He answered (this is my modest paraphrase):

> Love the Lord your God
> with all your heart, soul, mind, and strength;
> and your neighbor as yourself.
> On these hang all the law and the prophets.

This twofold love command is embodied in the Decalogue. If you keep the latter, you'll find that you're doing the former.

*Yours in Christ,*
*a fellow pilgrim*

## 78

*Dear future saint,*

Jesus emerges from the desert, gaunt and famished yet full of the Spirit's power. He begins to preach the good news of God's kingdom. He sees the crowds already beginning to form. He goes up on a mountain, like Moses so long before. His disciples come to him. He opens his mouth and begins to teach them, saying:

> "Blessed are the poor in spirit,
>     for theirs is the kingdom of heaven.
> Blessed are those who mourn,
>     for they shall be comforted.
> Blessed are the meek,
>     for they shall inherit the earth.
> Blessed are those who hunger and thirst for justice,
>     for they shall be satisfied.
> Blessed are the merciful,
>     for they shall obtain mercy.
> Blessed are the pure in heart,
>     for they shall see God.
> Blessed are the peacemakers,
>     for they shall be called sons of God.
> Blessed are those who are persecuted for justice's sake,
>     for theirs is the kingdom of heaven.

"Blessed are you when people revile you and persecute you and utter all kinds of evil against you falsely on my account. Rejoice and be glad, for your reward is great in heaven, for so people persecuted the prophets who were before you."

These are the Beatitudes, so called because they are Jesus's pronouncement of *happiness* (Latin *beatitudo*) upon his followers; or rather, his pointing us in the direction of where, and in whom, true happiness is found. Not in the places we might expect, is the short answer.

Here, in the Beatitudes, is the promised upside-down kingdom of God.

The rest of the Sermon consists of a series of teachings on different matters: the high calling of God's people; the lasting truth of the Scriptures; anger, adultery, divorce, oaths, and violence; how to give generously; how to pray; how to fast; what to do with money; worrying about ourselves and judging others' behavior and seeking God with perseverance; finally, bearing fruit, following Jesus, and doing his word (as opposed to merely politely listening to it—giving it lip service, we might say).

If you haven't noticed by now, there are no corners of the Christian life exempt from God's interest. God is all up in your business. Whatever it is, however great or small, it concerns him. There is nothing so huge that he cannot handle it; nothing so minute that he cannot understand it. To be a Christian is to let the will of God touch every part of your life. Nothing can be sealed off. It may hurt at first, but in the end it is all for your good.

Jesus shows us the Way in the Sermon; we see what it means to be good and do good in his teachings, which he then lives out in the rest of his ministry. I know a group of young men at my university who memorize the Sermon and pledge to one another to live it out, together and in the world. They wear a small cross around their necks to show their commitment. They take Jesus at his word: he wants us to live this way, to live as he did and as he taught. They are right.

I wrote in an earlier letter that Christianity is not first of all about "being a good person." That remains true. Christianity is about God rescuing you from the clutches of Sin and Death and transferring you into the kingdom of his Son. But Sin and Death cling closely, as the author of Hebrews puts it. They nip at our heels. Like the Israelites at the Red Sea, we begin to long for our old chains. They weren't so bad, were they?

When God rescues us in Christ, his Spirit works a *transformation* in us. It begins in baptism and ends in death. We must be changed. He does it for us. But not without us. Discipleship and sanctification go hand in hand.

It is in this sense that being a Christian entails "becoming good," inasmuch as being a Christian entails becoming like Christ. Over time, to be sure—and by the Spirit's help, and with the aid of the sacraments, and propped up by our sisters and brothers, and nourished by God's word, and sustained in prayer— but yes, in truth, more and more like Christ.

Not that every Christian, even every elderly Christian, is much like Christ. But every Christian ought to be more like Christ than she was when she *began* following him. Most of us start out in a bad place. We may not be far along, years down the road. But if we're no longer where we were, then that is nothing less than the miraculous work of God. It may not be much in the world's eyes, but it is everything in his.

Yours in Christ,
a fellow pilgrim

GOD MAKES HIS PEOPLE HOLY

## 79

*Dear future saint,*

You ask for specifics. Always specifics! Here I am, preaching and philoso-phizing, and you want to know how to live. I would have thought the Ten Commandments as practical as it gets!

The Christian life is marked simultaneously by the cardinal virtues (cour-age, prudence, temperance, justice) and by the theological virtues (faith, hope, love). Recall the fruit of the Spirit: love, joy, peace, patience, kindness, goodness, faith, gentleness, and self-control. Lives marked by such fruit are by definition free of envy, murder, adultery, theft, and dishonesty. Parents are honored and God alone is worshiped. This is the good life.

Jesus's life and teachings take this vision further. Here's what he says: Instead of merely avoiding murder, reject anger altogether. Instead of only shunning adultery, resist lust altogether. Instead of solely resisting lust, es-chew divorce altogether. Instead of making oaths to show you're being honest, never tell a lie whatsoever. Instead of calling for retaliation against those who harm you, give the evildoer even more than he wants. Instead of reserving your love for neighbor and kin, love your enemies and pray for those who persecute you.

If you do all this, Jesus says, you shall be whole, complete, or perfect, as is your Father in heaven.

Later in the Sermon, Jesus adds the following about forgiveness (pre-sumably of enemies, though God knows our friends and family often hurt us more than anyone else):

> "If you forgive others their sins,
> your heavenly Father also will forgive you;
> but if you do not forgive others their sins,
> neither will your Father forgive your sins."

Later still in the Gospel, Saint Peter approaches Jesus and asks him, "Lord, how often shall my brother sin against me, and I forgive him? As many as seven times?" Jesus answers him, "I do not say to you seven times, but seventy times seven." In brief, there's no limit to Christian forgiveness.

This is a hard teaching. Christian lives are to be known for loving enemies, praying for persecutors, forgiving without end, telling the truth no matter the cost, freedom from all violence, and not a hint of sexual impropriety. As Jesus teaches elsewhere, his followers are to marry for life. "What God has joined together, let no one put asunder."

I worry I have become, if possible, *too* specific. But these are the teachings of Jesus. We are bound to obey them. Let me try to unfold their implications and how we are meant to find life in them.

First, they are not a condition for being saved. They are the shape of our salvation, *having been* baptized into Jesus. We are carried by the church into the adventure of following Jesus. This is what following him looks like, *beginning* with our baptism into his life and death.

Second, they are not an impossible call to perfection. The Spirit of Jesus in us is what makes obedience possible. The fact that we will inevitably falter and fail and fall in our walk does not mean Jesus is not asking us to walk in the first place. The Spirit carries us along the path.

Third, they are not for individuals. They are for a community of his disciples. We know the name of this community! The church. The Sermon is the charter for the body of believers whose head is Christ. It is not a general constitution for people who do not know the Lord.

Fourth, the Sermon encapsulates an important rule that characterizes all of Jesus's teaching as well as Christian ethics as a whole: it is not natural but supernatural. It is not human but divine. It does not make sense in a fallen world. Even in an unfallen world, parts of Jesus's teaching would transcend strictly natural human living. His words are the keys to the *kingdom*, and the king of that realm is God. The Sermon is our Way into life eternal—not a path to earthly happiness or worldly success. By those terms, the Sermon is a scandal. Even a kind of joke.

Fifth, while few among us will embody the teachings of the Sermon in a truly exemplary manner, it is possible for the church as a whole to show the world the Way of Jesus by adhering to the Sermon as best she can, with the Spirit's help. This is exactly what Jesus wants:

> "You are the light of the world. A city set on a hill cannot be hid. Nor do people light a lamp and put it under a bushel, but on a stand, and it gives light to all in the house. Let your light so shine before others, that they may see your good works and give glory to your Father who is in heaven."

The "you" and "your" there are second-person plural. *Y'all*, as we say in Texas. Most instances of "you" in the Bible should be rendered "y'all," as they are in other languages. The point is that Jesus isn't talking to you, an individual. He's talking to y'all, the church. *Us*, God's people. *We* are the light of the world. I could never be that light all on my own.

In the next letter, I want to think about how the church is God's light to the world and in the world regarding three areas of human life: money, sex, and power. Buckle up.

*Yours in Christ,*
*a fellow pilgrim*

## 80

*Dear future saint,*

So: money, sex, and power. Our world thrives on these. Or rather, on distorted versions of them. As a result, the gospel has much to say about them. The church teaches quite concretely about all three. Her teaching follows Jesus's closely, here in the Sermon and elsewhere in his ministry. Let's take them each in turn.

*Money.* At times Jesus appears to teach that his followers shouldn't hold possessions at all. At a minimum, Jesus pronounces blessings upon the poor—in Saint Luke's Gospel, it is not the poor in spirit but just the poor—and gives the following severe warning about wealth:

> "No one can serve two masters;
> for either he will hate the one and love the other,
> or he will be devoted to the one and despise the other.
> You cannot serve God and mammon."

Following Jesus, Christians believe money to be a rival deity to the true God, and therefore an idol to be spurned. For this reason Saint Paul writes that envy is idolatry, and "the love of money is the root of all evils; it is through this craving that some have wandered away from the faith and pierced their hearts with many pangs." No believer lives out these convictions perfectly, but our common life ought to show it forth with clarity and beauty.

Saint James ups the ante, though. He does not speak *about* the wealthy. He speaks to them directly:

> Come now, you rich, weep and howl for the miseries that are coming upon you. Your riches have rotted and your garments are moth-eaten. Your gold and silver have rusted, and their rust will be evidence against you and will eat your flesh like fire. You have laid up treasure for the last days. Behold, the wages of the laborers who mowed your fields, which you kept back by fraud, cry out; and the cries of the harvesters have reached the ears of the Lord of hosts. You have lived on the earth in luxury and in pleasure; you have fattened your hearts in a day of slaughter. You have condemned, you have killed the righteous man; he does not resist you.

I trust you can see that anyone who connects Christian faithfulness with financial prosperity is lying. God does not want you to be rich. Wealth is not a reward from God for your obedience to him. What you have, it is true, comes from him. It is a blessing *in the sense* that it is an unmerited gift and that it is meant to be used in the Lord's service.

But do not forget two things. First is Jesus's teaching that "it is easier for a camel to go through the eye of a needle than for a rich man to enter the kingdom of God." He goes on to say that, humanly speaking, such a thing is truly impossible, but with God anything is possible. In other words, it takes a divine miracle to save a single rich person!

Second, the more faithful to Christ you are in this life, the more likely you are to suffer for him. This rule applies to money and possessions as much as, or perhaps more than, anything else. Jesus did not come to relieve us of our earthly suffering but to join us in it. Unite your suffering to his—unite your need, your lack, your poverty to his cross—and he will give you joy *in the midst of it*, not instead of it.

Our treasure is in heaven, not on this earth.

*Sex.* Jesus is both traditional and revolutionary in his teaching on sex. The following vignette is representative:

> Pharisees came up to him and tested him by asking, "Is it lawful to divorce one's wife for any cause?" He answered, "Have you not read that he who made them from the beginning made them male and female, and said, 'For this reason a man shall leave his father and mother and be joined to his wife, and the two shall become one flesh'? So they are no longer two but one flesh. What therefore God has joined together, let not man put asunder."
>
> They said to him, "Why then did Moses command one to give a certificate of divorce, and to put her away?" He said to them, "For your hardness of heart Moses allowed you to divorce your wives, but from the beginning it was not so. And I say to you: whoever divorces his wife, except for unchastity, and marries another, commits adultery."

At the same time, Jesus was himself single, as was Saint Paul. Each of them commended this form of life to believers. The early church saw in this teaching and example a higher path than natural marriage, good and God-ordained as marriage is. For, as Jesus taught, we will not be married in heaven. Those called to lifelong celibacy make a kind of sacrifice, but it is a sacrifice in service to a higher love and thus a higher happiness: union with Christ alone. Such a life anticipates, even tastes in advance, the marriageless life of heaven.

Or rather, heaven's marriage-*consummated* life. For as Paul tells us, marriage on earth is a window or image or sacrament of Christ's relationship to the church. A man and a woman bound together in lifelong fidelity speaks volumes; what it tells of is God's own faithfulness to his people. It turns out that marriage, like everything else, is about Jesus. Marriage, therefore, will be *fulfilled* when Jesus returns, not abolished. Nevertheless, ordinary marriage as we know it will no longer exist.

So Christians either marry for life or are celibate for life. What they may not do is commit any kind of *unchastity*, which refers to sexual immorality, including sex outside of marriage. "Chastity" is the sexual virtue proper to every Christian, without exception. It takes one of two forms. Which of the two is your calling is a matter of careful discernment.

*Power*. We have seen, time and again, God's relationship to earthly power, whether physical or political or otherwise. Because God is not threatened by us, he need not play by our rules. When he comes to earth, he does not come bearing a sword, much less flanked by martial ranks of angels.

He comes instead as a helpless child, the son of a virgin. He comes to the desert, alone and hungry. He comes to the city, riding on a humble donkey. He comes to the Garden, praying in such anguish that he sweats blood. He comes to the Praetorium, whipped with lashes, scourged and mocked and crowned with thorns. He comes to Calvary, nailed to a cross, a spectacle for onlookers and a victim of empire. He comes at last to a tomb, a corpse like any other man or woman. He comes to be buried. He was born to die.

Now remember what Jesus told Paul: "My grace is sufficient for you, for my power is made perfect in weakness." This is what Jesus showed us in his own life and death. Divine power is manifested in human weakness. The pitiful Jesus is the vessel of almighty God.

If it was true for him, all the more so for us. In our weakness, we are strong. The world worships power, but we worship a crucified Messiah. His power is real, but it is the secret power of the Spirit. So long as we are on this earth, it is this power, the power of God's grace, that is our strength.

*Yours in Christ,*
*a fellow pilgrim*

## 81

*Dear future saint,*

Here is where the saints enter in. (I know you've been wondering about them!) The saints are little Christs dotting the landscape of the church's history. Her tradition holds them close, for they refract the light of Christ in ten thousand ways, each one precious. Look to the saints when you want to see how any of this works in practice.

For example, think of Saint Anthony and Saint Benedict, fathers of the monastic life. "Monastic" refers to *monks*. Monks and nuns are men and women who give up marriage and possessions in order to live for Christ alone, whether by themselves (in some desert hideout) or with others (in a monastery or convent). Living in community, they make three vows: poverty, celibacy, and obedience (to the leader of the community). These dispossessions and abstentions are not forms of masochism. They are a taste of heaven on earth. And like living signs, they show the rest of us what lies in store for all of us, the whole church, when Christ returns.

Nothing is better for growing in the spiritual life than visiting a monastery or convent. There are dozens in the States. There are far more overseas. I've been to a bunch. I once spent two nights on Mount Athos, the most magnificent monastic community on the planet. Simply observing the monks in their prayers and their labors has the power to change your life. It has changed the lives of many. It might even make you want to take vows and join them yourself.

Now think of Saint Monica. Her son, Saint Augustine, wrote a whole book about her. Not everyone realizes this. They think the *Confessions* are Augustine's story, or at least God's. It's true that the narrative's divine protagonist is Jesus. But the human protagonist—the chief instrument of Jesus's will and work—is Monica. And what does she do in the book, which is to say, in her son Augustine's life?

She prays.

That's all. She prays, and prays, and prays, and weeps tears like blood, and prays some more. She is the widow from Jesus's parable who refuses to stop pestering a judge for justice. The judge is not himself a just man. But because he cannot stand to hear her continue banging on his door, demanding justice, he gives it to her. She knocks, and he answers.

That's Monica. She's my hero. My patron saint. Ever since I read Augustine's *Confessions* as a father, she became my model as a parent. I want to be like Monica when I grow up. I want to pray my children into heaven, like she did. I want God to get so fed up with my *bang bang bang*-ing on his door that he opens it wide and lets in my kids. If I do nothing else, my life will have been worth it. Monica showed me that.

Now think of Saint Perpetua. She was a young convert to the faith who lived in Rome about 140 years after Saint Peter and Saint Paul were martyred there. She was also a new mother, her infant still nursing, when she was arrested and taken to the Colosseum. She had a vision of Christ that gave her the courage she needed to face the lions. Though her father begged her to recant for the sake of her child, she entrusted him to God, and walked willingly to her death.

About a century earlier, Saint Ignatius had died the very same death. A bishop of Antioch, which was a major hub of the church at the time, Ignatius was taken in chains from that great city (in modern-day Turkey) across the empire to Rome. While traveling, he wrote seven letters to seven congregations, including Corinth, Ephesus, and Rome. In this he was like both Paul and Saint John, who likewise began the book of Revelation with letters to seven churches. Among other things, Ignatius urged no one to intervene. Rather he sought to glorify God by his witness in death:

> Let me be food for the wild beasts, through whom I can reach God. I am God's wheat, and I am being ground by the teeth of the wild beasts, so that I may prove to be pure bread.

More than a millennium later, Saint Francis of Assisi did not die a martyr, but he lived as one. He sold all he had and gave it to the poor. He kickstarted a mass movement in medieval Europe. Women and men of every class and rank followed his example. The Franciscan order of monks persists to this day. Their love for the poor—for Christ in the poor, Christ in creation, Christ in the birds and the trees, in brother sun and sister moon—is a living testimony in history to the power and person of Jesus.

Think, finally, of Saint Thérèse of Lisieux. She entered a convent as a young teenager. She died of tuberculosis before the age of twenty-five. By every worldly standard, her life was unimportant, unremarkable, insignificant: not public but private, not visible but hidden, not loud but quiet, even silent.

Yet, as is so often the case, her holiness became renowned, not only in France but around the world. Her holiness was simple in the extreme. She loved Jesus. Only Jesus. Nothing but Jesus. Men and women sought her counsel through letters. Her sisters cared for her and nursed her in bad health.

On September 30, 1897, she died. Her last words: *Je vous aime, ô mon Dieu, je vous aime!*

Translation: I love you, O my God, I love you!

A little over 125 years later, Pope Emeritus Benedict XVI—born Joseph Ratzinger—was on his deathbed. At ninety-five years old, he had lived a full life. He survived the Nazis; he attended a great church council; he rose in the ranks of the German university system; his international influence in theology was peerless; he policed the boundaries of church doctrine; eventually he became the bishop of Rome.

What were the words of this great mind, this surpassing intellect, just before he closed his eyes?

*Jesus, ich liebe dich!* Jesus, I love you!

May we all be so fortunate. Howsoever we reach our end in this life, may similar words of faith and affection for our dear Lord pass our lips, just before we meet him face-to-face.

*Yours in Christ,*
*a fellow pilgrim*

## 82

*Dear future saint,*

The flip side of looking to the saints is that it can trick us, in one of two ways. In both cases we imagine that faithful Christian living is heroic living. If I am to love and honor Christ in all that I do, then my life should look *impressive* as a result; surely I will be famous, or visibly virtuous, or highly regarded, or worth telling a story about. My Christlikeness should make me stand out from the crowd.

I want to relieve you of this mind-set. It isn't true. Thomas à Kempis, a priest from the Netherlands whom I quoted in a previous letter, gave us a precious book about six hundred years ago. It's called *The Imitation of Christ*, and it's full of wisdom about the spiritual life. About one's reputation, he writes that "he who seeks passing fame or does not in his heart despise it, undoubtedly cares little for the glory of heaven." He goes on:

> Praise adds nothing to your holiness, nor does blame take anything from it. You are what you are, and you cannot be said to be better than you are in God's sight.
>
> Never desire special praise or love, for that belongs to God alone who has no equal. Never wish that anyone's affection be centered in you, nor let yourself be taken up with the love of anyone, but let Jesus be in you.
>
> Do not let your peace depend on the words of men. Their thinking well or badly of you does not make you different from what you are. Where are true peace and glory? Are they not in Christ?

In my last letter I mentioned Saint Thérèse. She is sometimes called Thérèse of the Little Way. From childhood, she wanted to be a saint. Not just a saint, but an apostle and priest and martyr. Yet she entered a convent, hidden away from the world, and never married, never preached, never published in her lifetime. She felt small; she felt *ungreat*. Yet where did these desires for greatness come from?

Here is the conclusion Thérèse reached. Because, she writes, "God cannot inspire unrealizable desires," it is not wrong, "in spite of my littleness, to aspire to holiness." So she searched for "a means of going to Heaven by a little way, a way that is very straight, very short, and totally new." In her time, elevators had just been invented, and they fascinated Thérèse. She imagined her quest as one for an elevator to heaven—an elevator for little souls like herself, not great souls like saints and martyrs.

Eventually she came to a discovery: "The elevator which must raise me to heaven is Your arms, O Jesus! And for this I [have] no need to grow up, but rather I [have] to remain *little* and become this more and more." In other words, far from being an obstacle to growing in the holiness of Jesus, littleness is the Lord's own means of doing so. Our littleness does not leave Jesus unimpressed. Rather, Jesus loves our littleness, loves us *in* our littleness, since it does not deceive us into believing that we must be great in order to earn his grace.

As a matter of fact, Jesus himself became little, shared in our littleness, in order to give us his greatness. We follow him most faithfully when we do not spurn his little way but embrace it. We do not need magnificent deeds and awesome works. Thérèse herself realized what her calling from God was. Not to martyrdom or the priesthood, not to the missionary field, not to fame or recognition. Here's how she wrote it, shouting it in a letter only a year before she died:

My Vocation Is Love!

"Thus," she concludes, "I shall be everything, and thus my dream will be realized." What she means is that, even in the tiniest, most insignificant situations, in the smallest of daily interactions, in the most mundane and seemingly unimportant encounters and relationships, if you act for love, then in that moment you might as well be giving your body over to the flames for Christ. What Christ wants is your love: for him and for those *he* loves. Whom does he love? Whoever crosses your path. Love them and you love him. Christ sees your love and delights in it. You delight the Lord whenever you love, whomever you love, however you love. You are loving him by loving those he has given you to love. (As Julian of Norwich says: "Failure of love on our part is the only cause of all our suffering.")

This is the little way, the way available to all, no matter one's station, status, health, wealth, fame, virtue, family, race, class, gender, job, or age. Follow Thérèse in the little way of love. If you follow her, you'll be following Christ.

*Yours in Christ,*
*a fellow pilgrim*

## 83

*Dear future saint,*

In the last letter I spoke of two temptations, though I didn't name them. Both mistake saints for heroes and littleness for greatness. They fear, I think, being stuck with a *boring* life.

This is the temptation of thinking "true" Christians are never ordinary. The second temptation supposes "true" Christians are never failures. Let me say a word about each.

Between us, my wife and I have many grandmothers. Right now I'm thinking about four of them. We called them Nama, Granji, Mom Pat, and Marnie. All were born between the two world wars; none is still with us.

They lived good but hard lives. They were married a total of nine times and gave birth to sixteen children. All but one went through multiple divorces. Two lost children at a young age. One died abruptly as the result of an accident in her late sixties. Two died from illness in their seventies. One died a few months before turning ninety-eight.

Each of these women, for all their differences, was a Christian. A couple wandered from the faith in middle age but eventually returned. All died in the faith. They fought the good fight, they finished the race. They left this world in the arms of Jesus, honored by the church and surrounded by family and friends.

Very few people know the names of these women. Within one or two generations, aside from a handful of memories passed on to their great- and great-great-grandchildren, no one will remain who knew them. No one will remember them as they were when they lived: their wry humor, the pleasure they took in their families, their indomitable resolve.

If the gospel is false, then this is a sad and tragic end—the type of end that comes for just about everyone. And even if the gospel is true, we may be tempted to imagine that Nama, Granji, Mom Pat, and Marnie were, Christianly speaking, "nothing special." After all, none of them is likely to be declared a saint by the church. (They would have found that notion hilarious!)

But here's what I want you to hear. *These four women lived exemplary Christian lives.* Precisely in their ordinariness, in the littleness of their inconspicuous, unexceptional, and unheroic lives, these women are what Christianity is all about. You must get it out of your head that Christianity is about upstanding, inspiring folk. It's not. It's about normal people. Normal people whom Jesus loved so much he died for them. Normal people for whom the grace of Jesus is enough. Sinners in need of God's mercy as much as you and I. Sinners about whom no biographies will be written, no film adaptations made—but sinners nonetheless beloved by the Lord and filled with his Spirit.

Christians, in a word, are *normies*. And these normie grandmas are the ones I look up to in the faith. I want to make it to the end of my life just like they did, having wrestled for decades with God and, yes, having been wounded in the process, but having also received his blessing. These ladies were blessed. Don't you forget it.

*Yours in Christ,
a fellow pilgrim*

## 84

*Dear future saint,*

Some of us fear being *normie* Christians (or, worse, we look down on others who seem to fit the bill). And some of us fear being *bad* Christians. What do I mean by the latter?

Simply this. No one wants to be Judas. Everyone wants to be King David or Saint Peter or Saint Paul. As it happens, though, there's not a lot of daylight between Judas and these great saints. I can't say it better than Luci Shaw, in her poem "Judas, Peter":

> because we are all
> betrayers, taking
> silver and eating
> body and blood and asking
> (guilty) is it I and hearing
> him say yes
> it would be simple for us all
> to rush out
> and hang ourselves
> but if we find grace
> to cry and wait
> after the voice of morning
> has crowed in our ears
> clearly enough
> to break our hearts
> he will be there
> to ask us each again
> do you love me?

Every one of us, it turns out, is a Judas. Every one of us is a failed disciple, a betrayer and denier and traitor. That's not what marks the difference between Judas and Peter. The only difference is that Peter returned to Jesus. (Better: *Jesus returned to Peter*, appearing to him personally after he rose from the dead. Yet he came not in judgment but in the mercy of God himself. And within days Peter was up in front of his countrymen, declaring the good news of what he'd witnessed with his own eyes: the Messiah, risen from the grave, eager to forgive—even those responsible for his death!)

Peter returned to Jesus, but Judas did not. Judas gave in to despair. Likewise David sinned against God but received the prophet Nathan's rebuke with contrition and sorrow. As for Paul, he persecuted Jesus's followers, seeking their arrest and punishment and even death. Yet he, too, accosted by Christ, repented and received his grace.

That is all you must do. Turn to Christ, return to Christ, over and over and over again. Each and every time, he will meet you with his love—never his rejection or condemnation. If, as I quoted early in our correspondence, the only tragedy in this life is not to become a saint, it is also true, in the words of Georges Bernanos, that "the only final grief is one day to stand impenitent under Merciful Eyes." The Lord is ready to forgive. Are you and I ready to be forgiven? Are we *penitent*?

There is a character in *Silence*, a novel about persecuted believers in seventeenth-century Japan, that exemplifies this Judas/Peter dynamic. His name is Kijichiro. He is the textbook definition of a failed Christian. He's earnest and well meaning, but every time the authorities come knocking, he opens the door and tells them everything. He betrays his fellow Christians. He betrays the Portuguese priests in hiding among them. People suffer torture and death as a result of his actions.

Yet every time—*every time*—Kijichiro is sorry for his actions, and means it. He comes to the priest, begging for forgiveness. Pleading for absolution. He wants to hear the voice of Christ grant him pardon for his sins.

Now here's the question. Is Kijichiro a Christian? A "real" or "true" Christian? Is he what we have in mind when we talk about the Christian life?

I'll give you my answer: *Yes.* Kijichiro is a true Christian. He's Judas—but he's also Peter. He's Judas because he betrays Jesus; he's Peter because he returns to him. And just as every one of us is Judas, so all of us are Kijichiro. *We are all "bad" Christians.* There is no other kind. What makes us Christian is our need, not our lack of need; our sins, not our spotless spiritual hygiene. We keep asking God's forgiveness in the Lord's Prayer for the simple reason that we need it, every single day.

On the shore of Galilee, the risen Jesus asks Peter three times: "Simon, son of John, do you love me?" Charcoal burns between them, just as Peter warmed himself over a charcoal fire the night he denied knowing Jesus. Yes, he betrayed the Lord; yes, he loves the Lord. Both are true. This is what made him weep that awful night. What brings him back to himself—back from the dead, you might say—is Jesus's piercing, painfully honest gaze. A gaze that sees the magnitude of the crime and somehow still forgives.

The same gaze meets us, too, along with the same power to forgive. The wickedest and most faithless of believers, decades removed from anything resembling obedience, has only to turn and meet this gaze, to look on the face of Christ. To see it—to be seen by it—is the very moment of our peace. It shatters and breaks us, even as it remakes us.

Look on him. Never stop looking on him. "Seek his face always," as one psalm puts it. Seek the face of Jesus in all things, and never stop returning to him. He will say to you what he said to Peter, which in the Gospels are Jesus's final, parting words to his chief apostle:

*"Follow me!"*

Yours in Christ,
a fellow pilgrim

## 85

*Dear future saint,*

If I understand your question—is it an objection?—you're wondering about
the *point* of all I've described. Or perhaps that's not quite right. You want to
know who is in view; the audience in mind; the direction of the church's ar-
row of witness. If I'm not mistaken, you want to know which way the saints
are facing.

Is the holiness of the church *inward facing*, apart from the world? Or is it
somehow *for* the world? Are the saints a model and inspiration for believers
alone? Or also for those outside the circle of faith? What, in short, is the
church's holiness *for*? Solely for her members? Or is the liturgical and moral
life of the church somehow part of her mission to the world?

The answer is yes. To all of it. We need not choose. No multiple choice.
All of the above.

The worship and ethics of the church are at once God's gift to God's people
and God's gift, through his people, to the world. The church's walls (literal in
the case of buildings; metaphorical in the sense of people) are Janus-faced:
they have two sides, and both are important.

The inner life of the church has its own integrity. The church cannot exist
*merely* for the sake of her mission to the world. She is Christ's bride, beloved
from the foundation of the world. Christ died for *her*. He loves *you* and *me*,
not only "them," while "they" are on the outside looking in. That wouldn't
make any sense.

But his love overflows the boundaries of the church. The church is sent
into the world: "for God so loved the world." The church does have a mission.
Her mission is to bear witness to the good news of her Lord. How? In word
and deed, above all in her common life of worship and mutual care and in
her service to the least of these, Christ's sisters and brothers. She models the
divine alternative in a world of lies and violence, of illness and pain. She is an
outpost of God's kingdom in Satan's territory.

The question that arises here is twofold. What is the role of evangelism in
this picture? And what is the concrete goal of the church's mission?

Evangelism comes from *evangel*, Greek for "gospel." To evangelize is to
share the good news with others, typically with the aim of converting them
to the faith. Evangelists (in the plural) are women and men who take up this

task as a personal calling. All believers are expected to be ready to share the reason for the hope they have in Jesus. In between lies the challenge.

It seems to me that we should place "evangelism" under "witness" and "witness" under "mission." Evangelism is *one of the things* the church does, since making converts falls under Christ's commission to make disciples from all nations. But discipling is more than baptizing new members. It also includes teaching, thereby growing believers in the maturity of their faith and walk with the Lord. Moreover, counting converts can be a tricky game to play. It's tempting to quantify our faithfulness with good numbers. That way lies danger.

Better to focus on what we can control and leave the rest to God. We cannot force others to come to Christ. What we can do is bear witness as a community to the Way of Christ, inviting any and all who see our life and hear this word to join us—freely, without condition or cost. Sometimes they will come in droves. Sometimes they will spurn the invitation. Either way, it is in the Lord's hands, not ours.

Now, what is the overall *effect* of the church and her mission on the world? I have heard a lot over the years that the church is supposed to change the world: to transform it, to restore it, to redeem or reclaim it.

Count me unpersuaded. When Christ returns in glory, the Lord will himself transform the world. Until that time, what we have to do is wait, pray, be patient, and bear witness. Sometimes the world will respond; sometimes it will ignore; other times it will turn hostile. I fail to see how the world's visible or measurable transformation could be a criterion of the church's fidelity to Christ's calling.

Having said that, the portrait I've painted of the church has, I hope, been sufficiently alluring that you might wonder: Who wouldn't want to sign up? That's how I feel. I've left plenty out, however. The church is far from perfect. She continues to ask for God's forgiveness because she knows, with Saint Paul, that of all sinners she is chief. Yet nothing can separate her from Christ's love. As Jesus said, "Those who are well have no need of a physician, but those who are sick; I have not come to call the righteous, but sinners to repentance." He also said, "My sheep hear my voice, and I know them, and they follow me; and I give them eternal life, and they shall never perish, and no one shall snatch them out of my hand." Thank God for that.

*Yours in Christ,*
*a fellow pilgrim*

## 86

*Dear future saint,*

There is so much more to say about the church. Her works of mercy for the poor: the imprisoned, the homeless, the migrant, the unborn. Her solidarity with the marginal, the maligned, the powerless and voiceless. Her patience with the suffering and the weak. Her accompaniment of the dying.

Wherever she goes, the gospel takes on flesh and blood. It is infinitely translatable. Babel continues to be undone by Pentecost. But not erased. Transfigured by the Spirit.

It is as if Christ were becoming incarnate *in each and every culture on earth*. This happens almost literally when the Bible is translated into a new language. And when women and men are baptized from some new people group, the body of Christ expands, mutates, diversifies. It now encompasses the globe.

In the prophecy of Habakkuk:

> The earth will be filled
> > with the knowledge of the glory of the LORD,
> > as the waters cover the sea.

This is true even as I write, just like the promise of God to Abraham that all the families of the earth would be blessed in him. For all the promises of God are Yes and Amen in Christ, and the church is Christ's body on earth. The prophecies of Scripture are not bound to past or future. Many of them are present tense: fulfilled, here and now, in our time.

Along these lines, the Creed has four words to describe the church: one, holy, catholic, and apostolic. These are sometimes called the "marks" of the church. They illuminate her mission and identity, including her triumphant march through the centuries, curiously resilient as civilizations rise and fall. She herself endures to the end by the promise of Christ, who spoke the following to Simon, chief of the Twelve:

"I tell you, you are Peter,
and on this rock [*petra*] I will build my church,
and the gates of Hades shall not prevail against it."

Nor have they, in the two millennia since. The church is what Christ wants her to be, granting all her faults.

1. The church is *holy* in all the ways we've canvassed in previous letters. Christ sets her apart from the nations by his effective word, imbuing her with his own Holy Spirit.

2. The church is *one* as her Lord is one; as he is one with the Father. One flock, one shepherd. One faith, one hope, one baptism in the one Spirit of God. In his last night on earth, just hours before being crucified, Jesus prayed that his followers might be *completely one*. For this visible unity we ought to be praying and working every single day.

3. The church is *apostolic* in the sense, first, that she was founded by the apostles; second, that her leaders form a chain of succession with the apostles; third, that the teaching of the apostles is authoritative in the church; and, fourth, that her entire existence is defined by having been sent, which is what *apostolos* means: "one who is sent."

4. The church is *catholic* because she is comprehensive. The Greek *katholikos* means "whole" or "universal." The church isn't merely one people the way Kenya or Canada is a single country. She embraces the human race. She includes and incorporates every tribe and tongue. She is universal in scope. No other people is like her.

In the book of Revelation, Saint John sees two groups in sequence. First, twelve thousand from each of the twelve tribes of Israel. These stand for Jewish believers in Jesus. Second:

> After this I looked, and behold, a great multitude which no man could number, from every nation, from all tribes and peoples and tongues, standing before the throne and before the Lamb, clothed in white robes, with palm branches in their hands, and crying out with a loud voice, "Salvation belongs to our God who sits upon the throne, and to the Lamb!"

This is the catholicity of Christ's church. It is a picture of the end that tells us what the people of God *will* look like and therefore *should* look like, on the way.

In a later vision, John hears a trumpet blown and loud voices in heaven crying out:

"The kingdom of the world
has become the kingdom of our Lord
and of his Christ,
and he shall reign forever and ever!"

This is the beginning of the end. We turn now to final things in my final set of letters to you.

*Yours in Christ,*
*a fellow pilgrim*

# *twelve*

# God Makes All Things New

From the heights of heaven Jesus Christ mercifully looks down upon you and graciously invites you there. He says, "Come, dear soul, and find everlasting rest in my bountiful arms where I have prepared undying delight for you in the abundance of my life." With your inward eyes behold the Blessed Virgin who maternally bids you: "Courage, my child, do not spurn my Son's desires or the many sighs that I have cast forth for you as I yearn with him for your eternal salvation." Behold the saints who exhort you and the millions of blessed souls who sweetly invite you and wish only to see your heart one day joined with theirs in praising and loving God forever. They assure you that the way to heaven is not as difficult as the world makes it out to be. "Be of good heart, dear brother," they say. "He who carefully considers the way of devotion by which we ascended hither will see that we acquired these delights by pleasures incomparably sweeter than those of the world."

—Saint Francis de Sales

## 87

*Dear future saint,*

The philosopher Immanuel Kant once asked a very famous question: *For what may we hope?*

This question is bedrock for the gospel. The good news about Jesus is the Creator's answer to it. For only he can answer it. Our great error is supposing the question is ours to answer. Our attempts are doomed from the start. And sometimes the nobler our intentions, the worse the consequences.

What we may hope for is Jesus Christ. He alone is our hope. When we look to him in hope, we long not just for his person—though God knows that is enough—but for his presence, his power, his mercy. We yearn for him to *reign*. When Jesus is Lord, and his will is done on earth as it is in heaven, all is right. All is well. Justice and peace kiss. The poor are honored and the hungry fed. No one is afraid. The world is as God intended it from the first. A world in which God may dwell and, by his Spirit, be all in all.

Few things capture these mingled feelings—dissatisfaction with the world as it is, desire for it to become what it is meant to be—than Christmas hymns. Though we wrap them in sentimentality, they are often quite profound. Consider the words of "Hark! the Herald Angels Sing":

> Hark! the herald angels sing,
> "Glory to the new-born King;
> Peace on earth, and mercy mild;
> God and sinners reconciled."
> Joyful, all ye nations, rise,
> Join the triumph of the skies;
> With angelic hosts proclaim,
> "Christ is born in Bethlehem."
> Christ, by highest heav'n adored,
> Christ, the everlasting Lord:
> Late in time behold Him come,
> Offspring of a virgin's womb.
> Veiled in flesh the Godhead see,
> Hail th' incarnate Deity!
> Pleased as man with man to dwell,

Jesus our Immanuel.
Hail the heav'n-born Prince of Peace!
Hail the Sun of righteousness!
Light and life to all He brings,
Ris'n with healing in His wings:
Mild He lays His glory by,
Born that man no more may die;
Born to raise the sons of earth;
Born to give them second birth.
Come, Desire of nations, come!
Fix in us Thy humble home:
Rise, the woman's conqu'ring seed,
Bruise in us the serpent's head;
Adam's likeness now efface,
Stamp Thine image in its place:
Final Adam from above,
Reinstate us in Thy love.

This hymn understands that Christmas is political, because the incarnation is political. What makes it political? It is the announcement of the birth of a new King!—in a world of kings who are not pleased to hear the news. If he is King, then they are not. If his justice will be meted out, then they might be on the wrong side of it. If his kingdom is advancing, then theirs must be in retreat.

The birth of Christ is a kind of D-Day in God's war against evil. The end is in sight. It has entered the field. It has made its way from the final chapter to the middle of the story. Everything from here on out is assured. The journey to victory begins now.

*Come, desire of nations, come!* This is Christian hope. The phrase comes from the prophet Haggai. The Lord says through him: "I will shake all nations, and the desire of all nations shall come: and I will fill this house with glory." The same confident exultation rings out from the Psalms. Here is the ninety-sixth psalm in full:

O sing to the Lord a new song;
sing to the Lord, all the earth!
Sing to the Lord, bless his name;
tell of his salvation from day to day.
Declare his glory among the nations,
his marvelous works among all the peoples!
For great is the Lord, and greatly to be praised;
he is to be feared above all gods.
For all the gods of the peoples are idols;

but the LORD made the heavens.
Honor and majesty are before him;
    strength and beauty are in his sanctuary.
Ascribe to the LORD, O families of the peoples,
    ascribe to the LORD glory and strength!
Ascribe to the LORD the glory due his name;
    bring an offering, and come into his courts!
Worship the LORD in holy array;
    tremble before him, all the earth!
Say among the nations, "The LORD reigns!
    Yea, the world is established, it shall never be moved;
    he will judge the peoples with equity."
Let the heavens be glad, and let the earth rejoice;
    let the sea roar, and all that fills it;
    let the field exult, and everything in it!
Then shall all the trees of the wood sing for joy
    before the LORD, for he comes,
    for he comes to judge the earth.
He will judge the world with righteousness,
    and the peoples with his truth.

I want to add only two things. The first you know: this psalm is about Jesus. How could it not be? It is the song the church sings every day, praying for the Lord to return. (His return, or second coming, is also called his "epiphany" or "Parousia"; the latter is a Greek word for *presence* or *arrival*.)

Second, remember that "nations" in both Hebrew and Greek may also be translated "gentiles." This gives us some perspective, as we approach the End. God promised Israel that through her the gentiles would come to worship him as the one true Lord of all. And so they have; so they do. Alter the words and it becomes clear.

> *Come, desire of the gentiles, come!*
> *Declare his glory among the gentiles!*
> *Say among the gentiles, "The Lord Jesus reigns!"*

Indeed, the Lord Jesus does reign. He shall reign forever. He is King of the Jews, but also of the gentiles. He is King of the world.

*Yours in Christ,*
*a fellow pilgrim*

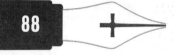

88

*Dear future saint,*

The Nicene Creed has two comments about the End. The first concludes the section on Jesus:

> He will come again in glory to judge the living and the dead,
> and his kingdom will have no end.

The second concludes the section on the Spirit and the church:

> I look for the resurrection of the dead,
> and the life of the world to come. Amen.

That about sums it up. Christian beliefs about last things—what theologians call "eschatology"—are surprisingly uncomplicated. I realize this may come as a shock. Our culture lives and breathes kooky conspiracy theories and whisper-told best sellers about "the end times." *Who is the antichrist?* The Internet will tell you.

The church, especially certain subcultures and corners of the church, has not helped in this area. So let me try to clear away the tangles, not to say the cobwebs.

Begin with Jesus's own words:

> "Truly, truly, I say to you, the hour is coming, and now is, when the dead will hear the voice of the Son of God, and those who hear will live. For as the Father has life in himself, so he has granted the Son also to have life in himself, and has given him authority to execute judgment, because he is the Son of Man.
>
> "Do not marvel at this; for the hour is coming when all who are in the tombs will hear his voice and come forth, those who have done good, to the resurrection of life, and those who have done evil, to the resurrection of condemnation."

The risen Jesus is in heaven. He will come again. When he returns, it will be to stay. He will raise the dead: the wicked to damnation, the righteous to eternal life. He will destroy Death and bury Sin forever. He will strip the Devil and his demons of their power and silence them for good. He will wipe away every tear. He will right every wrong. He will transform the lowly bodies of the baptized into glorious bodies like his own: never to die again, no longer subject to pain, injury, decay, or illness.

He will make all things new: a new creation; what Scripture calls "a new heaven and a new earth." Just as we are baptized, put to death and made alive again, purged of our fallenness and filled with God's own life, so will the whole universe. In and by and through Jesus, it will be baptized, crucified, raised, transfigured. It will shine with divine light.

We will be with him and with one another. His happiness will be ours. The marriage supper of the Lamb will be our feast. The betrothal of Israel to her Lord will at last be consummated, world without end.

This, in so many words, is the End for which we hope. There is always more to say, but for now it is enough.

*Yours in Christ,*
*a fellow pilgrim*

## 89

*Dear future saint,*

No, don't take my word for it. Take Saint John's. Here is the book of Revelation, from the Bible's final chapters:

> The devil who had deceived the saints was thrown into the lake of fire and sulphur, and he will be tormented day and night forever and ever.
>
> Then I saw a great white throne and him who sat upon it; from his presence earth and sky fled away, and no place was found for them. And I saw the dead, great and small, standing before the throne, and books were opened. Also another book was opened, which is the book of life. And the dead were judged by what was written in the books, by what they had done.
>
> And the sea gave up the dead in it, Death and Hades gave up the dead in them, and all were judged by what they had done. Then Death and Hades were thrown into the lake of fire. This is the second death, the lake of fire; and if anyone's name was not found written in the book of life, he was thrown into the lake of fire.
>
> Then I saw a new heaven and a new earth; for the first heaven and the first earth had passed away, and the sea was no more. And I saw the holy city, new Jerusalem, coming down out of heaven from God, prepared as a bride adorned for her husband; and I heard a loud voice from the throne saying:
>
>> "Behold, the dwelling of God is with men.
>> He will dwell with them,
>> and they shall be his peoples,
>> and God himself will be with them;
>> he will wipe away every tear from their eyes,
>> and death shall be no more,
>> neither shall there be mourning
>> nor crying nor pain any more,
>> for the former things have passed away."
>
> And he who sat upon the throne said, "Behold, I make all things new."
> Also he said, "Write this, for these words are trustworthy and true."

GOD MAKES ALL THINGS NEW

And he said to me, "It is done! I am the Alpha and the Omega, the beginning and the end. To the thirsty I will give from the fountain of the water of life without payment. He who conquers shall have this heritage, and I will be his God and he shall be my son. But as for the cowardly, the faithless, the polluted, as for murderers, fornicators, sorcerers, idolaters, and all liars, their lot shall be in the lake that burns with fire and sulphur, which is the second death."

Then came one of the seven angels, saying, "Come, I will show you the Bride, the wife of the Lamb."

And in the Spirit he carried me away to a great, high mountain, and showed me the holy city Jerusalem coming down out of heaven from God, having the glory of God, its radiance like a most rare jewel, like a jasper, clear as crystal. It had a great, high wall, with twelve gates, and at the gates twelve angels, and on the gates the names of the twelve tribes of the sons of Israel were inscribed; on the east three gates, on the north three gates, on the south three gates, and on the west three gates. And the wall of the city had twelve foundations, and on them the twelve names of the twelve apostles of the Lamb.

I expect much of this imagery and symbolism to dazzle and even befuddle. What I want it to do is enchant and delight. As if you peeked through the narrow window of a door to a private theater, on whose screen played a movie you'd never seen before. A movie whose sights and sounds were nothing like you'd ever seen. *I must find a way to see that as soon as possible. I want it to wash over me like a flood.*

Revelation is meant to produce such a feeling in its readers. John saw and heard things no one on earth has seen or heard, and he put them into sparkling but unavoidably paltry words while exiled by Rome on the island of Patmos. (You can go there, by the way; I've visited the cave where tradition says he received his visions and composed the book. Just one more reminder that we're not telling tall tales here, but talking about real people in real times and places, most of which receive pilgrims such as yourself.)

What John sees is this. Everything bad will be banished from God's good creation. Everything beautiful and right will be rescued, retrieved, restored, re-created, reimagined, renewed, remade. Your Sin-soaked, Death-haunted self will be shot through with the very Light and Life of God. His plan will be complete. What he said on the cross, on the lips of Jesus, will find its final purchase:

"It is finished."

*Yours in Christ,*
*a fellow pilgrim*

## 90

## Dear future saint,

I will not, sad to say, be answering any of your questions about who's going to heaven and who's going to hell. Or rather, I will not be designating categories of humankind destined for damnation. Why? For many reasons, all of which are theologically *and spiritually* significant.

First, the church teaches that hell is real and that eternal separation from God is a possibility for one reason and one reason only: Jesus himself taught it, as reported and elaborated by his apostles. You can look to many places for this, including the excerpt in the previous letter, but the simplest is the twenty-fifth chapter of Saint Matthew's Gospel.

Second, the church forbids speculation about the status of other souls before God. You simply do not know, cannot know, and have no right to know, much less to presume to know. So don't! Don't do it.

Third, the church even discourages, at least in a certain sense, an overweening certainty about your own status. By this I *don't* mean that you have any reason to lose sleep over your salvation. If you are a baptized believer in Christ and member of his body, I take it for granted (as does the church) that you are saved.

No, what I mean is: the habit and virtue in question is *hope*, not assurance. As Saint Paul writes, "in this hope we were saved. Now hope that is seen is not hope. For who hopes for what he sees? But if we hope for what we do not see, we wait for it with patience." In other words, hope leads us to set all our trust in Christ, him alone and nothing and no one else. I do not draw confidence from something in myself; I do not deceive myself into supposing I am anything other than a sinner in need of God's unmerited grace.

Fourth, the gospel has stakes. Perhaps the greatest temptation facing the church in our day is to proclaim a message without stakes. But a message without stakes cannot be a matter of life and death. If death is not a possibility, how is life an offer? If none of us is *saved from anything*, then how is the news that Jesus saves us good? Following in Paul's wake, all of the apostles and saints in history worked themselves to the bone, usually suffering greatly and dying young, "that by all means some might be saved."

Pascal's wager is useful here. I've quoted Pascal before; he is famous for many reasons, one of which is his metaphor of the "bet" or "wager." Often this is watered down to suggest that, given the eternal stakes, it is better to bet that God exists (and go to heaven) than to bet otherwise (and go to hell), when the consequence of doing so in a godless world would mean neither heaven nor hell. A sort of probabilistic, statistical theology.

That's not quite the whole picture, though. What Pascal says is that your *life* is a wager, because *just by being born*, you're a part of the game. It follows that there is no abstaining from making the bet: "you must wager. There is no choice, you are already committed." You can't opt out. Your life is your bet. Even taking your life is itself a way to play the game. So don't kick against the goads, pretending you're not opting in. Your mother opted you in. The only question is how you will play the cards you were dealt.

Within *this* framework, Pascal urges you: Bet your life on Christ. I'm with him. Go all in on red. You can't check forever. And you can't win by folding.

Fifth, the New Testament is crystal clear about a handful of things. Jesus is Lord. Jesus rose from the dead. Jesus forgives us our sins. And so on. Another thing about which there is no confusion: *how and by whom human beings are saved*. Jesus's words are plain: "I am the way and the truth and the life. No one comes to the Father except through me." Saint Peter echoes Jesus in a sermon early in the book of Acts: "There is salvation in no one else, for there is no other name under heaven given among mortals by which we must be saved." Anyone who is saved—anyone whom Jesus raises on the last day to reign with him and in him in the new creation—is and will be saved by Jesus. No exceptions.

Sixth, however, the New Testament is *also* adamant that we will be surprised by whom we meet in heaven. This is another way of reiterating the earlier point, that we are not God, much less the Savior. We are neither judge nor jury. God alone knows; God alone decides; God alone saves. Avoid presumption and judgmentalism at all costs!

Seventh and finally, there is a long-standing minority tradition in Christian history that wonders whether all might be saved. Occasionally this wonder becomes more than a question; sometimes it moves from mystical contemplation to quiet trust to outspoken certainty. I have never been convinced that any Christian can have such sure knowledge (aside, I suppose, from private revelation). We cannot know that God will save all.

I do believe it is permissible to hope and pray for it. Paul teaches that God "desires all to be saved and to come to the knowledge of the truth." If this is God's desire, let it be ours. If our desire is holy and true, God will not only bless it; he will use it as a means of bringing the world to Christ. If our desire is errant or imperfect, God will show us, in this life or the next. He will make straight the crooked timber of our longings, in this area as in every other.

I do not believe we may *preach* or *teach* this, however. Nor does doing so seem wise. How could we preach and teach what we merely want to be true?

Jesus has given us the gospel, which is more than sufficient for making disciples. We cannot gainsay what so much of Scripture and tradition appear to teach, plainly and continuously. Whoever we supposed was unsaved that turns out to be saved, we will delight in. Let us not form our hearts or our neighbors' to be cranky or resentful at *him* or *her* or *them* "making it in." The whole point is that none of us belong. You don't. They don't. I certainly don't.

That's the beauty of it. Heaven is an island of misfit toys. There are no others, in all of humanity. Our salvation is accepting that we, too, are misfits, and delighting in God's delight in us, misfits that we are. "The last shall be first and the first shall be last." Jesus is nothing if not consistent.

*Yours in Christ,*
*a fellow pilgrim*

**91**

*Dear future saint,*

You write, with poignant urgency: *So what do we do in the meantime?* Simply asked, simply answered.

We wait.

There are few things more Christian than waiting. The Bible is full of models of waiting and even commands to wait:

> I wait for your salvation, O LORD.
> I wait for the LORD, my soul waits,
>   and in his word I hope.
> No eye has seen a God besides you,
>   who works for those who wait for him.
> For God alone my soul waits in silence,
>   for my hope is from him.
> My soul waits for the LORD
>   more than watchmen for the morning,
>   more than watchmen for the morning.
> The LORD is good to those who wait for him,
>   to the soul that seeks him.
> The LORD is a God of justice;
>   blessed are all those who wait for him.

These are only a few of the countless passages in Scripture where God's people must wait on the Lord. To wait is not merely to pass the time while the future approaches. It is to rest in the peace and confident trust that God is as good as his word; that he will do what he has promised; that he will act at just the right time.

Waiting is a spiritual discipline—patience is a virtue—because it is a theological act rooted in hope. It says: *I am not God. I cannot fix what must be fixed. God alone can do it. He has said he will. He never lies. I will stake my life on his promise.*

I understand that waiting sounds passive. In a sense it is! Christianity means passivity *in the sense* that we let go, once and for all, of our delusions of mastery and myths of control. Stanley Hauerwas says Christians are people who live "out of control." Indeed. We know who is in control. It ain't us.

Waiting is also a matter of the clock. Christian hope knows what time it is. It's *after* Pentecost, *before* Parousia. "The night is far gone, the day is at hand," writes Saint Paul: "salvation is nearer to us now than when we first believed." We tell time, not by seasons or dates or presidents or wars or famines or plagues or paydays. We tell time by Christ. His time is resurrection time. Time looks different in the church. His kingdom has come, but not yet in full.

Until then, we hope. Until then, we wait.

*Yours in Christ,*
*a fellow pilgrim*

## 92

*Dear future saint,*

Just before entering the promised land, Moses faces the people of Israel and offers them a choice. He says:

"See, I have set before you this day life and good, death and evil.

"If you obey the commandments of the LORD your God which I command you this day, by loving the LORD your God, by walking in his ways, and by keeping his commandments and his statutes and his ordinances, then you shall live and multiply, and the LORD your God will bless you in the land which you are entering to take possession of it.

"But if your heart turns away, and you will not hear, but are drawn away to worship other gods and serve them, I declare to you this day, that you shall perish; you shall not live long in the land which you are going over the Jordan to enter and possess.

"I call heaven and earth to witness against you this day, that I have set before you life and death, blessing and curse; therefore choose life, that you and your descendants may live, loving the LORD your God, obeying his voice, and cleaving to him; for that means life to you and length of days, that you may dwell in the land which the LORD swore to your fathers, to Abraham, to Isaac, and to Jacob, to give them."

*Therefore choose life.* This is the call and command given to everyone who hears the gospel. *Love the Lord Jesus, obey his voice, and cleave to him; for this means life to you, even life eternal.*

I referred to stakes two letters ago. These are the stakes: life and death, good and evil, what lasts versus what fades. "Jesus Christ is the same yesterday and today and forever." He is life. Death has no sway over him.

Choose him. Choose him who is life. His life is the light of humankind, for it is the light that shone on the first day of creation and the eighth day of new creation. His light is good, for "God is light and in him is no darkness at all." His light is love, for "love is of God," and "he who loves is born of God and knows God. He who does not love does not know God."

Why? Because "God is love." The gospel in three words! *God. Is. Love.*

Saint John continues:

In this the love of God was made manifest among us, that God sent his only Son into the world, so that we might live through him. In this is love, not that we loved God but that he loved us and sent his Son to be the expiation for our sins.

Beloved, if God so loved us, we also ought to love one another. No one has ever seen God; if we love one another, God abides in us and his love is perfected in us.

John concludes:

By this we know that we abide in him and he in us, because he has given us of his own Spirit. And we have seen and testify that the Father has sent his Son as the Savior of the world.

Whoever confesses that Jesus is the Son of God, God abides in him, and he in God. So we know and believe the love God has for us.

God is love, and he who abides in love abides in God, and God abides in him. In this is love perfected with us, that we may have confidence for the day of judgment, because as he is so are we in this world.

There is no fear in love, but perfect love casts out fear. For fear has to do with punishment, and he who fears is not perfected in love.

We love, because he first loved us.

Choose this love. Choose his light. Choose life in him over every alternative. *Choose Christ.* "For what, without Jesus, can the world give you?" asks Thomas à Kempis. "Life without Him is a relentless hell, but living with Him is a sweet paradise. If Jesus be with you, no enemy can harm you."

*Yours in Christ,*
*a fellow pilgrim*

## 93

*Dear future saint,*

Between December 2014 and January 2015, twenty-one men were kidnapped by the Islamist terrorist group called ISIS. The men were working construction in Sirte, Libya, far away from their families in Egypt. All but one (who was from Ghana) were Coptic Christians.

The Copts are a religious minority in Egypt. They trace their lineage all the way back to the time of the apostles; they are one of the oldest Christian communities in the world. For nearly fourteen centuries, following the fall of Christian Egypt to Muslim armies, the Coptic Church has lived under Islamic rule in one form or another. At times beset by active persecution, they have always lived as second-class citizens, comprising about 10 percent of Egypt's population. It is illegal for them to evangelize their neighbors.

In February 2015 ISIS released a video recorded in Libya, on the shore of the Mediterranean Sea. The twenty-one men, all in orange jumpsuits, are invited to recant their faith in Christ. They refuse. In response the masked, black-garbed men at their backs behead each and every one of them.

These are the twenty-one Coptic martyrs, or "the twenty-one" for short. They were immediately recognized as martyrs and saints by the leader of the Coptic Church, Tawadros II. In 2023 Pope Francis invited Tawadros to Rome to honor the twenty-one by granting them their own feast day on the Catholic liturgical calendar. Tawadros gave Francis a relic of the martyrs as a gift to the Roman Church. This meeting was an extraordinary sign of unity between two communions long divided by doctrine and sacrament.

The twenty-one Copts were ordinary young men. They were not monks or priests, pastors or scholars. They were in a big city looking for work to provide for their families. Had they never been kidnapped, it is unlikely you or I would ever have heard about them.

So what sets apart these ordinary young men? One simple but remarkable thing.

In the face of death, they were faithful to their Lord.

That's it. But "it" is everything. It's the sum total that Christ asks of us. Here is what he said when sending out the Twelve to preach the gospel in the towns of Israel:

"Have no fear of them; for nothing is covered that will not be revealed, or hidden that will not be known. What I tell you in the dark, utter in the light; and what you hear whispered, proclaim upon the housetops.

"And do not fear those who kill the body but cannot kill the soul; rather fear him who can destroy both soul and body in hell. Are not two sparrows sold for a penny? And not one of them will fall to the ground without your Father's will. But even the hairs of your head are all numbered. Fear not, therefore; you are of more value than many sparrows.

"So everyone who acknowledges me before men, I also will acknowledge before my Father who is in heaven; but whoever denies me before men, I also will deny before my Father who is in heaven."

The twenty-one knew these words in their bones. They would not and did not fear those who kill the body, and so they would not and did not deny the name of Jesus. We know, therefore, that Jesus himself received the twenty-one into heaven as the sainted martyrs they are. They are there even now, their souls rejoicing in the presence of the One for whose sake they gave their lives. Do you doubt that they are praying for us who remain on earth? I don't.

These men grew up in normal families in small villages far from centers of power and fame. They were baptized as infants, brought to the church's lit-

"21 New Martyrs of Libya," an icon commissioned to honor the Coptic martyrs. © Tony Rezk. Used by permission.

GOD MAKES ALL THINGS NEW

urgy, given the body and blood of Christ in the sacrament. While still young, they received a tattoo of a small black cross on the wrist. Why? To mark them for life with the cross of Christ.

Truly they were marked, body and soul. Their church prepared them to follow Christ in this world. They followed him to the shore of the Mediterranean, and there they showed the world the power of God. They chose life by submitting to death. They found life *in* death: the life of God in the cross of Jesus Christ.

May you and I, dear friend, strive to imitate their imitation of our Lord. May each of us know in our daily life, however ordinary, the goodness and power of God. May all God's people discover together that his grace is sufficient, for his strength is perfected in our weakness.

This is my prayer for you and for the whole church, which is the body of Christ, "the fullness of him who fills all in all." Amen. The Lord's peace be with you.

Yours in Christ,
a fellow pilgrim

# Acknowledgments

There are three sets of people responsible for this book's existence.

First, the children to whom it is dedicated. I've been writing letters to my own children since their first month of life. Later on I wrote letters to my nephews and to my godchildren on the days of their baptism. This practice got me in the habit of writing short, accessible letters to young people about the hope we share in Christ. The habit stuck. I don't recall when I *first* had the idea for this book, but the notion that it should be in the form of letters was present from the beginning. I have Sam, Rowan, Paige, Liv, Isaiah E., Malachi, Ezra, Eli, Evelyn, Simon, Isabella, Naomi, and Isaiah F. to thank for that.

Second, my students over the last six years and counting. I have taught thousands of them at this point, mostly eighteen-to-twenty-two-year-old undergraduates. They want to know Christ. They are hungry for him. But all too often they've been fed milk at best, empty calories at worst—though not always for lack of trying on the part of pastors and parents. Like Saint Paul, I have made it my singular purpose in the classroom to teach them Christ and nothing but Christ, to give them *him* in all his richness and beauty. This book is the result of seeing their hunger and being moved by it. I hope this is a book they can read with profit. It was written with them in mind. I thank them for showing up, eager to learn, and for opening their hearts and minds to the joys and stressors of theological learning. I've got the best job in the world.

Third, James Ernest at Eerdmans. In 2021, just before Thanksgiving, I sat down with James in San Antonio. I give him a rundown of what I was working on. When I mentioned the idea for this book, he told me to drop everything and get it to him as soon as humanly possible. So I did. I hope it approximates the spontaneous elevator pitch I made in that SBL/AAR book hall. Thanks to him for the encouragement and, as I've said to him more than once, for lighting a fire in my bones to get this thing into the world.

Special thanks to friends and family who spent time with the manuscript or aided in its conception, development, and completion: Garrett and Stacy East, Mitch and Allison East, Ray and Georgine East, Matt Fisher, Caroline Kennemer, Matthew Loftus, Ross McCullough, Dan McGregor, Luke Roberts, and Chris and Jenny Thompson. A second word of thanks to the entire

East family, who not only read what I write but also serve as my biggest cheerleaders, even as they keep me honest. They love what God has called me to do, but they are not impressed by me. Rightly so.

Thanks to my colleagues here at Abilene Christian University, particularly my dean Ken Cukrowski and (former) chair Rodney Ashlock, who have made my writing possible. Thanks also to Richard Beck, John Boyles, Conner Crawford, Jamie Dunn, Ian Gibson, Layne Hancock, Justin Hawkins, Amy McLaughlin-Sheasby, Jake Meador, Amanda Pittman, Riley Simpson, Kester Smith, Bradley Steele, and Myles Werntz for conversations germane to the subject of this book. Thanks, finally, to those persons so far unnamed—living and dead, writers and ministers, teachers and saints—who handed on to me the faith I hope to hand on here. Some of them you know; they have names like Lewis and Bonhoeffer, Barth and Augustine. Many you don't; they have names like Spence and Toni, Craig and Randy. I cannot list each of them, but I owe every one of them my enduring gratitude.

Under God, my wife, Katelin, is the reason any of this is possible. By the time this book is published, we will have been together for two decades. Thanks to her for grace, love, patience, and support. And thank God for her. Anyone who's met her knows which of us is the lucky one.

Brad East
Feast Day of Saint Maximilian Kolbe, 2023

# Notes and Resources

As the reader will have noticed, there are no footnotes, citations, or even scriptural references in the correspondence just completed. I did not want such things to clutter the text, especially for newcomers to the Bible. It can be distracting and even overwhelming for the eye constantly to see "Rom. 12:10" and "Lev. 19:18" and "Rev. 3:16" in parentheses. Besides, who would include formal citations in personal letters? I wouldn't.

For readers interested in tracking down references, however, I have included them below. Not only references to the Bible but quotations and allusions to nonbiblical authors and books. They do not contain commentary but are almost entirely limited to bibliographic citations. So let me say a few words before they begin.

First, the default translation of the Bible throughout this book is the Revised Standard Version. I have taken the liberty, though, of regularly modifying the translation, paraphrasing or summarizing between different versions of the same story, or amending the quoted version with a nod to the King James Version, the New International Version, the New Revised Standard Version, or the English Standard Version. These occasions should be obvious to the trained eye and, I hope, unobtrusive to the untrained.

Second, early on I mention other catechisms the reader might consult. Most of the texts I would recommend can be found online for free or for an affordable price. In no particular order, I suggest looking at Martin Luther's Small and Large Catechisms; the Heidelberg Catechism; The Catechism of the Catholic Church; The Shorter and Longer Catechisms of Saint Philaret of Moscow; and *To Be a Christian: An Anglican Catechism* (Wheaton: Crossway, 2020). I'll also mention Ben Myers's little book *The Apostles' Creed: A Guide to the Ancient Catechism* (Bellingham, WA: Lexham, 2018), a recent classic and a favorite of my students. Tim Keller's *The Reason for God: Belief in an Age of Skepticism* (New York: Penguin, 2018) is worth reading, too. For something a little spicier, see Francis Spufford's *Unapologetic: Why, Despite Everything, Christianity Can Still Make Surprising Emotional Sense* (New York: HarperOne, 2013). Other entry-level or trustworthy writings may be found in the notes below.

Third and finally, my aim in this book has been *ecumenical.* I have not sought to tell the reader which tradition, movement, or denomination is the right one. I am not sure that is possible in the state of a divided church. At the very least, so long as we Christians are not united, we should pitch as big a tent as possible in our writing, preaching, teaching, and practice. I have attempted something like that here. Nevertheless, choices must be made. As evidenced by my language, my sources, my influences, and some of my emphases, I have neither succeeded nor attempted being all things to all people. One cannot be Methodist *and* Baptist *and* Catholic *and* Reformed *and* Orthodox. My hope instead was to be true, as best I could, to the church's doctrine and liturgy across all twenty centuries of her existence: to be biblical, creedal, evangelical, and catholic all at once. I did not want to give readers a sampling of Texan-American Christianity from the twenty-first century. I wanted instead to provide a reliable representation of *the one faith of Christ's body* that would be as recognizable to Julian of Norwich (an English anchoress who died around 1416) as it would be to Theodore Abū Qurrah (an Arab Christian who died around 825) as it would be to Origen (a North African scholar who died around 253)—as indeed it would be to an ordinary Christian in modern-day Brazil, Nigeria, or Greece. That, in any case, was the goal. I leave to readers whether I have succeeded.

# *Notes*

vi  *"Julian of Norwich"*  Malcolm Guite, *The Singing Bowl* (Norwich, UK: Canterbury, 2013), 82.

*"Be dead in life"*  Saint Isaac of Nineveh, *On Ascetical Life*, trans. Mary Hansbury (Crestwood, NY: St. Vladimir's Seminary Press, 1989), 45.

*"It is never too late"*  François Mauriac, *The Eucharist: The Mystery of Holy Thursday*, trans. Marie-Louise Dufrenoy (Providence, RI: Cluny, 2018), 45.

1  *"Jesus wants to possess"*  Patrick Ahern, *Maurice and Thérèse: The Story of a Love* (New York: Image, 1998), 130 (from a letter dated June 9, 1897).

3  *There was once a very old man*  The account comes from *The Martyrdom of Polycarp*, which can be found in translation online.

*"to live is Christ, and to die is gain"*  Philippians 1:21.

5  *life in abundance*  John 10:10.

*Christ calls us to count the cost*  Luke 14:28.

6  *Unless a seed "dies"*  John 12:24.

*Jesus gives the name "witness"*  Acts 1:8.

*the blood of the martyrs*  The line goes back to Tertullian in his work *Apologeticus*, written before the year 200, though it is more of a generous paraphrase than a literal translation. He wrote, in effect, that the more believers are struck down, the more they multiply, because "Christians' blood is seed."

8  *"We love, because he first loved us"*  1 John 4:19.

10  *the whole world upside down*  Acts 17:6.

11  *"If anyone would come after me"*  Mark 8:34–37.

*"He who loves his life loses it"*  John 12:25–26.

12  *he constantly withdraws*  For example, see Luke 5:16; 6:12; 9:18; 11:1.

*"By the word of the LORD"*  Psalm 33:6.

*"Man shall not live by bread alone"*  Matthew 4:4. See the temptation scenes in Matthew 4:1:1–11; Mark 1:12–13; Luke 4:1–13.

*"Unless you eat the flesh of the Son"*  John 6:53–56.

12 *"This is my body"* Matthew 26:26, 28.

*"in Spirit and truth"* John 4:23.

14 *Alphonsus de Liguori* All the following comes from Alphonsus de Liguori, "Prayer, the Great Means of Salvation," in *Alphonsus de Liguori: Selected Writings,* ed. Frederick M. Jones (New York: Paulist, 1999), 296 (chap. 1).

15 *As one theologian puts it* John Webster, *The Grace of Truth,* ed. Daniel Bush and Brannon Ellis (Farmington Hills, MI: Oil Lamp, 2011), 133. Webster is drawing on a similar line by John Calvin.

*the Jesus Prayer* See further *The Way of a Pilgrim,* trans. R. M. French (New York: HarperOne, 1965).

16 *"Teach me to seek You"* Saint Anselm of Canterbury, "Proslogion," in *The Major Works,* ed. Brian Davies and G. R. Evans (New York: Oxford University Press, 1998), 86–87 (1).

17 *It's especially beloved of Paul* In Romans alone, see 1:7; 8:27; 12:13; 15:25–26, 31; 16:2, 15.

*They cry out to God in prayer* Revelation 6:9–11.

*a great cloud of witnesses* Hebrews 12:1.

18 *an eyewitness to the resurrection* See Acts 2:32; 3:15; 5:32.

*"The only real sadness"* The novel with which the quotation is associated was first published in 1897 as *La Femme Pauvre.* I have failed to find this exact phrasing in either the English or the French, though perhaps Bloy put it this way in popular lectures or essays.

*"I am sure that he who began a good work in you"* Philippians 1:6.

19 *whatever comes out of a person* Matthew 15:18–19.

20 *learning to speak Christian* See further Stanley Hauerwas, *Working with Words: On Learning to Speak Christian* (Eugene, OR: Wipf & Stock, 2011).

21 *"And one peculiar nation"* John Milton, *Paradise Lost,* bk. 12, ll. 111–113, 123–129, 147–148.

23 *there was a man named Abraham* Genesis 11:10–26 recounts the generations to Terah, Abraham's father; vv. 27–32 prepare the reader for the Lord's calling of Abraham in 12:1–3. Sarah's death and burial come in 23:1–20; Abraham's death comes in 25:7–11. All the chapters in between concern the election, travels, and fate of Abraham and Sarah and their household.

*"So Abram went"* Genesis 12:4.

24 *The name of Abraham's God is the Lord* This is a simplification, and possibly misleading. The Name of God revealed to Israel through Moses is YHWH. (See further the third chapter of the book of Exodus.) Observant Jews do not vocalize the Name or speculate regarding its vowels or pronunciation. Many gentile

Christians do, albeit imprudently and far too casually in my view. All who regard YHWH as the Name of God revere and venerate it. Traditional practice, Jewish and Christian alike, is to substitute "the Lord" (or "the LORD") for its appearance in Scripture. Many Jews also substitute "HaShem," which is "The Name" in Hebrew. In these letters I will use "the LORD" in direct quotations from the Bible.

24   *"The LORD our God, the LORD is one"*   Deuteronomy 6:4.

      *God's own friend*   Isaiah 41:8.

25   *all the promises of God*   2 Corinthians 1:20.

      *Abraham is the father of faith*   Romans 4:11.

27   *It's an everlasting promise*   Genesis 17:1–21; Romans 11:29.

      *stories of older and younger sons*   Nearly the whole of Genesis is taken up by such stories. Jesus's parable of the prodigal son—a parable about not one but two sons, one who stays and one who leaves and returns—is the consummation of this biblical motif.

      *"Because he loves you"*   Deuteronomy 7:6–8.

28   *he is love*   1 John 4:8.

29   *nearer to us than we are to ourselves*   Saint Augustine of Hippo, *Confessions,* trans. Henry Chadwick (New York: Oxford University Press, 1991), 43 (3.6.11).

30   *"a tissue of quotations"*   C. S. Lewis, *Reflections on the Psalms* (New York: Harcourt, 1958), 26–27.

      *"how constantly Our Lord repeated"*   Lewis, *Reflections on the Psalms,* 26–27.

32   *This ritual seals the relationship*   See the full sequence in Genesis 12–17.

      *The election of Israel is . . . irrevocable*   Romans 11:29.

33   *love is stronger than death*   Song of Songs 8:6–7. Love is "strong as death," but in context, it is presented as stronger, as indeed it is.

      *not in heaven or on earth*   Romans 8:38–39.

34   *Here's the story in a nutshell*   I'm summarizing the rest of the book of Genesis, beginning in chapter 21.

      *God hears their cries*   Exodus 2:23–25.

      *God shows himself*   Exodus 3:1–4:17.

      *"Let my people go!"*   Exodus 5:1.

35   *God wins in short order*   See Exodus 5:1–14:31.

      *the Lord's "mighty hand" and "outstretched arm"*   See Deuteronomy 5:15; 7:19; 11:2; 26:8; etc.

      *Sing with Miriam and Moses*   Exodus 15:1–21; the quotations come from vv. 11 and 2.

37  *"Let my people go"*  Exodus 4:23; see also 5:1–3; 7:16; 8:20; 9:1, 13; 10:3. The phrasing is "so they may serve me" or "hold a feast to me."

*the Lord leads Israel*  They leave the Red Sea in Exodus 15:22 and reach the foot of Sinai in 19:1. While Moses begins receiving the Law soon thereafter, within the larger biblical narrative Israel doesn't depart from Sinai until chapter 10 of the book of Numbers. Leviticus, in between Exodus and Numbers, is set entirely at Sinai; and Deuteronomy, although set later in the story, is told as a remembrance or recapitulation *of* Sinai.

*God tells Israel*  Leviticus 19:2.

38  *a light to the gentiles*  Isaiah 49:6.

*a priestly kingdom*  Exodus 19:6.

*"Salvation is from the Jews"*  John 4:22.

39  *the great cloud of witnesses*  Hebrews 12:1.

41  *After leaving Sinai*  See Numbers 10–36.

*Once the time is up*  See the book of Joshua, especially the opening eleven chapters.

*For some years*  See the book of Judges, especially the opening nine chapters.

*They want a king*  See 1 Samuel 1–8.

*Israel becomes a great kingdom*  The story takes place across 2 Samuel and 1–2 Kings, also recounted in 1–2 Chronicles.

42  *"When the Lord restored"*  Psalm 126:1–3.

*life becomes rather dismal*  See further the books of Ezra, Nehemiah, and 1–2 Maccabees.

*one great cosmic joke*  See Herman Melville, *Moby-Dick: An Authoritative Text, Contexts, Criticism*, ed. Hershel Parker, 3rd ed. (New York: Norton, 2018), 179–81.

44  *Saul is Israel's first king*  See 1 Samuel 9:1–31:13.

*it occurs to David*  See 2 Samuel 7:1–29.

45  *Here is the opening verse*  Matthew 1:1.

46  *One [group] is the prophets*  See further Deuteronomy 18:15–22; the stories of Elijah and Elisha in 1–2 Kings; and prophetic books like Amos, Hosea, Jonah, Isaiah, Jeremiah, and Ezekiel.

*"all the prophets"*  For example, see Luke 13:28; 24:27; Acts 3:18, 24; 10:43.

*The second group ... is the priests*  The second half of Exodus and all of Leviticus are concerned with the priests, their calling and their duties.

47  *God did end up dwelling in a temple*  See 1 Kings 5–8.

*the language of temple and sacrifice to describe Jesus*  1 Corinthians 5:7 may be the clearest (and even earliest) reference. The Gospels interpret Jesus's suffering, blood, and death *as* a sacrifice, though they render the offering of his life in the form of a story rather than the direct claims of a theological statement.

49   *the bride of his youth*   Proverbs 5:18.

51   *"May God who"*   Saint Basil the Great, "Hexaemeron," in *Basil: Letters and Select Works*, vol. 8 of *Nicene and Post-Nicene Fathers*, ed. Philip Schaff and Henry Wace, 2nd ser. (Peabody, MA: Hendrickson, 1895), 71 (homily 3, section 10).

53   *"In the beginning"*   Genesis 1:1.

     *The great Italian poet Dante Alighieri*   In Canto 33 of *Paradiso*, or the final line of the final (100th) canto of the entire *Divine Comedy*.

     *"lost in wonder, love, and praise"*   "Love Divine, All Loves Excelling," written by Charles Wesley in 1747.

55   *God alone exists*   For example, see Psalms 41:13; 90:2; 103:17; 106:48; Nehemiah 9:5; 1 Chronicles 16:36.

     *God creates "from nothing"*   There are many good books on this topic; an excellent recent one is Ian A. McFarland, *From Nothing: A Theology of Creation* (Louisville: Westminster John Knox, 2014).

56   *"Let there be light"*   Genesis 1:3.

     *"sub-creators"*   J. R. R. Tolkien, "On Fairy-Stories," in *The Tolkien Reader* (New York: Ballantine, 1966), 3–84.

58   *an old line attributed to J. B. S. Haldane*   There are many versions and origin stories of the anecdote; one comes in Arthur C. Clarke's foreword to *What I Require from Life: Writings on Science and Life from J. B. S. Haldane*, ed. Krishna Dronamraju (New York: Oxford University Press, 2009), x.

59   *The Nicene Creed*   The Nicene Creed comes in many forms, depending on liturgical tradition, translation, and so on. Here and in later letters I will use the version found in *The Book of Common Prayer and Administration of the Sacraments and Other Rites and Ceremonies of the Church* (New York: Church Publishing Incorporated, 2016), 358–59, with the exception of (1) changing the "we" to "I" and (2) excluding the *filioque* ("and from the Son") in the third article, being a later addition to the original conciliar text and not a matter of ecumenical agreement with Eastern Christians.

     *As the letter of Saint James . . . puts it*   James 1:17.

60   *the One "who was and is and is to come"*   Revelation 4:8; see also 1:8.

     *"I am that I am"*   Exodus 3:13–14.

61   *"The heavens are telling"*   Psalm 19:1–4.

62   *"conflict" between "faith" and "science"*   See further Ronald L. Numbers, ed.,

*Galileo Goes to Jail and Other Myths about Science and Religion* (Cambridge, MA: Harvard University Press, 2009).

63   *a theological statement . . . a confession of faith*    See Karl Barth, *Dogmatics in Outline*, trans. G. T. Thomson (New York: Harper & Row, 1949), 50–58.

66   *Julian of Norwich*    See further Denys Turner, *Julian of Norwich, Theologian* (New Haven: Yale University Press, 2011).

    *"Our Lord showed me"*    Julian of Norwich, *Revelations of Divine Love (Short Text and Long Text)*, trans. Elizabeth Spearing (New York: Penguin, 1998), 47–48 (section 5); both this and the following three quotations.

67   *an echo of Saint Augustine*    Saint Augustine, *Confessions*, 3 (1.1.1).

68   *"Do you want to know"*    Julian, *Revelations*, 179 (section 86), both this and the next quotation.

69   *"God is good"*    Saint Athanasius of Alexandria, *On the Incarnation*, trans. John Behr (Yonkers, NY: St. Vladimir's Seminary Press, 2011), 57 (section 3).

71   *"Then God said"*    Genesis 1:26–31.

73   *"He who has seen me has seen the Father"*    John 14:9.

    *the "second" or "last" Adam*    See Romans 5:12–21; 1 Corinthians 15:20–22, 45–50; Luke 3:23–38.

    *"Ask, and it will be given you"*    Matthew 7:7–8.

    *A philosopher once wrote*    John Stuart Mill, *Utilitarianism* (1863), chapter 2.

75   *the value of questions*    See now Matthew Lee Anderson, *Called into Questions: Cultivating the Love of Learning within the Life of Faith* (Chicago: Moody Press, 2023).

76   *there is already a rich tradition*    "Dryness" is a common term in the devotional and mystical tradition of Christian writers, some of whom I cite below. The "dark night" comes from Saint John of the Cross, a priest and friar from the second half of the sixteenth century who wrote both a poem about the experience and a treatise reflecting on it.

    *This is perfectly normal*    For believers struggling with doubt, suffering, or existential questions, the poetry and prose of Christian Wiman are a gift. See especially *My Bright Abyss: Meditation of a Modern Believer* (New York: Farrar, Straus & Giroux, 2013) and *Zero at the Bone: Fifty Entries against Despair* (New York: Farrar, Straus & Giroux, 2023).

78   *"So God created man in his own image"*    Genesis 1:27–28.

81   *the praying animal*    See Robert W. Jenson, *Systematic Theology*, vol. 2, *The Works of God* (New York: Oxford University Press, 1999), 53–72.

82   *what the rest of the Bible says*    See Romans 8:29; 1 Corinthians 15:49; Colossians 1:15–20; 3:10.

84 *They come later*   Genesis 9:1–7.

  *God speaks directly to Adam*   Genesis 2:16–17.

85 *"When Adam fell"*   Julian, *Revelations*, 121 (section 51).

88 *"puts him forth"*   See Romans 3:25.

  *an offering for sin*   See Isaiah 53:10.

  *although in God's wisdom*   Saint Thomas Aquinas, *Summa theologiae* III, q. 48, a. 1 ad 2.

  *"The saying is sure and worthy of all acceptance"*   1 Timothy 1:15.

89 *a primeval catastrophe*   Genesis 2:4–3:24.

92 *Their failure was their fall*   For speculative reflection, see John E. Hare, *God's Command* (New York: Oxford University Press, 2015), 261–308. For recent investigation of the empirical, historical, and theological questions involved, see William Lane Craig, *In Quest of the Historical Adam: A Biblical and Scientific Exploration* (Grand Rapids: Eerdmans, 2021).

93 *the very first thing that occurs after the exile*   Genesis 4:1–16.

94 *"My Father is always working"*   John 5:17.

95 *"Not my will, but yours, be done"*   Luke 22:42; see also Matthew 26:39; Mark 14:36.

96 *"Humble yourself"*   James 4:10.

97 *a choice between two options*   Here I follow the lucid treatment of Ian A. McFarland, *In Adam's Fall: A Meditation on the Christian Doctrine of Original Sin* (Malden, MA: Blackwell, 2010). For a succinct account, see his "Original Sin," in *T&T Clark Companion to the Doctrine of Sin*, ed. Keith L. Johnson and David Lauber (New York: T&T Clark, 2016), 303–18.

98 *Saint Paul calls Sin a tyrant*   See Romans 3–8.

  *"Everyone who commits sin is a slave to sin"*   John 8:34.

  *The Lord came for the sick*   Matthew 9:12; Mark 2:17; Luke 5:31.

104 *the metaphor of adultery*   The book of Hosea is one great meditation on this theme, especially the opening chapters. Idolatry and "harlotry" are so interwoven that one becomes inseparable from the other.

  *describes God as jealous*   Exodus 34:14.

  *"Hear, O Israel"*   Deuteronomy 6:4.

105 *"Imagine a number of men in chains"*   Blaise Pascal, *Pensées*, trans. A. J. Krailsheimer (New York: Penguin, 1995), 137 (section 2, series 4, number 434).

107 *Saint Augustine once remarked*   Saint Augustine of Hippo, *The City of God*, trans. Marcus Dods (New York: Modern Library, 1993), 418–21 (13.9–11). See also Augustine, *Confessions*, 6 (1.6.7).

107 *the final enemy of God's kingdom*   1 Corinthians 15:26.

   *death is a product of sin*   Romans 5:12–14.

   *Just as Paul describes*   See again Romans 3–8. Death "reigned" (5:14) through Adam's fall and "sin reigned in death" (5:21).

108 *"Fear not"*   Revelation 1:17–18.

109 *The best answer . . . runs in two directions*   See further the stimulating reflections on angels, the origins of Sin and Death, and other matters in Paul J. Griffiths, *Decreation: The Last Things of All Creatures* (Waco, TX: Baylor University Press, 2014).

110 *That could be true*   For speculative reflection, see C. S. Lewis, *Out of the Silent Planet* (New York: Scribner, 1938).

111 *I take this to mean*   See Kathryn Tanner, *Christ the Key* (New York: Cambridge University Press, 2010), esp. chapters 1–3. Compare the brief but helpful discussion in Thomas Joseph White, OP, *The Light of Christ: An Introduction to Catholicism* (Washington, DC: Catholic University of America Press, 2017), 98–104.

112 *"solitary, poor, nasty, brutish, and short"*   The line comes from Thomas Hobbes, *Leviathan* (1651), 1.13. In context, Hobbes is describing human life apart from society, government, culture, or civilization; when all one has is one's own strength to secure one's position.

   *We will not . . . make it out of life alive*   This is a standard Hauerwasian proverb; I'm not sure whether it is in print.

   *"God so loved the world"*   John 3:16–17.

113 *conclude either that there is no God or . . . that he must be evil*   The Latin is *aut nullum esse Deum, aut iniquum esse Deum*; see *De servo arbitrio*, in *D. Martin Luthers Werke: Kritische Gesamtausgabe*, 73 vols. (Weimar: Hermnan Böhlaus Nachfolger, 1883–2009), 18:784. For an English translation, see *Career of the Reformer III*, ed. Philip S. Watson, vol. 33 of *Luther's Works*, ed. Helmut T. Lehmann (Philadelphia: Fortress, 1972), 291.

   *"Although God is still pleased"*   John Calvin, *Institutes of the Christian Religion*, trans. Henry Beveridge (Peabody, MA: Hendrickson, 2008), 212–13 (2.6.1).

   *Fyodor Dostoevsky says as much*   Fyodor Dostoevsky, *The Brothers Karamazov: A Novel in Four Parts with Epilogue*, trans. Richard Pevear and Larissa Volokhonsky (New York: Farrar, Straus & Giroux, 1990), 236–46.

115 *"Man's greatness"*   Pascal, *Pensées*, 46–47 (section 1, part 11 ["APR"], number 149).

   *"God alone is man's true good"*   Pascal, *Pensées*, 45 (section 1, part 10 ["The Sovereign Good"], number 148).

   *"not only impossible but useless"*   Pascal, *Pensées*, 57 (section 1, part 14 ["Excel-

lence of This Means of Proving God"], numbers 191 and 192), both this and the
next quotation.

117 *"The Only Begotten Word"* Saint Cyril of Alexandria, *On the Unity of Christ*,
trans. John Anthony McGuckin (Crestwood, NY: St. Vladimir's Seminary Press,
1995), 54–55.

119 *An angel from God* Luke 1:26–38.

120 *"Behold, I am the handmaid of the Lord"* Luke 1:38.

121 *heaven is "where Christ is"* Colossians 3:1.

122 *They're called icons* See further Saint John of Damascus, *Three Treatises on the
Divine Images*, trans. Andrew Louth (Crestwood, NY: St. Vladimir's Seminary
Press, 2003); Saint Theodore the Studite, *Writings on Iconoclasm*, trans. Thomas
Cattoi (New York: Newman, 2015); Rowan Williams, *The Dwelling of the Light:
Praying with Icons of Christ* (Grand Rapids: Eerdmans, 2003).

*to see Christ in the life of Saint Francis* G. K. Chesterton, *Saint Francis of Assisi*
(New York: Image, 1957), 107–22.

*"Christ plays in ten thousand places"* Gerard Manley Hopkins, "As Kingfishers
Catch Fire," in *The Major Works*, ed. Catherine Phillips (New York: Oxford University Press, 2002), 129.

*Each of us is a little Christ* C. S. Lewis, *Mere Christianity* (New York: Harper-
Collins, 1952), 177.

*"Imitate me as I imitate Christ"* 1 Corinthians 11:1.

123 *Luke opens with Saint Elizabeth* Luke 1:5–25.

*Matthew opens with a genealogy* Matthew 1:1–25.

*Saint Mark opens with Jesus* Mark 1:1–11.

124 *"In the beginning was the Word"* John 1:1–5.

*"And the Word became flesh"* John 1:14, 16–18.

*In light of this mystery* See further Saint Cyril of Alexandria, *On the Unity of
Christ*. See also Brant Pitre, *Jesus and the Jewish Roots of Mary: Unveiling the Mother
of the Messiah* (New York: Image, 2018).

125 *the angel Gabriel says to Mary* W. H. Auden, *For the Time Being: A Christmas
Oratorio*, ed. Alan Jacobs (Princeton: Princeton University Press, 2013), 17.

127 *"Before Abraham was, I am"* John 8:58.

128 *"in which God keeps the church in the truth"* John Webster, *The Domain of the
Word: Scripture and Theological Reason* (New York: T&T Clark, 2012), 31.

129 *the Holy Spirit . . . would lead the church into all truth* John 16:13; 14:18.

*the gates of hell will never prevail* Matthew 16:18.

131 *the good news of "Immanuel"* Matthew 1:23.

131 *led by pastors and teachers* See further Lewis Ayres, *Nicaea and Its Legacy: An The Approach to Fourth-Century Trinitarian Theology* (New York: Oxford University Press, 2004); Khaled Anatolios, *Retrieving Nicaea: The Development and Meaning of Trinitarian Doctrine* (Grand Rapids: Baker Academic, 2011); John Behr, *The Formation of Christian Theology*, vols. 1–2 (Yonkers, NY: St. Vladimir's Seminary Press, 2001–2004).

*How could we be cleansed . . . ?* Saint Basil the Great, *On the Holy Spirit*, trans. Stephen Hildebrand (Yonkers, NY: St. Vladimir's Seminary Press, 2011), 55–59 (sections 10–12).

*"In the beginning"* Genesis 1:1–3.

132 *"By the word of the Lord"* Psalm 33:6.

*"In the beginning was the Word"* John 1:1–3.

*Jesus the Word is both God's self and God's fellow* D. A. Carson, *Jesus the Son of God: A Christological Title Often Overlooked, Sometimes Misunderstood, and Currently Disputed* (Wheaton, IL: Crossway, 2012), 40–41.

*Jesus is God's "second self"* N. T. Wright, *Simply Christian: Why Christianity Makes Sense* (New York: HarperCollins, 2006), 221.

133 *"Pray then like this"* Matthew 6:9–13.

134 *what happened to Jesus at his baptism* Matthew 3:13–17; Mark 1:9–11; Luke 3:21–22.

*"practicing" the Trinity* See further Robert W. Jenson, *Canon and Creed* (Louisville: Westminster John Knox, 2010), 48; Karen Kilby, *God, Evil, and the Limits of Theology* (New York: T&T Clark, 2021), especially chapters 1–4.

135 *"In the cross is salvation"* Thomas à Kempis, *The Imitation of Christ*, trans. Aloysius Croft and Harold Bolton (Mineola, NY: Dover, 2003), 41 (book 2, chapter 12).

138 *Jesus enters the public eye* Saint Mark's opening seven chapters are not unlike a movie trailer in this respect. A series of "smash cuts" to the next scene, one after another. Read them in a single sitting, and you'll get a quick sense of Jesus's ministry.

*"the word which [God] sent to Israel"* Acts 10:36–39.

*"The time is fulfilled"* Mark 1:15.

*"Thy kingdom come"* Matthew 6:10.

*His word is like God's* See again the opening chapters of Saint Mark's Gospel.

139 *The twelve followers he appoints* Matthew 10:1–4; Mark 3:13–19; Luke 6:12–16.

*Jesus is "the Messiah, the Son of the living God"* Matthew 16:16.

139 *The city of Jerusalem welcomes him*    Matthew 21:1–11; Mark 11:1–11; Luke 19:28–44; John 12:12–19.

*he is another Moses*    See Deuteronomy 18:15–22; Acts 3:17–26.

*Jesus of Nazareth, the King of the Jews*    John 19:19; see also Matthew 27:37; Mark 15:26; Luke 23:38.

140 *"We had hoped"*    Luke 24:21.

*Similar questions had arisen*    Ezekiel 37:1–14.

*"Can these bones live?"*    Robert W. Jenson, *Systematic Theology*, vol. 1, *The Triune God* (New York: Oxford University Press, 1997), 12.

141 *God raises Jesus from the dead*    See Matthew 27:57–28:20; Mark 15:42–16:8; Luke 23:50–24:49; John 19:38–20:29.

*a good infection*    Lewis, *Mere Christianity*, 172–77.

143 *God will wipe away every tear*    Revelation 21:4.

*"All the promises of God"*    2 Corinthians 1:20. I have substituted "Christ" for "him" in the first sentence of the verse.

144 *"Why do you seek . . . ?"*    Luke 24:5 (adapted; "the Living One" is my translation); see also Mark 16:6; Matthew 28:6.

145 *thirty different ways of understanding*    For curious readers, see the theories online at https://www.bradeast.org/blog/2019/09/an-atonement-typology.html. For far weightier reflections than mine, see Fleming Rutledge, *The Crucifixion: Understanding the Death of Jesus Christ* (Grand Rapids: Eerdmans, 2015).

*One theory to rule them all . . .*    See J. R. R. Tolkien, *The Lord of the Rings* (Boston: Houghton Mifflin, 1966).

146 *"For our sake"*    2 Corinthians 5:21.

*And unlike the sacrifices of birds and goats*    Hebrews 9:1–10:18.

*"It is finished"*    John 19:30.

*"What can wash away my sin?"*    "Nothing but the Blood of Jesus," written by Robert Lowry in 1876.

*Its track record . . . is 100 percent*    Enoch and Elijah are biblical exceptions, as is the Blessed Virgin Mary (according to Catholic and Orthodox tradition). All were mortal by nature, though; if they or any others have been kept from death, it is by a special gift of God.

*"For this reason the Father loves me"*    John 10:17–18.

*"For we know"*    Romans 6:9–10.

147 *"Do you not know"*    Romans 6:3–8.

*"The Father has delivered"*    Colossians 1:13–14.

147 *"He who commits"*  1 John 3:8.

    *"Since therefore the children share"*  Hebrews 2:14–18.

148 *"Then I saw an angel"*  Revelation 20:1–3, 10, 14.

    *"Fear not"*  Revelation 1:17–18.

    *"Worthy are you"*  The vision fills the whole fifth chapter; the quotations come from Revelation 5:9–14.

150 *"Death, be not proud"*  *The Complete English Poems of John Donne*, ed. C. A. Patrides (London: J. M. Dent & Sons, 1985), 440–41.

152 *salvation comes from the Jews*  John 4:22.

    *As he said not once but twice*  Matthew 15:24; see also 10:6.

    *"recapitulation"*  See Saint Irenaeus, *Against Heresies*, trans. Alexander Roberts and James Donaldson, vol. 1 of *Ante-Nicene Fathers* (Peabody, MA: Hendrickson, 2012).

153 *"He has helped his servant Israel"*  Luke 1:54–55.

    *"Blessed is the Lord"*  Luke 1:68–71.

    *"I have asked to see you"*  Acts 28:20.

155 *"Were the Spirit not to be worshiped"*  Saint Gregory of Nazianzus, *On God and Christ: The Five Theological Orations and Two Letters to Cledonius*, trans. Frederick Williams and Lionel Wickham (Crestwood, NY: St. Vladimir's Seminary Press, 2002), 139 (*Oration* 31, section 28).

157 *"So when they had come together"*  Acts 1:6–11.

158 *Glory, glory, hallelujah!*  "Battle Hymn of the Republic," written by Julia Ward Howe in 1861.

159 *"All authority in heaven and on earth"*  Matthew 28:18–20.

160 *Luke opens Acts*  Acts 1:1.

162 *Pentecost . . . is an annual Jewish festival*  For a brief overview, see Deuteronomy 16:1–17.

    *Jesus appeared to his followers*  See Acts 1:1–2:47.

163 *"all flesh"*  Joel 2:28–29.

    *repents and is "baptized"*  The second chapter depicts the whole event; the quotation comes from Acts 2:38.

    *"He blows where he wills"*  John 3:8.

    *"it is to your advantage"*  John 16:7.

    *a "seal"*  See 2 Corinthians 1:22; Ephesians 1:13; 4:30.

    *mistaken for a gardener*  John 20:15.

164 *His ascension is his exaltation*   For example, see Acts 2:33; 5:31; Philippians 2:9; Hebrews 7:26.

*"[Israel's] former priests"*   Hebrews 7:23–28.

165 *"we have such a high priest"*   Hebrews 8:1.

*Yes, they continue*   For a recent accessible treatment, see Andrew Wilson, *Spirit and Sacrament: An Invitation to Eucharismatic Worship* (Grand Rapids: Zondervan, 2019). For historical discussion, see Carlos Eire, *They Flew: A History of the Impossible* (New Haven: Yale University Press, 2023).

*his own special fruit*   Galatians 5:22–23.

166 *"Now the Lord is the Spirit"*   2 Corinthians 3:17.

*"For freedom Christ has set us free"*   Galatians 5:1.

*"no one speaking by the Spirit of God"*   1 Corinthians 12:3.

167 *"On this mountain"*   Isaiah 25:6–8.

*the people are now the temple*   1 Corinthians 3:16–17.

*a kind of micro-temple*   1 Corinthians 6:19–20.

*he spoke of his own body*   John 2:21.

*now called the body of Christ*   See Romans 12:5; 1 Corinthians 12:27; Ephesians 5:23; Colossians 1:24 (and those passages' larger contexts).

168 *"I ask, then"*   Romans 11:1–2.

169 *We see what Paul means*   Romans 11:28–29.

*"according to the flesh"*   See Romans 1:3; 4:1; 8:4–5; 9:5; etc.

*"Think not that I have come"*   Matthew 5:17–18.

*More than a few writers have suggested*   See further Joseph Cardinal Ratzinger, *Many Religions—One Covenant: Israel, the Church, and the World*, trans. Graham Harrison (San Francisco: Ignatius, 1999), especially 69–71; Robert W. Jenson, *The Triune Story: Collected Essays on Scripture*, ed. Brad East (New York: Oxford University Press, 2019), especially 223–326; Mark S. Kinzer, *Postmissionary Messianic Judaism: Redefining Christian Engagement with the Jewish People* (Grand Rapids: Brazos, 2005).

*He is the head of his body*   Ephesians 4:15–16; 5:23; Colossians 1:18; 2:19.

170 *"For this reason"*   Ephesians 3:1–6.

*"separated from Chist"*   Ephesians 2:12.

*"But now . . . in Christ Jesus"*   Ephesians 2:13, 17–22; 3:9. Here and in other biblical quotations I have made "gentiles" lowercase.

171 *the calling and promise to Abraham*   Genesis 12:1–3.

*the initial event of gentiles coming to faith*   Acts 10:1–48.

171  *whether gentiles could join Jews*    Acts 15:1–29.

172  *with one voice*    Romans 15:6.

    *The answer is adoption*    Romans 8:14–17; Galatians 3:23–4:7.

    *"But to all who received him"*    John 1:12–13.

    *Christ's body and bride*    Ephesians 5:21–33; 2 Corinthians 11:2; Revelation 19:4–9; 21:1–3, 9–11.

    *"cannot have God as his father"*    Saint Cyprian of Carthage, *On the Church: Select Treatises*, trans. Allen Brent (Crestwood, NY: St. Vladimir's Seminary Press, 2006), 157 (*The Unity of the Catholic Church 6*).

    *there is no salvation apart from Abraham's covenant family*    See Saint Cyprian, *On the Church: Select Letters*, trans. Allen Brent (Crestwood, NY: St. Vladimir's Seminary Press, 2006), 211–13 (*Letter* 73).

173  *he is the father of faith*    Romans 4:11.

175  *"I accept the bait"*    Saint Cyril of Jerusalem, *Lectures on the Christian Sacraments: The Procatechesis and the Five Mystagogical Catecheses Ascribed to St. Cyril of Jerusalem*, trans. Maxwell E. Johnson (Yonkers, NY: St. Vladimir's Seminary Press, 2017), 69 (*Protocatechesis 5*).

177  *"Very truly, I tell you"*    John 10:9–16.

178  *"there is one body and one Spirit"*    Ephesians 4:4–6.

    *"The truth itself"*    Saint Augustine, *City of God*, 346–47 (11.2).

179  *we find ourselves at last*    Matthew 10:39; 16:25.

180  *in the words of "Amazing Grace"*    "Amazing Grace," written by John Newton in 1772.

    *Wise teachers in Eastern Christianity*    The clearest and most suggestive teaching in Scripture is found in 2 Peter 1:4. For discussion, see Kallistos Ware, *The Orthodox Church: An Introduction to Eastern Christianity* (New York: Penguin, 2015), 225–31.

182  *"Work out your own salvation"*    Philippians 2:12–13.

    *"Grant what you command"*    Saint Augustine, *Confessions*, 202 (10.29.40).

    *a moving story in Saint Matthew's Gospel*    Matthew 8:5–10, 13.

183  *"That insane asshole is dead"*    Franz Wright, "Baptism," in *Walking to Martha's Vineyard* (New York: Knopf, 2008), 44–45.

    *"unless a person is reborn from above"*    John 3:3.

    *"unless a person is born of water and the Spirit"*    John 3:5–6.

    *"It is the Spirit that gives life"*    John 6:63.

    *"So, then, sisters and brothers"*    Romans 8:12–17.

184 *"When Christ calls a man"*   Alas, the newer translations render the German more literally (and thus less poetically). For the older translation, see Dietrich Bonhoeffer, *The Cost of Discipleship*, trans. R. H. Fuller (New York: Touchstone, 1959), 89.

*"If anyone would come after me"*   Mark 8:34–35.

185 *"ascetic" practices*   For brief introduction, see Saint Isaac of Nineveh, *On Ascetical Life*. For detailed treatment, see Saint John Climacus, *The Ladder of Divine Ascent*, trans. Colm Luibheid and Norman Russell (Mahwah, NJ: Paulist, 1982). Readers might also benefit from *Charity and Its Fruits* by Jonathan Edwards, published in 1749 and widely available online for free.

186 *First, we fast because*   Fasting occurs throughout Israel's history; Jesus fasts for forty days and forty nights following his baptism; in the book of Acts, the church in Antioch enters a time of fasting and praying in order to discern the Lord's will. *While* they are doing this, the Spirit tells them, "Set apart for me Barnabas and Saul for the work to which I have called them." Then, after *more* praying and fasting, "they laid their hands on them and sent them off" (13:1–3).

*"If you carry the cross"*   Kempis, *The Imitation of Christ*, 41–43 (book 2, chapter 12). See further Saint Bonaventure, *The Journey of the Mind to God*, especially chapter 7; English translations are available for free online.

188 *"the one thing needful"*   Luke 10:38–42.

*when her brother, Saint Lazarus*   John 11:1–44; the quotation comes from verses 32–36.

*Mary appears once more*   John 12:1–8.

190 *Human beings are made to worship*   See further James K. A. Smith, *You Are What You Love: The Spiritual Power of Habit* (Grand Rapids: Baker Academic, 2016); Tish Harrison Warren, *Liturgy of the Ordinary: Sacred Practices in Everyday Life* (Downers Grove, IL: InterVarsity Press, 2016).

*He spoke with pride*   1 Thessalonians 1:9–10.

*a perpetual factory of idols*   Calvin, *Institutes of the Christian Religion*, 55 (1.11.8): "the human mind is, so to speak, a perpetual forge of idols."

191 *To him who sits on the throne*   Revelation 5:13.

192 *A sacrament is a symbolic practice*   See further Andrew Davison, *Why Sacraments?* (Eugene, OR: Cascade, 2013).

*"[God] likes matter"*   Lewis, *Mere Christianity*, 64.

*"earthen vessels"*   2 Corinthians 4:7.

193 *"My grace is sufficient for you"*   2 Corinthians 12:9–10.

*He opposes the proud*   James 4:6; 1 Peter 5:5.

194 *Like the younger brother*   Luke 15:11–32.

195 *"from above"*  John 3:3, 5.

*up through the present day*  See further Peter J. Leithart, *Baptism: A Guide to Life from Death* (Bellingham, WA: Lexham, 2021).

196 *After celebrating Passover*  See further Brant Pitre, *Jesus and the Last Supper* (Grand Rapids: Eerdmans, 2017). For an accessible biblical and theological re-flection on Holy Communion, see the same author's *Jesus and the Jewish Roots of the Eucharist: Unlocking the Secrets of the Last Supper* (New York: Image, 2016).

*"Jesus took bread"*  Matthew 26:26–29.

*"The Lord Jesus on the night"*  1 Corinthians 11:23–26.

*"I am the bread of life"*  John 6:48–51, 53–58.

197 *Let us keep the feast!*  1 Corinthians 5:8.

*The Bible is the word of the living God*  See further John W. Kleinig, *God's Word: A Guide to Holy Scripture* (Bellingham, WA: Lexham, 2023). See also Ben-edict XVI, *Verbum Domini*, available online for free and in translation.

198 *"As the rain and the snow"*  Isaiah 55:10–11.

*the phrase "the word of the Lord"*  1 Thessalonians 1:2–2:13; Acts 4:4, 31; 6:2–4; 8:4, 14, 25; 11:1; 13:5–7, 44–49; and so on.

*In the middle of his Gospel*  John 12:41; 5:46; 8:56.

199 *"It was because God made us"*  Saint John of Damascus, *On the Orthodox Faith: A New Translation of* An Exact Exposition of the Orthodox Faith, trans. Norman Russell (Yonkers, NY: St. Vladimir's Seminary Press, 2022), 239 (82).

201 *"for whom Christ died"*  Romans 14:15; 1 Corinthians 8:11.

*"Christ also suffered for you"*  1 Peter 2:21.

*"All of Christ's action"*  The Latin is *omnis Christi actio nostra est instructio*; see Saint Thomas Aquinas, *Summa Theologiae* III, q. 40, a. 1 ad 3.

*"Do nothing from selfishness"*  Philippians 2:3–11.

202 *"You know that among the gentiles"*  Mark 10:42–44, NRSVue.

*"always carrying in the body"*  2 Corinthians 4:10–11, 16–18.

203 *the Ten Commandments*  Exodus 20:1–20; Deuteronomy 5:1–21.

*the Sermon on the Mount*  Matthew 5–7.

204 *the gospel clothed in an imperative*  See Karl Barth, *Church Dogmatics* II/2, *The Doctrine of God*, trans. Geoffrey W. Bromiley et al. (Peabody, MA: Hendrick-son, 2010 [1942]), 509–781.

*"Love the Lord your God"*  Matthew 22:34–40; Mark 12:28–34; Luke 10:25–28.

205 *Jesus emerges from the desert*  Matthew 4:11–25; the Beatitudes are found in Matthew 5:1–12.

206 *Sin and Death cling closely*   Hebrews 12:1.

*Like the Israelites at the Red Sea*   Exodus 14:10–12.

207 *the fruit of the Spirit*   Galatians 5:22–23.

*Instead of merely avoiding murder*   Matthew 5:21–48.

*"If you forgive others"*   Matthew 6:14–15.

*"Lord, how often . . . ?"*   Matthew 18:21–22.

208 *"What God has joined together"*   Matthew 19:6; Mark 10:9.

*"You are the light of the world"*   Matthew 5:14–16.

210 *just the poor*   Luke 6:20.

*"No one can serve two masters"*   Matthew 6:24.

*envy is idolatry*   Ephesians 5:5.

*"the love of money is the root of all evils"*   1 Timothy 6:10.

*"Come now, you rich"*   James 5:1–6.

211 *"it is easier for a camel"*   Matthew 19:24.

*"Pharisees came up to him"*   Matthew 19:3–9.

*Each of them commended*   Matthew 19:10–12; 1 Corinthians 7:1–40, especially v. 7.

*we will not be married in heaven*   Matthew 22:29–32.

*marriage on earth is a window*   Ephesians 5:31–32.

212 *marriage . . . fulfilled when Jesus returns*   See Revelation 19–22.

*"My grace is sufficient for you"*   2 Corinthians 12:9.

213 *Saint Anthony and Saint Benedict*   Saint Athanasius wrote *The Life of Saint Anthony* around the year 360; less than a century later, Saint Benedict wrote his *Rule*, which is still in use to this day. Both are available in translation online.

*Saint Monica*   See Saint Augustine, *Confessions*, especially 49–51 (the end of book 3), 82–84 (the middle of book 5), 150–54 (the end of book 8), 166–78 (the second half of book 9).

*the widow from Jesus's parable*   Luke 18:1–8.

214 *Saint Perpetua*   The account comes from *The Passion of Saints Perpetua and Felicity*, available in translation online.

*he wrote seven letters to seven congregations*   See Saint Ignatius of Antioch, "The Letters of Ignatius," in *The Apostolic Fathers in English*, ed. and trans. Michael W. Holmes (Grand Rapids: Baker Academic, 2006), 87–129.

*"Let me be food for the wild beasts"*   Saint Ignatius, "Letters," 113–14 (*Letter to the Romans* 4.1).

214 *Saint Francis of Assisi*   There are many books about Saint Francis; one of the most readable is the one I cited earlier by Chesterton, called *Saint Francis of Assisi*.

*Saint Thérèse of Lisieux.*   See Saint Thérèse of Lisieux, *Story of a Soul: The Autobiography of Saint Thérèse of Lisieux*, trans. John Clarke, 3rd ed. (Washington, DC: ICS Publications, 1996).

215 *Pope Emeritus Benedict XVI*   See Gerard O'Connell, "Pope Benedict XVI's Last Words: 'Jesus, I Love You,'" *America*, December 31, 2022, https://www.america magazine.org/faith/2022/12/31/pope-benedict-final-words-244442.

216 *"he who seeks passing fame"*   Kempis, *The Imitation of Christ*, 33–34 (book 2, chapter 6), 36 (book 2, chapter 8), 76 (book 3, chapter 28); both this and the following three quotations.

*"God cannot inspire unrealizable desires"*   Saint Thérèse, *Story of a Soul*, 207 (chapter 10), both this and the next quotation.

217 *"My vocation is love!"*   Saint Thérèse, *Story of a Soul*, 194 (chapter 9), both this and the next quotation.

*"Failure of love on our part"*   Julian, *Revelations*, 94 (section 37).

220 *"Judas, Peter"*   Luci Shaw, "Judas, Peter," in *Polishing the Petoskey Stone: Selected Poems* (Vancouver, BC: Regent College, 2003), 201.

*the difference between Judas and Peter*   See their intertwined stories in Matthew 26:14–27:10; John 18:1–27; 20:1–21:23; Acts 1:1–42.

221 *David sinned against God*   See 2 Samuel 11:1–12:23.

*[Paul] persecuted Jesus's followers*   See Acts 7:54–9:31.

*"the only final grief"*   Georges Bernanos, *The Diary of a Country Priest*, trans. Pamela Morris (New York: Carroll & Graf, 1965), 192. This is a direct quote, unlike with Bloy, but it is worth noting that the translation is less than exact. It is possible the translator meant to echo Bloy in English, whether or not Bernanos meant to do so in their shared French.

*a character in* **Silence**   Shusaku Endo, *Silence*, trans. William Johnston (New York: Taplinger, 1969). In the 2016 film adaptation by Martin Scorsese, the character is played by Yôsuke Kubozuka.

*"Simon, son of John, do you love me?"*   John 21:1–19; compare John 18:15–18.

222 *"Seek his face always"*   Psalm 105:4 NIV.

*"Follow me!"*   John 21:19.

223 *"for God so loved the world"*   John 3:16.

224 *"Those who are well"*   Luke 5:31–32.

*"My sheep hear his voice"*   John 10:27–28.

225 *"The earth will be filled"*   Habakkuk 2:14.

226 *"I tell you, you are Peter"*   Matthew 16:18.

    *In his last night on earth*   See the full prayer in John 17:1–26.

    *Saint John sees two groups*   Revelation 7:1–17; the quotation comes from vv. 9–10.

    *"The kingdom of the world"*   Revelation 11:15.

229 *"From the heights of heaven"*   Saint Francis de Sales, *Introduction to the Devout Life*, trans. John K. Ryan (New York: Image, 1966), 57 (1.17).

231 *For what may we hope?*   Kant formulates it in the first-person singular, following "What can I know?" and "What should I do?" Found in his first *Critique* (published then revised in the 1780s).

    *"Hark! the Herald Angels Sing"*   "Hark! the Herald Angels Sing," written by Charles Wesley and George Whitefield in 1739 and 1754.

232 *"I will shake all nations"*   Haggai 2:7 KJV.

    *"O sing to the* LORD *a new song"*   Psalm 96:1–13.

234 *"Truly, truly, I say to you"*   John 5:25–29.

235 *"a new heaven and a new earth"*   Revelation 21:1–4.

236 *"The devil who had deceived"*   Revelation 20:10–21:14.

237 *"It is finished"*   John 19:30 (*tetelestai*); compare Revelation 21:6 (*gegonan*). The Greek translation of the original Hebrew of Genesis 2:1–2, when God "finishes" the work of creation on the sixth day, reads *synetelesthēsan* and *synetelesen*.

238 *Jesus himself taught it*   Especially Matthew 25:31–46.

    *"in this hope we were saved"*   Romans 8:24–25.

    *Following in Paul's wake*   1 Corinthians 9:22; my quotation renders passive what Paul says in an active voice.

    *Pascal's wager*   Pascal, *Pensées*, 121–125 (section 2, series 2, number 418).

239 *"I am the way and the truth and the life"*   John 14:6.

    *"There is salvation in no one else"*   Acts 4:12.

    *whether all might be saved*   Associated with figures such as Origen, Saint Gregory of Nyssa, and Saint Isaac of Nineveh. For a recent argument in favor of Christian universalism, see David Bentley Hart, *That All Shall Be Saved: Heaven, Hell, and Universal Salvation* (New Haven: Yale University Press, 2019).

    *God "desires all to be saved"*   1 Timothy 2:4.

240 *"The last shall be first"*   Matthew 20:16.

241 *"I wait for your salvation"*   Genesis 49:18; Psalm 130:5; Isaiah 64:4; Psalms 62:5; 130:6; Lamentations 3:25; Isaiah 30:18, respectively.

242 *people who live "out of control"*   See Stanley Hauerwas, *The Peaceable Kingdom:*

*A Primer in Christian Ethics* (South Bend, IN: University of Notre Dame Press, 1983).

242 *"The night is far gone"*    Romans 13:12, 11.

243 *"See, I have set before you"*    Deuteronomy 30:15–20.

*"Jesus Christ is the same"*    Hebrews 13:8.

*"God is light"*    1 John 1:5; 4:7, 8, 9–12, 13–19.

244 *"For what, without Jesus, can the world give you?"*    Kempis, *The Imitation of Christ*, 35 (book 2, chapter 8).

245 *twenty-one men were kidnapped*    See further Martin Mosebach, *The 21: A Journey into the Land of Coptic Martyrs*, trans. Alta L. Price (Walden, NY: Plough, 2019).

**Pope Francis invited Tawadros to Rome**    See Devin Watkins, "Pope Francis Adds 21 Coptic Orthodox Martyrs to Catholic List of Saints," *Vatican News*, May 11, 2023, https://www.vaticannews.va/en/pope/news/2023-05/pope-francis-tawadros-ii-coptic-orthodox-martyrs-egypt.html.

246 *"Have no fear of them"*    Matthew 10:26–33.

247 *"the fullness of him who fills all in all"*    Ephesians 1:23.

# Index

196–97, 199, 220, 247; shed on the cross, 145–48, 165, 168–73, 257

Bloy, Léon, 18, 254, 271

body, 14, 100, 147, 157–58, 164, 183, 185–86, 246–47; as dwelling for Christ's Spirit, 163, 181, 192–96, 202; ecclesial, 13, 158, 167–70, 172, 178, 190, 194, 208, 225, 238; eucharistic, 12–13, 189, 196–97, 220, 247; good, 143–44; human, 72, 94, 199; incarnate, 120, 124, 128, 152; risen, 17, 143–44, 235

Bonhoeffer, Dietrich, 184

Caesar, 42–43, 139, 153

Calvary, 146, 187, 212

Calvin, John, 113, 190, 254

Carson, D. A., 132

catechesis, 7–10, 19–20, 251

catholicity, 195, 225–26, 252

charismatic gifts. See signs and wonders

Chesterton, G. K., 122

Christ. See anointing; king(s); Messiah

church, 6–9, 12–13, 76, 84, 92, 100–101; and Israel, 29–31, 39–40; life, mission, and worship, 157–227; traditions and doctrines, 121–22, 128–31

command(s). See discipleship; ethics; law of Moses; obedience

communion. See Eucharist

contingency, 60–61, 102

Coptic martyrs, 245–47

councils, ecumenical, 128–29

covenant(s), 32–34, 37–38, 45, 73, 167–73, 196

creation, 51–84, 143–44, 158, 234–35, 239, 243

creed(s), 252; Apostles', 7; Nicene, 59, 127–29, 157, 162, 194, 225–26, 234, 257–58

cross. See crucifixion

crucifixion, 226, 235, 237; of Jesus, 108, 126–27, 135, 139–43, 146–47, 163, 167–68, 201–2; as pattern of Christian life, 3, 5–6, 11, 182–89, 201–2, 206, 211–12, 247; of sinful self, 146–47, 193–94

Cyprian of Carthage, 122, 172–73

Cyril of Alexandria, 117, 121, 131

Cyril of Jerusalem, 175

Dante Alighieri, 53

David, 30, 44–47, 92, 119–23, 139, 151–53, 220–21

death: of believers in baptism, 147, 168, 182–84, 194–96, 208; of Christ for sinners, 3, 5–6, 108, 126–27, 135, 139–50, 160, 163, 167–68, 196–202, 212; of death, 33, 108, 121–22, 150, 188, 234–44; of fallen creatures, 72, 85–89, 104–16, 188; of martyrs for Christ, 3–6, 18, 19, 76, 164, 214, 245–47; of self as way to life, vi, 3–6, 11–12, 18, 95–96, 104, 159, 175, 177, 183–87, 190, 206, 212, 247

deification, 145, 180–81

demons, 110, 138, 165, 186, 235

desire, 33, 46, 60, 76, 95–96, 186, 239; for Christ, 16, 216–17, 231–33; for earthly things, 103–4

devil. See Satan

discipleship, 10, 121, 168, 171, 177–78, 195, 202; and failure, 220–22; and mission, 159–61, 223–24; and Sermon on the Mount, 133–34, 205–12; and spiritual practice, 11–13, 185–89

disciplines, 11–16, 185–93

divinization. See deification

doctrine, 9–10, 19–20, 57, 97–98, 113–14, 130–34

dominion, 71, 77, 80, 83, 138, 146–47

Donne, John, 150

Dostoevsky, Fyodor, 113–14
doubt, 75–76, 259

Eden, 89–93, 110, 111, 177
election, 21–40, 48–49, 151–53, 168–73
Elijah, 39, 121, 151–52, 257, 264
Elisha, 152, 257
Elizabeth, 121, 123
Endo, Shusaku, 221
Enoch, 264
eternal life, 1, 66, 68, 191; through
    death, 3–4, 6, 11–12, 135, 245–47;
    through grace, 111–12, 196, 199, 224,
    243–44; through resurrection,
    107–8, 142–44, 234–35
ethics, 9–10, 37–38, 63, 80, 98, 99–101,
    178–79; and the Christian life,
    201–27; and the cross, 182–87
Eucharist, 12–13, 191–98
evangelism, 178, 223–24, 245
Eve, 73, 83–84, 89–93, 109–11, 145
evolution, 91–94, 111–12
Exodus, 34–37, 42, 139, 162
Ezekiel, 30, 140

failure, 18, 39, 44, 92–93, 103, 127,
    217–22
faith, 250, 252; as belief, doctrine, or
    confession, 5, 20, 23, 30, 34, 59, 62–
    65, 124, 127–32, 178, 226; as theologi-
    cal virtue, 17, 76, 127, 165, 168, 207; as
    trust in God's promise, 9, 16, 21, 25,
    76, 120, 164, 172–73, 179–83, 214–15;
    as way of life, 5, 9, 15, 19, 39–40, 76,
    82, 189–98, 218–19, 245–47
Fall, the, 73, 92–93, 97–98, 109–14, 177
fasting, 12, 66, 186, 206, 268
Father, God the; and adoption, 26–28,
    134, 145, 172–73, 177–84, 194–96; and
    the Son, 12, 119, 134, 162, 164, 190,
    202, 206, 244; and the Trinity, 59,
    130–34, 190–91

finitude, 60, 103
forgiveness, 139; of others' sins against
    us, 133, 207–8; of our sins against
    God, 88, 102, 147, 157, 163, 165, 194,
    196, 220–22, 239; as a petition in the
    Lord's Prayer, 133, 224
Francis (pope), 245
Francis de Sales, 229
Francis of Assisi, 214
freedom: in Christ, 76, 85, 102,
    104, 108, 139, 143, 147, 158, 165–66,
    194–97; in the exodus, 34–36, 139;
    for obedience, 37, 76, 185–87, 203–4,
    207–8; of the will, 80, 96, 99–101, 195
friendship, 8, 9, 101, 127, 143, 249–50;
    between God and Abraham, 24,
    48–49; between us and Christ,
    187–88, 195

Gabriel, 119–20, 125
Galilee, 119, 137–38, 141, 157, 159, 164,
    221–22
Genesis, 21–114, 123, 131, 254–55
gentiles, 26–31, 38, 40, 152, 182, 190,
    202, 233; adopted through Christ,
    168–73, 177–78
Gethsemane, 144, 152, 163, 212
gift. See grace
Golgotha. See Calvary
gospel. See atonement; crucifixion;
    faith; grace; hope; incarnation;
    kingdom of God; Messiah; prom-
    ise(s); resurrection; salvation
grace, 41, 111; and God's free gift, 102,
    124, 138, 145, 170, 172, 188, 218–22,
    238; and God's love, 15–16, 217; and
    God's power, 121, 177, 182, 212, 247;
    and the sacraments, 191–94, 199
Granji, 218–19
gratitude, 15, 27, 249–50; and the
    Eucharist, 196–97; to God, 11, 35, 54,
    76, 78–79, 114, 181

Judas Iscariot, 188, 220–22

judgment, 41, 46, 127, 213, 220, 233–36, 239, 244

Julian of Norwich, vi, 66–68, 85, 96, 217, 252

justice, 41, 77, 119, 151–52, 204–7, 213, 231–32, 241

Kant, Immanuel, 231

Kijichiro, 221

king(s), 208; Adam, 83; Israel, 30, 41–45, 47, 83, 151, 220; Jesus, 3, 45, 84, 119, 123, 127, 138–40, 151–52, 164–65, 169, 231–33

kingdom of God, 13, 19, 138–39, 183, 205–6, 211

land, 23, 41–43, 168, 177, 198, 243

language, 66, 109, 121, 137, 208, 251–52; at Babel and Pentecost, 92, 162, 167, 180, 225; for Christian mysteries, 19–20, 80–81, 127, 171

law of Moses, 27–28, 72, 124, 152; and gentiles, 169–73; and Israel, 34–41, 162, 243, 256; and Scripture, 30, 46, 92, 139, 198, 203–5, 211

Lewis, C. S., 30, 122, 141, 192

liturgy, 12–13, 189, 190–91, 192–98, 223, 245

Lord's Prayer, 7, 133–34, 138, 143, 221

Lord's Supper. See Eucharist

love: and Jesus, 8, 73, 79, 88, 102, 112, 125, 146, 172; the Lord's for Abraham's children, 24, 27–28, 32–36, 42, 45, 48–49, 87, 168–69, 197, 224, 243–44; the Lord's for humankind, vi, 8, 16, 29, 53, 57–63, 66–68, 76, 81, 112, 125, 168, 194, 201, 219–24, 243–44; ours for the Lord, 8, 15–16, 37–38, 44, 53–54, 57–58, 103–4, 115, 133, 164, 179, 190, 204, 211–22; ours for others, 98, 103, 133, 191, 201, 204,

207, 211–12, 214, 243–44; as a virtue, 17, 165, 207

Luke the Evangelist, 119–20, 123, 137–40, 159–61, 210

Luther, Martin, 113, 251

marks of the church, 225–27

Mark the Evangelist, 123, 137–39, 263

Marnie, 218–19

marriage, 37, 119, 218; and the Lord, 32, 66, 213, 216, 235; and sex, 78–79, 211–12

Martha of Bethany, 188

martyrdom, 17–18; as dying for Christ, 3, 76, 164, 214, 245–47; as living for Christ, vi, 3–6, 159, 177–78, 186–87, 216–17

Mary, Blessed Virgin, 73, 84, 141, 153, 189, 264; and the incarnation, 88, 119–28, 137, 151, 177

Mary Magdalene, 141

Mary of Bethany, 188–89

Matthew the Evangelist, 137–39, 159, 182–83, 196, 238; opening chapter of his gospel, 45, 123, 131; and Sermon on the Mount, 133–34, 203, 205–12

Mauriac, François, vi

Melville, Herman, 42–43

mental health, 99–101

Messiah, 45, 139–40, 167–68, 171, 202, 212, 221

Mill, John Stuart, 73

Milton, John, 21

miracles. See signs and wonders

Miriam, 35–36

mission: and anointing, 44–45; of the church, 159–61, 164, 168, 178, 223–27; and dominion, 77; of Jesus, 139, 152, 202

Mom Pat, 218–19

money, 104, 186, 188, 192, 206, 209–11

Monica of Hippo, 121, 213–14

monks, 15, 19, 213–14, 245
morality. *See* ethics
Moses: and the exodus, 34–37; and
   Israel, 27–28, 41, 46, 171–72, 243; and
   Jesus, 124, 139, 151–52, 169, 198, 205,
   211, 243; and the law, 30, 37–38, 72,
   124, 139, 162, 169–72, 203–4, 211, 243
*munus triplex*. *See* threefold office
mystery, 72, 89, 96, 114, 120–27, 130,
   169–71

Nama, 218–19
Nathan, 44–45, 221
New Testament, 30–31, 45, 46, 89, 123,
   197–98, 239
Nicene Creed. *See* creed(s)

obedience, 211, 213; and Abraham,
   21, 32; and Jesus, 152, 202; and the
   Lord's wise commands, 5, 10, 38, 110,
   130, 138, 186, 204, 208, 243; and sin,
   75, 90, 111, 221–22
Old Testament, 30–34, 45–46, 121, 151,
   169, 197–98, 203–4
Origen, 131, 252, 272
Our Father. *See* Lord's Prayer

parousia. *See* second coming
Pascal, Blaise, 105, 115–16, 238–39
Passover, 137, 162, 167–68, 196
patience, 165, 207, 225, 238, 241–42
Paul: his gospel for the gentiles,
   167–73; his life and death, 3, 92,
   121, 153, 160, 211–12, 214, 220–21; his
   writing, 3, 17–18, 25, 32, 88, 98, 107–8,
   121–22, 143, 146–47, 163, 166, 182–84,
   190, 192–93, 196–98, 201–2, 210, 212,
   224, 238–39, 242, 249
peace, 55, 113, 121, 205, 241, 247; of
   Christ, 138, 170, 216, 222, 231–32, 247;
   of the Spirit, 165, 207
Pentecost, 159–68, 180–84, 225, 242
Perpetua, 122, 214
Peter: and the church, 225–26; and

forgiveness, 207, 220–22; and the
   gentiles, 171–72; and the good news
   of Christ, 138–39, 163, 201, 207, 239;
   and Saint Paul, 3, 121, 160, 214
people of God. *See* Abraham; church;
   election; Israel
philosophy, 63, 72, 80, 115
Pilate, 126, 140
Polycarp, 3
poverty. *See* money
power: of God, 10, 35, 51, 53, 57, 60,
   65, 95, 100–101, 119, 133, 141, 182, 247;
   of God's servants, 121, 172, 192–93,
   212; of God's Son, 73, 85, 107–8, 139,
   146–49, 177, 234–35; of God's Spirit,
   12, 126, 132, 138, 157, 160, 163–66, 186,
   190, 205, 212; of God's word, 12, 55,
   69, 183, 197, 221
prayer: intercessory, 17, 39, 188, 195,
   213–14, 226, 229, 239, 246–47; the
   Lord's, 7, 133–34, 138, 143, 221;
   monastic, 15, 66–67, 213; place of,
   in Christian life, 11–17, 76, 81, 130,
   182–87, 191, 206–8, 224, 233
priest(s), 19, 216–17, 221; Adam, 80,
   83, 89–90; Israel, 38, 44–48, 83, 151;
   Jesus, 47, 84, 147–48, 151, 164–65
promise(s): for/to Abraham's children, 23, 25, 27, 32, 34, 41–43, 45,
   167–73, 225, 243; of/about Christ,
   25, 73, 129, 143, 158, 167–73, 198,
   225–26, 241; of/about the gentiles,
   26–27, 167–73, 225, 233; of/about the
   Holy Spirit, 162–63
prophet(s): Adam, 83–84; Israel, 30,
   41, 44–46, 83, 151, 170, 205, 221; Jesus,
   84, 138, 151, 164–65; Scripture, 30–31,
   38, 131, 140, 153, 162–63, 167, 169, 193,
   197–98, 204, 232
providence, 108, 113, 164
Psalms, 15, 30, 42, 46, 61, 132, 222,
   232–33

of God; incarnation; saint(s); resurrection

Spirit (of God/Christ). *See* Holy Spirit

suffering. *See* atonement; death; discipleship; eternal life; faith; hope; saint(s); providence; resurrection

tabernacle, 44, 165, 167

temple, 37, 44–47, 83, 90, 152, 164–71

temptation, 39–40, 100, 218–22, 224, 238; of Adam and Eve, 109–10, 152; of believers, 133, 148, 186, 201; of Jesus, 12, 148, 152

Ten Commandments, 7, 203–4

Theodore Abū Qurrah, 252

Thérèse of Lisieux, 1, 214–17

Thomas à Kempis, 135, 186–87, 216, 244

Thomas Aquinas, 75, 88, 122, 201

threefold office, 44–47, 83–84, 151–53

Tolkien, J. R. R., 56, 145

Torah. *See* law of Moses

tradition, 72, 76, 92, 99, 121, 137, 160, 252; examples, practices, and doctrines, 190–98, 213–15, 238–40; task of handing on the faith, 19–20, 80

Trinity, 130–34, 159–60, 185

types, 84, 151–53, 188–90

unity, 23–24, 27, 130–32, 162–63, 171–73, 177–78, 226–27, 245

universalism, 239–40, 272–73

universe, 23–24, 29, 35, 53–65, 73, 91–92, 109–10, 132, 235

violence, 83–84, 87–88, 107, 141, 203, 206–9, 212

virtue, 76, 135, 165–66, 179, 207–9, 210–12, 238, 241–42

wealth. *See* money

Webster, John, 15, 128

Wiman, Christian, 259

witness. *See* martyrdom; mission; resurrection

Word of God: and God's power, 12, 25, 46, 83–84, 131–32, 138–39, 167, 182–83, 192, 206, 241; and the good news, 25, 138–39, 151–52, 178, 191, 198; and Holy Scripture, 12, 46, 131, 138–39, 191–93, 197–98

worship: due to God alone, 3, 37–38, 58, 104, 110, 111, 122, 130, 155, 162, 203, 207, 233, 243; overflowing in grateful joy, 54, 66, 108, 148–49, 233; as part of human nature, 92, 104, 190; with God's people, 12–13, 59, 130, 133–34, 185, 189–99, 212, 223

Wright, Franz, 183

Wright, N. T., 132

YHWH, 255

Zechariah, 153